English Catholic
Heroes

English Catholic Heroes

edited by

John Jolliffe

GRACEWING

First published in 2008

Gracewing
2 Southern Avenue, Leominster
Herefordshire HR6 0QF

ISBN 978 0 85244 604 1

Front Cover: St Edmund Campion, SJ
from the Venerable English College, Rome

Typesetting by
Action Publishing Technology Ltd, Gloucester, GL1 5SR

Contents

Introduction

John Jolliffe

The purpose of this book is twofold. First, it is to remind believers and non-believers alike of the enormous part played by the great men of the Catholic Church not only in the spiritual life of the country, but, initially, in bringing to an end the Dark Ages and spreading literacy and civilization over a largely barbaric land. Since so little history is now taught in schools, only a tiny minority of children are ever told anything about St Aidan and St Cuthbert, the founders of the great monastic tradition which produced the sole pioneers of education in England. This led to the triumphs of Romanesque and Gothic ecclesiastical architecture, not only in abbeys and cathedrals but in many hundreds of smaller parish churches. Our great source for these early lives, the Venerable Bede, is often regarded as the Father of English History. These three are together the subject of our first chapter, and at one level, therefore, this book goes on to tell the story of a series of influential lives, many of them quite unfamiliar to most modern readers.

Secondly, after the Reformation, and above all the Dissolution of the monasteries, a new version of the nature of England was craftily invented by the Tudor monarchs and their ruthless henchmen, starting with Thomas Cromwell, in order to protect their claim to the throne, which was by no means the only one, or even perhaps the strongest. At first this partly mythical version was rigorously imposed, and later, under the plausible threat of real or imagined subjugation by Spain and later France, it became so genuinely popular that to deny it or even doubt it became treasonable and was often punished by a gruesome death. By the nineteenth century, thanks to the genius of Macaulay as a stylist and a twister of inconvenient facts, it was accepted as the Whig interpretation of history. Although those who doubted it were no longer murdered, there were precious few historians who could correct the traditional picture, and the great nineteenth-century pioneer John Lingard, the first to examine English history with proper attention to the primary sources (see chapter 9) was either ignored for many years, or else his findings were airbrushed out of the prevailing picture, while Burnet, Macaulay and the Trevelyans fed the popular appetite with overwhelming success. Eventually, however, led by Herbert Butterfield (and much interrupted by the Second World War) a reconsideration of the Reformation and its consequences in separating England from Europe has made enormous advances. J. J. Scarisbrick, Eamon Duffy and John Bossy have led the way in correcting the misconceptions about the period which had been accepted almost without question for four hundred years, William Cobbett being the greatest and most eloquent exception to the general line. All these historians deserve to be read with care by anyone, Catholic and non-Catholic alike, who is interested in discovering why and how life in England developed as it did. An excellent new book by Lewis Jones, *The English Myth*, is also worth reading in this context.

In the sixteenth century what the Church needed, like many human institutions, was some measure of well-judged reform, which was nearly brought about by Cardinal Pole and his allies (see chapter 3). What it got instead was abolition, proscription and replacement under the self-appointed domination of the King. It has become increasingly clear that Henry VIII became England's most destructive and controversial king. Amoral, treacherous and ruthless, vainglorious and restless, he was eaten up first by largely futile extravagance, which led to the looting of the monasteries, the abolition of the only existing welfare system by which so much was provided for the poor, the sick and the helpless (which is also referred to in Disraeli's great novel *Sybil*) and not least, to the destruction of the glories of medieval painting and sculpture which had adorned churches all over the country. But this was a separate issue from his divorce from Queen Catherine and the brutality arising from his desperate desire, untimately unsuccessful after other divorces and judicial murders, to produce a male heir to carry on his succession. By attacking France, and cutting England off from Rome he literally isolated his country from the whole integrated culture of Europe. Loyal Catholics were continuously ostracized and penalized for the next two centuries, and strong personal prejudice against them continued long after that. It was not until 1945, and another dissolution, this time of the British Empire, that attempts began to reconnect Britain with a very different Europe, not a task to be achieved easily or quickly, as we now know.

However, things did begin to improve in the eighteenth century. Whatever the shortcomings of the so-called Enlightenment, it did as a rule reject torture and judicial murder. Chapters 7 and 8 on Challoner and the ninth Lord Petre explain how disabilities were, very slowly, lifted. But so successful was the earlier falsification of English history that it was only comparatively recently that it has been revealed and attacked. Those who had taught history in Catholic schools are not without varying degrees of blame in this matter, and one of the aims of this book is to open eyes that should have been opened before. Nevertheless, it has often been shown that the Church gains long-lasting strength from persecution. If anything could have snuffed out Catholicism in England, one would have thought that Henry VIII and his younger daughter would have succeeded in doing so. Yet neither Thomas Cromwell and his KGB-style system, nor Queen Elizabeth's set-up with the Cecils and their professional spies and torturers managed it. This is why a quarter of the heroes described here lived in the severest of the penal times.

Sadly, the enemy within has recently been more successful, witness the falling-off in vocations, though many feel, following St John Chrysostom, that at parish level there could be married priests, up to the level of bishop, as in the Orthodox Church. There have also been various dismal attempts to make the Church accommodate itself to the modern world, rather than vice versa. However, Cardinal Hume (chapter 16) and Leonard Cheshire (chapter 15) are undoubtedly the great recent heroes. It should also be stressed that heroic deeds on an international, corporate scale are now more important, and more effective, than ever. CAFOD is perhaps the best known example. Similarly, Aid to the Church in Need operates all over the world, now with a strong British contribution under Neville Kyrke-Smith. The Sovereign and Military Order of Malta not only raises huge sums for the sick and wounded in various theatres of war, but several of their staff have recently been killed on their own form of active service.

Readers may be dismayed to find no heroines included here. Fortunately, plans are going ahead for a female sequel to this book, and no doubt Julian of Norwich, Margaret Pole, Mary Ward and many others will be celebrated in due course. Others will be disappointed to find their personal favourites missing. Adrian IV, the only English pope, perhaps deserves a mention, though he is chiefly remembered for his approval of the conquest of Ireland by Henry II. William Byrd, the great Tudor composer of church music who somehow managed to work with a foot in the Protestant as well as the Catholic camp; Elgar has strong claims, though his faith was uncertain at the end. Gerard Manley Hopkins and Francis Thompson all have their strong admirers; so has G. K. Chesterton, but delightful though they often are, his verbal somersaults and paradoxes did not equal the achievements of his great friend Belloc (chapter 13).

Monsignor Ronald Knox was certainly one of the greatest Catholic intellects of modern times, and he was for years the most celebrated priest (as well as one of the most modest) in England. Cardinal Heenan described him as 'perhaps the greatest figure in the Church of the twentieth century'. Though deeply conservative in many ways, he nevertheless understood that after two world wars the winds of change were blowing, and observed 'We do not want a place for old men to dream their dreams; young men, here, shall have their visions instead.' He was described by a friend as 'a shepherd rather than a fisherman', guarding his flock rather than going out to make converts. But his nature was so self-effacing, and his actual life so largely uneventful, that it is much more valuable to read his numerous brilliant books, such as *The Belief of Catholics, A Spiritual Aeneid, The Hidden Stream* and *Enthusiasm*, than to linger over his biographical details. Evelyn Waugh's great novels, especially *Helena*, and more indirectly the *Sword of Honour* trilogy were certainly inspired by his faith; but his cruelty, malice and unresisted urge to despise and snub the harmless narrowly disqualify him, though he once claimed that 'You don't know how much worse I would have been if I hadn't been a Catholic.' As for his friend Graham Greene, his Catholicism was of a distinctly à la carte nature, and it is even harder to see how it affected his way of life. There are also a number of exceptional men who only joined the Church after their great achievements were over, such as Malcolm Muggeridge.

Next, I must thank those who have helped me most in this task. First and foremost Dom Aidan Bellenger, the Abbot of Downside, for his crucial editorial advice, and also for arranging for this book to be published under the auspices of the English Catholic History Association, thereby qualifying it for subventions from several charities. I particularly thank the Craigmyle Trust, the Derwent Trust, the Clover Trust, the Bisgood Trust and the Waterside Trust; and among individuals Sir Anthony Bamford, John Boss, Sir Rocco Forte, the Earl of Gainsborough, Dermot Gleeson, my nephew William Jolliffe, Andrew Knight and Peter MacCann of Castlecraig for their generosity. It has enabled the book to be published at a low enough price to be affordable by schools as a text and for their libraries as well as for many individuals who would otherwise have found it beyond their reach. I am also grateful to Sir Peter Ramsbotham for his suggestions about the chapter on Leonard Cheshire.

Finally, I would like to pay tribute to my patient publisher, Tom Longford of Gracewing, a wonderfully well informed, resourceful and acute professional who more than anyone else is keeping the flag of Catholic publishing flying at a time when many other firms have disappeared.

Chapter 1

St Aidan, St Cuthbert, and the Venerable Bede

Andrew Breeze

Aidan, Cuthbert, and Bede are three saintly figures from early Northumbria, who are so closely linked that it is hard to think of one of them minus the others. Without the work of Aidan and Cuthbert in converting Northumbria to Christianity, we might not have had Bede the historian: without Bede, we should know very little of Aidan and Cuthbert. Let us look at them one by one.

First, Aidan. Although he appears in a book of English Catholic heroes, Aidan (d. 651) was not English at all. He was a Celt from Iona, who spoke the Gaelic language then common to Ireland and western Scotland. His name is Irish (it means 'little fire', from *áed*, 'fire'), and he arrived in Northumbria barely able to speak English. We do not know where he was born or when, or who his family were. The first we hear of him is in 635, after Northumbria had gone through political and religious crisis. The Roman mission to Northumbria began with the baptism of King Edwin by Paulinus in 627. At first all went well. Yet Edwin was killed in 632 by Penda of Mercia at Hatfield, near Doncaster, and the armies of Penda and his Welsh ally Cadwallon began ravaging Northumbria, which relapsed into paganism.

Recovery came thanks to Oswald, Edwin's nephew. The hostility of his uncle had forced Oswald into exile at Iona, where he became a Christian. In 633 he returned to Northumbria, killed Cadwallon of Gwynedd in battle near Hexham, and resumed power as King of Bernicia or northern Northumbria (County Durham, Northumberland, and south-east Scotland). Oswald then asked the Irish of Iona to take over the work of conversion. But the first monk they sent was a failure. He was severe, regarded the English as savages, and had to be sent back. He was replaced by Aidan, who was a tremendous success.

Oswald gave Aidan the island of Lindisfarne, where he set up a monastery and began the work of evangelization, travelling up and down the coast of Bernicia by boat. It is true that Aidan's English was at first so weak that Oswald sometimes had to translate for him. Yet Aidan went on as first Bishop of Lindisfarne to found monasteries (including Melrose, Gateshead, and Whitby) and churches. Although there was a shortage of priests, that did not defeat Aidan. He freed slave-boys and trained twelve of them for the priesthood. One of them, Eata, actually ended up as Abbot of Melrose and eventually Bishop of Lindisfarne. So the Church in Northumbria began to grow again.

Like all missionaries, Aidan was a practical man. He was good at organizing and knew how to deal with people. Yet he was also famous for humility and simplicity of life. Two famous stories in Bede's *Ecclesiastical History* bring this out. The first of them describes what Oswald did one Easter Day at a royal banquet.

> When he had sat down to dinner with Bishop Aidan, a silver dish full of rich foods was placed on the table before him. They had just raised their hands to ask a blessing on the bread when there came in an officer of the king, whose duty it was to relieve the needy, telling him that a great multitude of poor people from every district was sitting in the precincts and asking alms of the king. He at once ordered the dainties which had been set in front of him to be carried to the poor, the dish to be broken up, and the pieces divided amongst them. The bishop, who was sitting by, was delighted with this pious act, grasped him by the right hand, and said, 'May this hand never decay.' His blessing and his prayer were fulfilled in this way; when Oswald was killed in battle, his hand and arm were cut off from the rest of his body, and they have

remained uncorrupt until this present time; they are in fact preserved in a silver shrine in St Peter's church, in the royal city [Bamburgh, Northumberland] which is named after Queen Bebbe and are venerated with fitting respect by all.

It is a curious story: the King's amazing generosity on Easter Day, when he and his Court would be looking forward to a really good meal after the long fast of Lent; the way the King's body was, years later, hacked to pieces like his silver dish, and the strange way his hand and arm, after the saint had blessed them, did not rot or decay, but remained intact. The silver shrine at Bamburgh has long vanished. But part of St Oswald (his head) still exists. It is now at Durham, having been kept in the coffin of St Cuthbert. It is not often one can see the bones of someone mentioned by Bede, but there it is.

The second story is about Oswin, who was Oswald's second cousin. After 642, when Oswald was killed in battle by Penda near what is now Oswestry in Shropshire, Oswin became King of Deira (southern Northumbria, approximating to modern Yorkshire). Aidan moved south from Bernicia to work with him, and Oswin honoured the saint and gave him gifts, with unexpected results.

He had given to Bishop Aidan an excellent horse so that, though he was normally accustomed to walk, he could ride if he had to cross a river or if any other urgent necessity compelled him. A short time afterwards Aidan was met by a beggar who asked him for an alms. He at once alighted and offered the horse with all its royal trappings to the beggar; for he was extremely compassionate, a friend of the poor and a real father to the wretched.

The king was told of this and, happening to meet the bishop as they were going to dinner, he said, 'My lord bishop, why did you want to give a beggar the royal horse intended for you? Have we not many less valuable horses or other things which would have been good enough to give to the poor, without letting the beggar have the horse which I had specially chosen for your own use?' The bishop at once replied, 'O King, what are you saying? Surely this son of a mare is not dearer to you than that son of God?' After these words they went in to dine. The bishop sat down in his own place and the king, who had just come in from hunting, stood warming himself by the fire with his thegns. Suddenly he remembered the bishop's words; at once he took off his sword, gave it to a thegn, and then hastening to where the bishop sat, threw himself at his feet and asked his pardon. 'Never from henceforth,' said he, 'will I speak of this again, nor will I form any opinion as to what money of mine or how much of it you should give to the sons of God.' When the bishop saw this he was greatly alarmed; he got up immediately and raised the king to his feet, declaring that he would be perfectly satisfied if only the king would banish his sorrow and sit down to the feast.

The king, in accordance with the bishop's entreaties and commands, recovered his spirits, but the bishop, on the other hand, grew sadder and sadder and at last began to shed tears. Thereupon a priest asked him in his native tongue, which the king and his thegns did not understand, why he was weeping, and Aidan answered, 'I know that the king will not live long; for I never before saw a humble king. Therefore I think that he will very soon be snatched from this life; for this nation does not deserve to have such a ruler.' Not long after, the bishop's gloomy forebodings were fulfilled in the sad death of the king which we have already described. Bishop Aidan lived for only twelve days after the murder of the king whom he loved; for he was taken from the world on 31 August |651| and received from the Lord the eternal reward of his labours.

Again, another strange story. The bishop's apostolic generosity; the King's compunction, as he warmed himself by the fire at York or Catterick (or wherever the royal court was); and the bishop's consternation at the king's act of humility, since he knew as a practical administrator that what was fitting for a cleric was not so for a king, who must govern and rule and maintain authority; and the saint's prophetic (and correct) sense that Oswin would die tragically.

Despite political change in Bernicia, Aidan continued to go during Lent to Farne Island (six miles south-east of

Lindisfarne) for prayer and penance. In 651 the island proved an unexpected vantage-point for the destruction of Bamburgh by the pagan king Penda, plundering Northumbria once again. Aidan survived Oswin's death at Bamburgh by a few days only. He died at the end of August and was buried at Lindisfarne. Like missionary bishops in some parts of the world today, Aidan had the sad knowledge that political leaders he knew and respected were likely to die young, murdered by their rivals.

By the time Bede was born Aidan had long since died. But Bede was still able to collect stories about him when he came to write his *Ecclesiastical History*, which he finished in 731, eighty years after Aidan's death. It is curious that many of the anecdotes about him are set at court, as if Bede's informants were courtiers, not monks. In any case they bring out Aidan's practical awareness that he must overcome natural inclinations and appear amongst the King's household, the seat of power, to feast with the King and encounter men and women of the Court whose lives were, perhaps, not exactly remarkable for sanctity. Otherwise the mission would have no success. Aidan could not live all the time as a hermit. He had to raise money to build churches and establish monasteries, organize the training of priests, make sure they were sent where they were needed, and so on. To do that he had to work with the King and other people in the government, who had their hands on the levers of power. No wonder Aidan gained spiritual refreshment in his retreats on Farne Island, where his neighbours were not courtiers and politicians but razorbills and kittiwakes, who were not constantly testing his practical wisdom.

Bede praises Aidan warmly, regarding him as an exemplary bishop, except for one thing: his errors on the dating of Easter. Like all the Irish and Welsh of his time, Aidan's calculations of this used a system of reckoning which had become obsolete. This was not a real problem while Aidan was alive. But in 664 (long after his death) it was to cause trouble at Whitby. For some it still causes trouble even now, as we shall see when we come to Cuthbert.

Although Aidan's humility and generosity to the poor made him much loved, the cult of Aidan has had its ups and downs. Only one ancient English church is dedicated to him, at Bamburgh, on the Northumberland coast. After Lindisfarne was sacked by the Vikings in 793, his relics are said to have been taken to Iona, for greater safety, but are now lost. Presumably they lie buried somewhere on the isle of Iona. Still, he has another kind of monument known to millions. In the British Library in London are the Lindisfarne Gospels, written at Lindisfarne by Bishop Eadfrith (698–721) and others, but with wonderful colours and loops and spirals that owe much to the art of Ireland and Celtic Scotland. So they are an indirect but lasting tribute to Aidan, an Irish or Scottish-Irish priest who helped bring Christianity to England.

After Aidan, Cuthbert. If Aidan was an Irishman, Cuthbert (born about 634, died 687) was an Englishman, a Northumbrian born in what is now Scotland, near Melrose, into a family of prosperous sheep-farmers. Most of what we know of him is thanks to Bede, who was only 14 when Cuthbert died and never met him, but who revered his name, gave him a major place in the *Ecclesiastical History*, and wrote lives of him in verse and prose. So Bede had a large role in the cult of the saint. In 651 Cuthbert entered the monastery of Melrose, now called Old Melrose, which is a mile from the later and more famous monastery. He was then sent to Ripon, where there were difficulties about his refusal to accept the Roman Easter, so that in 661 he was back at Melrose as prior. At the synod of Whitby in 663–4 he accepted the Roman Easter and became prior of Lindisfarne, but gave that up in 676 to become an anchorite on Farne Island or Inner Farne. In 685 he was consecrated Bishop of Lindisfarne. He retired to Farne Island again in 686, and died in that solitude above the waves on 20 March 687.

Stories were told of Cuthbert's miraculous and prophetic powers. There is a strange tale of him when he was in Carlisle on 20 May 685, visiting his diocese while Ecgfrith of Northumbria was invading the land of the Picts.

On the following day, when the people of the city were showing him its wall and a well in it wonderfully built long before by the Romans, he suddenly became anxious, leaned on his stick, and looked down sorrowfully at the ground. Then, raising himself up again and looking up to the sky, he groaned deeply and said in a quiet voice, 'Something terrible seems to have happened in the battle'.

A priest standing by him asked how he knew, and Cuthbert said, 'Do you not see how changed and stirred up the air is? What man can search out the judgements of God?' And Cuthbert hurried to speak to the queen, who was nearing the end of her pregnancy. Cuthbert's forebodings were justified, because that very day King Ecgfrith and his army were massacred by the Picts in the battle of Nechtansmere, at a spot four miles from Forfar in eastern Scotland (though some now place it near Kingussie, in the Highlands).

So Cuthbert impressed people as someone with more than human authority. But other stories of him are less intimidating. He was remembered as a man with a special feel for nature, so that the eider is known in Northumberland as 'St Cuthbert's Duck'. The tameness of the birds nesting on Inner Farne, all around his cell, was attributed to the holiness of Cuthbert. A Durham monk of the twelfth century wrote of these sea ducks that the saint, while he watched and prayed on Farne, 'allowed nobody to touch them, slaughter them, or trouble them with any mischievous intention'. The monk went on to say that Cuthbert

> so tamed the aforesaid winged and swimming creatures that they gave him unquestioning obedience. He prescribed for them where they should nest, and exactly when they should arrive and when they should leave. So they still arrive at fixed times, and in the hour of need and adversity have recourse to the familiar protection of the Blessed Cuthbert.

Whether he knew it or not, this writer has made the ducks sound just like monks, who are also obedient, live regular hours, etc. Still, as few medieval people had much interest in any bird unless they could eat it, the story is charming; though it also underlines the power of the saint, as is usual in early hagiography.

There is another story to suggest Cuthbert's gentleness and sense of justice, as well as his power over the natural world.

> They were on a journey and became tired and hungry. Cuthbert and the boy who was his companion knew there was nobody likely to be able to help them, but Cuthbert told him not to despair. The man of God replied, 'My son, learn to have faith, and trust in God, who will never allow those who trust in him to perish with hunger.' Then, looking up and seeing an eagle flying in the air, he said, 'Do you perceive that eagle yonder? It is possible for God to feed us even by means of that eagle.' As they were talking, they came near a river, and saw the eagle standing on its bank. 'Look,' said the man of God, 'there is our good servant, the eagle I spoke to you about. Run, and see what provision God has sent us, and come again and tell me.' The boy ran and found a good-sized fish, which the eagle had just caught. But the man of God reproved him. 'What have you done, my son! Why have you not given part to God's servant? Cut the fish in two pieces, and give her one, as her service well deserves.'

Yet another story of him points to power over nature, as well as his austerities. Cuthbert had gone from his island refuge by night, standing in the sea with the water up to his neck and arms, praising God. One night a monk of the monastery followed him secretly.

> When the dawn of day approached, he came out of the water and, falling on his knees, began to pray again. When he was doing this, two quadrupeds, called otters, came up from the sea, and, lying down on the sand, breathed upon his feet, and wiped them with their hair; after which, having received his blessing, they returned to their native element. Cuthbert himself returned home in time to join in the accustomed hymns with the other brethren. The brother, who waited for him on the heights, was so terrified that he could hardly

reach home; and early in the morning he came and fell at his feet, asking his pardon, for he did not doubt that Cuthbert was fully acquainted with all that had taken place. Cuthbert replied, 'What is the matter, my brother? What have you done? Did you follow me to see what I was about to do? I forgive you for it on one condition: that you tell it to nobody before my death.'

There has always been a strong cult of Cuthbert, with fifty ancient churches are dedicated to him. In Domesday Book what we call County Durham was called 'St Cuthbert's Land', and his name survives to this day in south-west Scotland with the town of Kirkcudbright, meaning 'church of Cuthbert'. Cuthbert, a traveller revered in his life, carried on travelling and being revered after death. When Viking attacks in the ninth century made Lindisfarne too dangerous, his community brought his body first to Chester-le-Street and then finally to Durham, where his bones still lie. When his tomb was opened in 1827 his pectoral cross and other treasures were found inside. So one can be closer to him than to almost anyone else who lived in the seventh century.

Cuthbert can, like many saints, be seen in different ways. Because of his compassion for living things, some like to think of him as a pioneer of ecology or nature conservation. However, Bede saw him more seriously and without sentiment. He described Cuthbert as Christ's soldier, armed with the helmet of salvation, shield of faith, and sword of the spirit, who overcame the army of demons whose presence was felt to be close.

Finally, Bede himself (673–735). So many people have praised Bede that it seems hard to say anything new about him. Biographical facts are few. It has been said that a life devoted to learning passes quietly away, undiversified by events, and (on the whole) such a life was Bede's. He was born near Sunderland. When he was seven, he was given by his parents (whose names are unknown) to a monastery. His life of study and teaching was spent at the monasteries of Wearmouth and then Jarrow. Yet his writings were used throughout Europe, and he gave a list of them at the end of his greatest work, the *Ecclesiastical History*. They included books on metrics and singing, commentaries on the Bible, including the books of Genesis, Samuel, Kings, Proverbs, Song of Songs, Isaiah, Daniel, the Minor Prophets, Jeremiah, Ezra, Nehemiah, Habakkuk, Tobias, the Gospels of Mark and Luke, Acts, the Catholic Epistles, and the Apocalypse; lives of Cuthbert in verse and in prose; a history of the Abbots of Wearmouth-Jarrow; a martyrology; a book of hymns; a book of epigrams; books on chronology, spelling, and figures of speech; and a history of England which has never been forgotten. This last book shines a historical torch over early England for a period that some people, rather oddly, call the Dark Ages, though the impression given by Bede's history is rather of an Age of Light, so clear and luminous is his writing.

Since Bede's life was one given over to daily prayer, teaching, and writing, there are not many anecdotes about him. But there are two stories of him which are so famous that they must be told. They come from his early life and from its very end. Here is the first. It describes the monastery at Wearmouth in a time of plague, which virtually wiped out the monks there.

> In the monastery over which Ceolfrith presided, all who could read or preach or recite the antiphons were swept away, except the abbot himself and one little lad nourished and taught by him, who is now a priest of the same monastery, and both by word of mouth and by writing commends to all who wish to know them the abbot's worthy deeds. And the abbot, sad at heart because of this visitation, ordained that, contrary to their former rite, they should, except at vespers and matins, recite their psalms without antiphons. And when this had been done with many tears and lamentations on his part for the space of a week, he could not bear it any longer, but decreed that the psalms with their antiphons should be restored to their order according to the regular course; and by means of himself and the aforesaid boy, he carried out with no little labour that which he had decreed, until he could either train them

himself or procure from elsewhere men able to take part in the divine service.

Everybody agrees the 'little lad' was Bede. One cannot help thinking that the experience of plague, in which (barring the abbot) all other members of the community died one by one, would have permanent effects on him, and what he thought of life.

The other story is also memorable. It describes Bede's last afternoon alive. He had been unwell, the other monks were concerned for him, but he carried on dictating a translation of St John's Gospel into English. What happened then is told by a young monk called Cuthbert, who was there at the time.

> But they were heartened when he said, 'If it be the will of my maker, the time has come when I shall be freed from the body, and return to him who created me out of nothing when I had no being. I have had a long life, and the merciful judge has ordered it graciously. The time of my departure is at hand, and my soul longs to see Christ my king in his beauty.' He also told us many other edifying things, and passed his last day happily until evening. Then the same lad, named Wilbert, said again, 'Dear master, there is one sentence still unfinished.' 'Very well,' he replied, 'write it down.' After a short while the lad said, 'Now it is finished.' 'You have spoken truly,' he replied: 'It is well finished. Now raise my head in your hands, for it would give me great joy to sit facing the holy place where I used to pray, so that I may sit and call on my Father.' And thus, on the floor of his cell, he chanted 'Glory be to the Father, and to the Son, and to the Holy Spirit' to its ending, and breathed his last.

So these are two stories about Bede, as a small boy and as an old man. But what was he like as a writer? Here we may quote, not something from the *Ecclesiastical History* (which is easy enough to obtain in translation), but from his other writings, which are harder to find. Here he is explaining a particular verse in the strange tale of Tobias and the fish, in the Apocrypha.

The angel said to Tobias: 'Take the fish by the gill and pull him towards you.' The Lord seized hold of the Devil and by dying caught and conquered the one who wanted to catch him in death. Moreover, he seized him by the gill so that, with the right hand of his power, he might separate his most wicked head from his entrapped body, that is, that he might remove the wickedness of the ancient enemy from the heart of those whom he had wickedly allied to himself and had made, as it were, one body with them, and that, as a merciful redeemer, he might graft them into the body of his Church. For a fish has a gill at the joining of its head and body. Now, just as our Lord is the head of his Church and the Church is his body, so the Devil is the head of all the wicked and all the wicked are his head and members. The reason why the Lord seized the very savage fish by the gill, dragged it towards him and cast it up on dry land was that, in smashing them to pieces, he openly and boldly exposed the Devil's capabilities in public, and rescued from the powers of darkness those whom he foreknew to be children of light.

Bede also wrote verse. It is true nobody has ever said that he was a great poet, but at least his verses give us an idea of the man. Here a hymn of his in praise of 'Our Captain God'.

O God that art the only hope of the world,
The only refuge for unhappy men,
Abiding in the faithfulness of heaven,
Give me strong succour in this testing place.
O King, protect thy man from utter ruin
Less the weak faith surrender to the tyrant,
Facing innumerable blows alone.
Remember I am dust, and wind, and shadow,
And life as fleeting as the flower of grass.
But may the eternal mercy which hath shone
From time of old
Rescue thy servant from the jaws of the lion.
Thou who didst come from on high in the cloak of flesh,
Strike down the dragon with that two-edged sword
Whereby our mortal flesh can war with the winds
And beat down strongholds, with our Captain God.

The poem is important, not because it is original or especially beautiful (it is neither), but because it is useful. It sets out Bede's firm belief that God is with us, especially at times of danger. That is why it appears in Christopher Howse's book on Comfort.

Bede has been called the greatest of all English historians (a comment that puts Edward Gibbon and Lord Macaulay in their place). Yet, like most great historians, he fuels argument. English Catholics who resisted the Reformation published a translation of his *Ecclesiastical History* in 1565 at Antwerp. It was the work of Thomas Stapleton, and it was meant to show how early English Christians had been loyal to the pope and to the Church's universal authority. People argue even now about Bede's account of the Easter Controversy, when the English Church was divided between those who followed the Irish system of dating Easter (which was out of date), and the Roman party, who used the system we have now. The dispute was resolved in favour of the Roman calendar at the Synod of Whitby in 663–4. But it is still used by some critics of Catholicism, who like to see in Celtic Christianity a model for their own views on liturgy or freedom or spirituality. In many ways they carry on the arguments of Welsh, Irish, and Scottish Protestants in the sixteenth century, who were convinced that the earliest Christianity of their countries was an evangelical and scriptural faith identical with their own. To the old arguments against Bede can be added some new ones. He has been accused of being an English imperialist or a racist; this seems a little hard on a writer who wrote with such sympathy and admiration of the Irish (not a common English characteristic), and even of the mysterious Picts of northern Scotland, about whom we should know little except for him.

Coming as they do from the beginnings of English history, Aidan, Cuthbert, and Bede might seem rather far from the concerns of the twenty-first century. But it is strange how the opposite seems true. They showed courage and dedication in working for what they knew to be right, whether by teaching, organizing, writing in defence of the truth, or just living the Christian life. We hear much about the problems of Britain now, when paganism appears stronger than it has been for centuries. But these problems might seem rather small compared with those of the seventh and eighth centuries, when England was just emerging from barbarism, and the standards of health were below those of any Third World Country, so that most people died young. In social conditions that would appal anyone living today, Aidan, Cuthbert, and Bede all worked with resolution, both by precept and example, for a civilization of love. And if that is not a call to heroism, it is hard to see what is.

Chapter 2

St Thomas Becket

Bernard Green, OSB

On Saturday 13 July 1174, King Henry II of England, Duke of Normandy, Duke of Aquitaine, Count of Anjou, son of the Empress Matilda, grandson of Henry I and great-grandson of William the Conqueror, walked from the Church of St Dunstan to the Cathedral of Christ Church, at Canterbury. Clad in a poor woollen smock, the man who might fairly have claimed to be the most powerful man in Christendom walked barefoot, as a penitent. Already king for twenty years, forty-one years old, he must have seemed to bystanders at the full vigour of his strength – of medium height, with a strong square chest and legs bowed from incessant days in the saddle, his reddish hair cut very short, his face enlivened by his remarkable blue-grey eyes, so expressive of his mood. Everything about this man exuded energy and power. He preferred to stand rather than sit, and to move rather than stand. He was notorious for the speed with which he travelled the length and breadth of his vast domains and the suddenness with which he could appear, unexpected by friend or foe. His bad temper was legendary but he was just as famous for his instinctive generosity. Loyal to his friends, unforgiving to his enemies, Henry had come to do penance.

He entered the cathedral and made his way to the tomb of his former servant and enemy, St Thomas Becket. Becket, Archbishop of Canterbury, had met a violent death in this cathedral three and a half years earlier. He had been canonized as a martyr just over a year before. Henry had come to

atone for the murder. He lay prostrate before the tomb and
there he was scourged by all the bishops and abbots present
and every single monk of the monastic community who
served the cathedral. He remained in prayer all day and all
night, never once leaving to eat or to relieve nature. In the
early hours of the morning, after the monastic office of
Lauds, he went around the altars of the cathedral and prayed
at the shrines of the saints before returning to the tomb of
St Thomas Becket. At dawn, before leaving Canterbury, he
heard Mass and drank water from the well of the martyr and
was honoured by a gift of a phial of his blood.

Henry had come to atone for the murder because at his
Christmas Court in Normandy in 1170, in a bloody rage, he
had blurted out these or similar words: 'Will no one rid me
of this turbulent priest?' Within days, four of his knights had
crossed the Channel, cornered the Archbishop in his cathedral and hacked him down. Henry denied repeatedly that he
had wanted Becket dead, but he could not deny that it was
his words and his wrath that had led to the killing. He had
already admitted as much and formally done penance at
Avranches in front of the Pope's representatives and in turn
had been formally forgiven. But the horror of the crime was
such that Henry had to come to Becket's very tomb to do
penance again and there venerate his old enemy as a martyr.
How had Henry been humbled and how had the Archbishop
been martyred?

Just as Henry was an unlikely penitent, so Thomas Becket
was an unlikely martyr. Becket was just over fifty when he
died and in his life he had excelled in the arts of war and
peace, as a leader of men and as an administrator, as a
courtier and as a diplomat, and above all as a great churchman. A Londoner of Norman French background, the son of
a businessman, he had had an excellent and expensive
education though not one that took him to higher studies in
law or theology. People remarked on his competent but not
very fluent Latin – the international language which was the
key to any kind of career in administration or the Church.
Thomas had probably been destined to follow his father in

business but, at some point when he was still young, his father lost a great deal in a fire and the young man was forced to pursue just that kind of career for which his education had only partly prepared him. Fortunately, family connections smoothed his path. He learned the aristocratic arts of horses and hawking from the Lord of Hastings, Richard de l'Aigle. Throughout his life, Thomas was noted for his excellent, courtly manners. He began his career in the banking house of a relative, one of the richest men in London, Osbert Huitdeniers, and from there in about 1145 he was propelled into the service of one of the greatest men in the kingdom, who might also have been a cousin, Theobald, Archbishop of Canterbury.

People described him as a tall, slender man with fair skin and dark hair, with shining eyes and a broad forehead and regular features apart from a prominent, aquiline nose. He grew more handsome as he grew older. They noted his acute sense of smell and sharp hearing. He was clever and gifted with an exceptional memory. He had charm and was a very engaging conversationalist. Conscious of the impression he made on people, he dressed well and in his early years was an avid follower of fashion. But it seems too that he had something of a stammer and was afflicted by frequent bouts of illness, especially to do with his stomach, which might suggest that for all his charm he suffered from stress. Though people often commented on his vanity and his preoccupation with clothes, there was never any suggestion that he followed the easy sexual moral standards of the age. Was that because he was devout – no one thought so – or because he was self-contained, perhaps somewhat lacking in any desire for physical intimacy?

He rose quickly in the service of Archbishop Theobald of Canterbury. The Archbishop was one of the greatest landholders of the realm as well as its leading bishop. He had a large staff of highly trained officials, clerks, who were clergy though often of a minor rank. Becket showed such promise as a clerk in Archbishop Theobald's household that he was sent to study law for a year at Bologna and Auxerre. Though he was still not the equal of the best educated of the officials surrounding the Archbishop, he was at least equipped to manage business and to know how to use their expertise. In 1154, Theobald promoted him to the position of Archdeacon of Canterbury and ordained him deacon. This was a major appointment; his predecessor, Roger de Pont l'Evêque, had moved from the archdeaconry to be Archbishop of York. He was given a handful of rich church livings, by which he took the income of several churches while employing priests to do the work for him. He was now a significant man himself, but though he held high office in the Church he still dressed in the most colourful, fashionable style.

The year that Thomas Becket was made Archdeacon of Canterbury was the year that Henry II became King of England. Becket was about thirty-four years old; he had risen by his own talents and merit far beyond the openings that family contacts had initially given him. Henry's succession after a bitter civil war was negotiated by Archbishop Theobald, among others. Perhaps Theobald was rewarded by the surprising elevation in 1155 of his able servant Thomas Becket to the office of Chancellor of England, the head of the royal administration.

Henry was not only King of England but was also, by inheritance and by marriage, the ruler of vast territories in France. As Chancellor, Thomas accompanied the King on his exhausting and exhaustive travels around his domains. Though the son of a London businessman, Thomas was now a great man in his own right with his own retinue of servants and powers of patronage. Great sums passed through his hands as he administered royal policy. He acted on the King's behalf as a judge, travelling around England hearing major court cases. He represented the King as his ambassador; his entourage in the legation which he led to the King of France in 1158 was so numerous and splendid that people wondered what the King could be like if this was the servant. He even acted as a military commander, leading 700 knights in a campaign to subdue Toulouse in 1159 and afterwards policing the border of Normandy with knights he paid for himself. By all accounts, his service of the King was reinforced by bonds of friendship; it was said that they had but one heart and one mind.

If promotion from the staff of Archbishop Theobald to the office of Chancellor of England was a surprise, no doubt for Becket as much as for his contemporaries, his appointment as Archbishop of Canterbury was astonishing. Theobald died in the spring of 1161. Becket, at the time, was leading a campaign in France against the King of France; he fell ill and both kings, of England and of France, visited him on his sickbed. Despite his standing as a major royal official, he was a most unlikely choice to replace Theobald at Canterbury. A whole year passed before Henry secured Becket's appointment as Archbishop, but it was clear that his aim was to have his close ally, friend and trusted servant in the vital post of leader of the English Church. It was an appointment that met with great resentment and suspicion. Thomas Becket was not a monk, whereas most of his predecessors for centuries had come from monasteries – indeed, he seemed a very secular man indeed in dress and style and activities. He was too close to the King – would he really look after the interests of the Church? He was not even a priest; he had to be ordained priest the day before he was consecrated bishop at the start of June, 1162.

For well over a century, the papacy had led a reform of the Church that seemed inevitably to lead to a clash with the princes and magnates of Christendom. The popes wanted to free the Church from lay control and exploitation, from the abuse of church wealth by powerful lay authorities, from the subordination of the clergy to lay power, and from the comfortable but corrosive standards of clerical discipline by which many clergy were married and expected to be succeeded in office by their sons to whom they would pass on not only their position but also the property and income that went with it. This great movement is often named the Gregorian Reform after one of its most strident advocates, Pope Gregory VII, who had found himself pitched headlong against the German Emperor, whom he excommunicated and forced to do penance after standing waiting in the snow outside the papal palace at Canossa.

England had had its experience of these disputes. While churchmen were willing to accept that the King appointed the bishops, they still wanted to insist that they owed their authority not to the King but to God. This was in part a dispute about symbols and ceremonies, the investiture of bishops, but it crystallized the central issue of the relationship of the Church and society and the independence of the clergy and the property of the Church. At the end of the eleventh and beginning of the twelfth century, the great Archbishop Anselm of Canterbury, a brilliant theologian as well as a great churchman, had struggled against the kings of his day, including Henry II's grandfather, to defend the independence of the Church in the investiture of bishops. Anselm endured two lengthy exiles in defence of the papal line. The appointment of Thomas Becket in 1162 looked suspiciously like an audacious move by Henry II to reassert royal control of the Church and reverse the efforts and achievements of Anselm.

At first, Thomas Becket gave a rather mixed impression of his view of his new office. He still wore brightly coloured clothes; he seemed to exult in the massive retinue of knights and servants who surrounded him and the staff of fifty-two clerks who administered the legal and bureaucratic machine of the Canterbury Church. Though he resigned the office of Chancellor, he retained the Archdeaconry of Canterbury and other church appointments which brought him a good income. Yet on the other hand, he began a process of consolidating his control over Canterbury Church lands, risking friction with same barons and even the King. In 1163, he began a campaign to have the great Anselm of Canterbury canonized as a saint. He blocked the attempt of King Henry's brother to enter a marriage that would have needed a special dispensation. Above all, he showed himself to be intransigent on the question of legal jurisdiction over the clergy. The Church had its own courts in which cases concerning clergy and church property were heard in accordance with the law of the Church, canon law. The King insisted that clergy found guilty in the church courts and stripped of their orders should then be handed over to the lay power for punishment. The Archbishop refused to submit the clergy to lay authority, responding that 'God Himself does not judge his enemies twice'. Given that as much as a sixth of the population counted as clergy, this was not an unimportant issue.

In October 1163, at a council of the bishops at Westminster, Henry demanded that they observe the ancient customs of the realm. Led by Thomas, they replied that they would, 'saving our order', meaning that they would only follow ancient practice if it did not conflict with canon law. But in January 1164, when the bishops assembled again at Clarendon, Thomas agreed to swear without reservation to follow the ancient customs. Henry then produced a list of sixteen customs that he expected the bishops to accept. Thomas then declared them contrary to canon law and refused to put his seal to them. This muddled and inconsistent behaviour at Clarendon cost Thomas the confidence of his fellow bishops, who were now divided and disheartened. Thomas imposed penances upon himself for his actions at Clarendon and made several unsuccessful attempts to slip away from England into exile in France.

Thomas was now in a very difficult position. His fellow bishops for the most part no longer trusted him. Most of them had been suspicious from the start but, after he had given them leadership in a major confrontation with the King, he had then twice performed a volte-face. He had sought the support of the Pope, Alexander III, but his advice was chiefly to avoid any dispute with the Crown. Worst of all, he was now clearly not just Henry's opponent in a disagreement over church rights but his personal enemy. All the affection that Henry had once had for him had now turned to bitterness and it scarcely seemed likely under the circumstances that the Archbishop could effect any reconciliation or compromise. It seemed that Thomas was himself the problem.

The quarrel flared up anew in the autumn of 1164. Henry summoned the Archbishop to appear before his royal Court to answer a dispute concerning a manor which belonged to the Church of Canterbury. Unsurprisingly, Thomas refused to comply. Henry then convened a council of magnates at Northampton in October, at which he accused Thomas of contempt of court and of embezzlement of royal funds during his time as Chancellor. The King first demanded detailed accounts of his time as Chancellor and then demanded an immense sum of money, some said as much as 30,000 marks (when, thirty years later, Henry's son Richard the Lionheart had to be ransomed from captivity in Austria, the sum demanded for his release from captivity, literally a King's ransom, was 100,000 marks). All the bishops begged Thomas to submit to the King but Thomas, in a scene of high drama, confronted the lay magnates who wanted him condemned as a traitor, announced that he was appealing to the Pope, and with uplifted cross in hand made his way through the midst of them and out of the castle. He vanished that night and a few weeks later escaped in disguise to the Continent.

He was to be in exile for six years. During that time, he received lukewarm support from Pope Alexander III who feared that a row with Henry of England was the last thing he needed when he was already engaged in a bitter struggle with the Emperor Frederick Barbarossa, while at the same time finding that several of the leading English bishops were deeply critical of Thomas. While the Pope attempted to negotiate a rapprochement between King and Archbishop, Thomas showed himself in no mood for compromise. On Whitsunday 1166, at the great abbey of Vézelay in Burgundy, he excommunicated the servants of King Henry who had infringed his rights. It took the Pope a year to lift the excommunication. Then on Palm Sunday 1169, at the Cistercian abbey of Clairvaux, he excommunicated ten people including the Bishops of London and Salisbury. Though the Pope managed to delay the excommunication taking effect, it came into force at the end of September. Meanwhile, the

Pope made a series of attempts to bring the two sides together.

Thomas clarified his demands. He wanted the King to abandon the ancient customs which were in direct contradiction to canon law; he wanted the King to restore him and his followers to their former titles and possessions and to be given compensation for their losses in exile; he wanted those who had injured him to be punished. Henry offered concessions: he would allow learned clerks to scrutinize the customs he had put on paper at Clarendon and abandon any judged to be 'evil' and he would reduce the financial demands he had levelled against Thomas at Northampton. Thomas, for his part, had no trust in Henry now. He repeatedly asked for a kiss of peace from the King as a pledge of his sincerity, which Henry repeatedly refused to give. Thomas and Henry met twice in 1169, at Montmirail and at Montmartre, but both encounters failed to find any way towards an agreement.

Meanwhile, Thomas lodged in various monasteries in France where he adopted a more ascetic and rigorous style of life, eating the same meagre fare as the monks, devoting hours to prayer and meditation and stuyding the Bible. He seemed to have been trying to make up for his ignorance of scripture and theology while at the same time finding a deeper level of personal absorption in God. The Pope sent him a Cistercian habit, which he adopted under his outer clothes, while he was staying with the Cistercians at Pontigny in 1164; he was found to be wearing it when the corpse was undressed after his death. It represented his renewed dedication to the cause of church reform as well as his commitment to the life of prayer and recollection of the Cistercians.

Henry had one long-standing and pressing need: to secure the succession of his eldest son to the crown of England. His family was fractious and they were liable to fight each other in savage civil wars. To guarantee that his eldest boy would succeed him, he wanted him crowned an anointed as king, as his junior partner, and the coronation of a monarch was the prerogative of the Archbishop of Canterbury. Thomas was appalled when Henry cut the Gordian knot by staging the coronation at Westminster Abbey in the June of 1170, with Archbishop Roger of York assisted by ten English and Norman bishops crowning the young King. This act changed everything. It was an outrageous infringement of the rights of Canterbury; it offended the Pope who had recently endorsed the Archbishop of Canterbury's right to preside at a coronation; but it satisfied a deep need of the King. Somehow, both sides felt in the aftermath of the coronation that the time for rapprochement had finally come.

Another meeting took place at Fréteval in July and, while much was left unsaid and unresolved, the way seemed open now for Thomas to return to England. It proved a very unfortunate compromise. There was not enough trust on either side. Too many issues were still open – above all a new papal sentence against the bishops who had presided at the young King's coronation which it fell to Thomas to implement. The thorny question of the lands and revenues of Canterbury, taken over by others in the Archbishop's absence, was bound to prove intractable on his return. Nevertheless, Thomas crossed the Channel in late November and went back to Canterbury for the first time in six years.

As the Archbishop enacted the papal sentence against the bishops who presided at the coronation and issued his own condemnation of people who had violated the rights and properties of the Church of Canterbury, he saw the King as having failed to keep his undertakings to restore his lost properties and respect his rights while he felt that he was only acting on behalf of the Pope. As the King heard of the Archbishop's actions in the weeks leading up to Christmas 1170, he felt that Thomas was acting as outrageously and aggressively as ever. This was the context in which, in a tremendous rage, Henry uttered his damning words at his Christmas Court in Normandy: 'What miserable drones and traitors have I nurtured and promoted in my household who let their lord be treated with such shameful contempt by a low-born clerk.'

Four knights took this as a command to arrest and, if necessary, silence the Archbishop for ever. They crossed the Channel and reached Canterbury on 29 December 1170. Already, the royal official entrusted with custody of the properties and revenue of Canterbury had blockaded the Archbishop in the cathedral's precincts. They succeeded in entering the Archbishop's hall and had a rambling, inconclusive but angry conversation with him in his private chamber. Thomas's clerks, sensing the danger he was in, hustled him into the cathedral, but he would not allow the door to be bolted and the knights, who had now put on their armour, followed him and confronted him as he stood in the afternoon gloom, near a pillar opening onto the north transept. More angry words were exchanged and then a violent struggle followed in which Thomas forcibly resisted their attempt to seize him. Blows were struck. Ruthlessly and deliberately, the knights cut him down and killed him.

It was one of the most famous murders in history. Some people thought that Thomas had wanted or at least expected to die as a martyr, but his astonished anger both in his chamber and in the cathedral suggests the opposite. It was a shocking death which horrified Christendom but what amazed all the major players in the tragedy was the popular reaction to Thomas's death. People quickly began to come to the cathedral to pray at his tomb. Soon, remarkable numbers of miracles were reported – the first only a week after the murder. A vast groundswell of popular feeling took everyone by surprise. The Pope's decision to canonize Thomas on Ash Wednesday 1173, a little over two years after the murder, was the only possible response to the explosion of the cult at his shrine, just as Henry's penitential visit a little over a year later was the only possible royal response to the crime. Canterbury became one of the greatest pilgrimage sites in Europe and St Thomas became the canonized embodiment of resistance to royal tyranny over the Church. It is no surprise that the shrine was demolished by Henry VIII. Though the issues that inflamed so much passion in the years leading to Thomas's death were complex and local and specific, the issue for which he died is ultimately of perennial and universal significance: the liberty of the servants of God's Kingdom from the control of any earthly kingdom.

Chapter 3

St John Fisher and St Thomas More

The bluntest of bishops and the most outspoken Speaker

Edward Leigh, MP and Alex Haydon

I will not condemn any other man's conscience, which lieth in their own heart far out of my sight. *Sir Thomas More*

Not that I condemn any other men's conscience. Their conscience may save them, and mine must save me.
Bishop John Fisher

Thomas More, who was declared by Pope John Paul II to be patron saint of statesmen and politicians, is a man whom all MPs should celebrate, whatever their religious convictions. It is to him that all members of Parliament owe an eternal debt of gratitude, for it was he who, as Speaker, won for us for the first time the right to freedom of speech in debating any subject. This is nowadays known as 'parliamentary privilege'. Because of him, we can, in Shakespeare's words from *King Lear* 'speak what we feel, not what we ought to say'.

Thomas More really is a saint for our time. One doesn't need to descend into hagiography to see him as a fine example for all politicians. Of course he had his faults. After all he was a successful lawyer and politician. Is it possible for anyone to rise in our professions without any blemish? Nor do we need to go to the other extreme and dismiss him as a narrow-minded bigot and burner of heretics. True, he did burn some, as his modern-day detractors keep reminding us. But to condemn him for that is to take him out of his context and his century when religion was central to everyone's life and government was a kind of theocracy. The authorities felt they had to enforce orthodoxy. Before we get too critical perhaps we could recall those modern-day magistrates who enforce laws against racist comments on the grounds that the equilibrium of society is upset by them. Or consider the laws against Islamist preaching that inspires terrorism. Heresy was then seen as a threat of that order and worse. In Germany an uprising inspired by Protestant notions, known as the Peasants' War, led in More's lifetime to terrible bloodshed.

But enough of this carping. The true genius of Thomas More's memory and why he is immortalized is because he stood up for what he believed in. In a sense his stand and that of Fisher is all the more extraordinary because what Henry VIII was proposing was not so outrageous. After all it was considered one of the greatest disasters that could befall a nation for a girl to inherit the Crown. Henry knew that if Mary was to succeed him and marry perhaps the heir to France or Spain, England and her freedom would literally be her dowry. The sensible course for Catherine would have been to retire quietly to a convent after failing in her most important job of providing a male heir. Only two great public men, More and Fisher, stood against the notion that England must have a male heir. Their obstinacy in the face of all their peers is glorious. No doubt too the prospect of execution concentrated the minds of many of their friends, and the fact that alone of all the courtiers and bishops More and Fisher refused to renounce their beliefs even if it led to the scaffold has ensured that they are remembered when all the others are forgotten.

One last canard should be laid to rest. It is alleged that More wanted to be a martyr. In fact he used all his lawyer-like skills to put off the evil day. One is left with the inescapable conclusion that he was just a sincere man who could not renounce his religious beliefs for a political, even a national, convenience. Why can we not delight in and applaud him and hold his memory sacred?

Recently More has become more topical as once again the
state starts to impose its morality on the churches in order
to stop what it sees as discrimination.

At the heart of Henry VIII's great matter was an issue
concerning marriage and the family. This is not the place to
debate the merits or otherwise of the Blair government's
insistence that the Catholic Church open its adoption agen-
cies to gay couples. Suffice it to say that Archbishop Vincent
Nichols of Birmingham came out with a Fisher-like statement that needs preserving for posterity:

> Those who are elected to fashion our laws are not elected to
> be our moral tutors. They have no mandate or competence
> to do so. And the wise among them would not wish it either.

In the context of the dispute, Dr Rowan Williams, the
Archbishop of Canterbury, famously declared that

> Rights of conscience cannot be subject to legislation.

But there is a broader reason why modern politicians should
celebrate the life of Thomas More. We live famously in an
age of spin. But we are more worryingly in an age where
Parliament is remarkably quiescent to the executive. Most
MPs appear more interested in the dubious delights of office
than in speaking their minds. Perhaps this has always been
so, but at least in the past there were more MPs of independent means. Now more and more MPs have had no career
outside Parliament. They have little alternative earning
power, no second career, and often no managerial experience, so becoming one of the Queen's Ministers is their only
real chance of making a mark.

Very few – in fact only two – men in public life, More and
Fisher, were prepared to stand up for their beliefs against
Henry VIII. Sadly very few today are prepared to stand
against the orthodoxy of their own parties. That is why more
and more people are becoming bored, disillusioned and
apathetic about politics. It seems to make no difference. All
the parties seem much the same.

More should not then just be the patron saint of politicians. He should be the patron saint of politicians who are prepared to sacrifice ambition for what they believe in. He is then very much a saint for our time.

In his day, John Fisher was the older of the two martyrs, so our story begins with him. He always suffers by comparison with More as being more austere, a celibate, less witty and less gifted as a writer. But, apart form his obvious holiness and heroic courage, he had great scholarly abilities and played a vital part in the nation's history, both religious and educational, as well as being the only British cardinal to be martyred – so far.

He was born in Beverley, Yorkshire in 1469. His father was a wealthy cloth merchant, who died when he was eight. Fisher was sent to Cambridge at fourteen (then a normal age). Elected a Fellow of Michaelhouse (now Trinity), he was ordained priest in 1491. His progress was so rapid that he had to get a dispensation to be ordained below the normal age. But he excelled as much with people as at study. More would later call him 'a peacemaker ... a man of skill and resourcefulness.' At the age of twenty-five, he was elected university proctor (one of two university administrators).

More meanwhile, had been born in 1478 into similar middle-class comfort as Fisher, his lawyer father ending as a minor judge. By the time of Fisher's appointment as proctor, More, who at thirteen had joined the household of John Morton, the Archbishop of Canterbury, had already completed just two years of study at Canterbury College (later Christ Church), Oxford. He had then been called home by his father. In 1496, about two years after Fisher's appointment as proctor, More entered Lincoln's Inn, being called to the Bar in 1501.

In the same year that More began his legal studies, Fisher was made Master of Michaelhouse. By 1501, Fisher had become Vice-Chancellor of Cambridge University. He had met Lady Margaret Beaufort, the mother of Henry VII and grandmother of Henry VIII. In 1502, Fisher resigned his Mastership and became chaplain to Lady Margaret. In the same year he became the first Lady Margaret Professor of Divinity. There are Lady Margaret professorships to this day at both Oxford and Cambridge. She was a great patron of learning. Under Fisher's guidance, she founded Christ's College at Cambridge, and Fisher later used a bequest of hers to complete St John's there. Among improvements he effected with Lady Margaret's help were the restoration of Greek and Hebrew – essential for the proper study of the Bible; the invitation to Erasmus, the great Dutch humanist scholar and Catholic reformer, to lecture, and the endowment of scholarships.

In 1504, More entered Parliament. His constituency is unknown. For four years, he had lived at the London Charterhouse, trying his vocation as a Carthusian monk. This was – and still is – one of the most austere of all religious Orders. They eat no meat, and their staple diet in More's day was such that More thought they smelled 'like otters'.

More had been wondering whether to join them or the similarly strict Observant Franciscans – one can imagine him as a persuasive wandering preacher – or to become, like Fisher, a diocesan priest. In the end, he realized that God was calling him to marriage, the Bar and politics. But it was from this experiment with the possibility of a religious vocation that his lifelong practice of wearing a hair shirt, daily reciting the Little Office and the use of the 'discipline' or whip of knotted cords on himself dated. Fisher used the same mortifications, which were common for clergy and religious at this period, as for the more devout laity. As Fisher wrote 'Let no one ... say 'I am not in holy orders, I have taken no religious vows.' The least Christian person ... is heir to the kingdom of heaven, brother of Jesus Christ, and bought with his precious blood.'

In 1504 Fisher became both Chancellor of Cambridge and Bishop of Rochester. This was the smallest see in England. By refusing the offer of larger and richer ones, he left himself time for study and for building up a scholarly library which would in time become known as one of the best in Europe.

Those Catholics who today feel smug that whatever our

bishops' occasional faults, at least they are not appointed by the Prime Minister, may be surprised to discover that Fisher was appointed by Henry VIII's father, Henry VII.

As the ageing King faced up to his impending death, he began to think he had 'promoted many a man unadvisedly' and he wanted to 'now make some recompense by promoting some good and virtuous men'. He told his mother Lady Margaret that he wanted to appoint Fisher 'for none other cause than the great and singular virtue that I see in him'. With typical late medieval laxity, Fisher was given a dispensation to be absent from his diocese. He made little use of it. His brother bishops for the most part spent their time, in his words 'attending after triumphs, receiving ambassadors, haunting princes' courts and such like'. Fisher rode about his diocese whatever the weather, visiting and tending to his flock. He showed Christ's mercy in a way that is seldom done now: by being tough in ticking people off for sin. He thought most of the clergy were too soft, using 'all bypaths and circumlocutions in rebuking them. We go nowhere near the matter. And so in the meantime the people perish'. The blunt-spoken Yorkshireman was having none of it. Not if it sent people to hell.

But Fisher combined this severity to sin with outstanding charity to the poor, visiting them in their chimneyless houses, sitting with them in the smoke for hours 'when none of his servants could bear to stay in the house'. And he would back up his spiritual counsel with daily gifts of food sent by his steward.

In the same year, he was elected Chancellor of Cambridge. This was the only thing that did take him away from the diocese. He was re-elected annually for the next decade, attempting to resign in 1514 in favour of the future Cardinal Wolsey (then Bishop of Lincoln). Uncharacteristically, Wolsey turned down the offer. Unprecedentedly, the University then appointed Fisher Chancellor for life.

As for the young More, in 1505, aged about twenty-six, he got married. His bride was one Jane Colt of Netherhall. She was the eldest daughter of a wealthy Essex landowner. More had originally been more attracted to her younger sister, but, according to his son-in-law John Roper 'when he considered that it would be both great grief and some shame also to the eldest to see her youngest sister in marriage preferred before her, he then of a certain pity framed his fancy towards her'. The marriage brought happiness to both. In four years of marriage they had three daughters and a son, then in 1511 Jane died. Only a few weeks after her death, More married again. His second wife was a plain-looking widow, Alice Middleton. She was a seasoned housewife, down-to-earth and a good stepmother for his children.

1505 was also the year that More and Fisher first met. Each was swift to see the other's talents. But their affection was reciprocal too. More wrote to Fisher after staying at Rochester in 1519 when Erasmus was also a guest, asking Fisher to 'continue in your affection for me'. Their mutual friend Erasmus noted that Fisher had 'a delightful gift of language'. He urged him to start studying ancient Greek and Hebrew. The knowledge this gave him of scripture armed him for the dispute over divorce, with its references to the Hebrew texts of Leviticus and Deuteronomy.

From the meeting of the three, Fisher, More and Erasmus, came a meeting of minds and hearts of perhaps the three greatest intellectuals of Christian Europe.

By the time his first wife died in 1511, More had already befriended some of the leaders of the New Learning (Catholic humanism). In addition to Erasmus, there were Linacre, Grocyn and Colet (the founder of St Paul's School). These men were part of a Catholic movement for reform in the Church which recognized the need both for holy living by the clergy and of sound theological training based on study of scripture in the original languages, rather than a reliance on the Latin Vulgate. Fisher himself acknowledged that the Vulgate contained errors. More famously gave his daughters a full academic education, a thing not heard of in the previous generation.

Meanwhile More's reputation both as a barrister and a

man of honesty, brilliance, loyalty to the King and love of his wife, children and friends, was growing. In 1509, the seventeen-year-old Henry VIII became king. He soon promoted More to a range of public offices. In 1510, he became Under-Sheriff of London (legal adviser to the mayor). In 1516 he was sent as envoy to Flanders. In the same year he published, to great international success his best-known work *Utopia* (in Latin), on which more below. Higher offices soon followed: Privy Councillor and Master of Requests (1518), Speaker of the House of Commons (1523–29); High Steward of Oxford University (1524); High Steward of Cambridge University and Chancellor of the Duchy of Lancaster (1525). More became so popular with the King and Queen that he was asked to dine with them every night, which meant he missed out for a time on seeing his family. But somehow he gradually changed his manner, though with utter tact, until the King reduced his calls on his time.

At this point, although there is not space to do justice to such a rich and complex work in this brief chapter, we must address the old chestnut of *Utopia*. Written in the long months of his embassy to Flanders in 1516 to negotiate the terms of treaties regulating the trade in woollen cloth, this book has been the source of much misunderstanding. Readers hungry for a simplistic ideology have underestimated More's irony, humour, playfulness and subtlety.

In his description of an imaginary island, *Utopia* (Greek for 'Not place'), inhabited by pagans of an advanced civilization, More deliberately laid several false trails. A conscious variation on Plato's *Republic*, the island is used as a vehicle for discussing political theories and criticizing contemporary institutions. More's method is a dialogue between himself, Peter Gilles (then town clerk of Antwerp) and his fictional explorer Hythlodaye.

More says he thinks one can adapt philosophy for statesmen. He then produces a profoundly un-utopian – one might even say a High Tory – piece of pragmatic wisdom (in the words from the later sixteenth-century translation):

You must with a crafty wile, and subtle train study and endeavour yourself, as much as in you lieth, to handle the matter wittily and handsomely for the purpose, and that which you cannot turn to good, so order that it be not very bad: for it is not possible for all things to be well, unless all men were good; which I think will not be yet these good many years.

Here is a recognition that political aims must be adaptable to human nature, which in the Catholic as in the traditional Tory understanding is fallen due to original sin.

Other ideas aired in *Utopia* include a form of religious communism; suicide as a form of euthanasia; divorce by consent; opposition to corporal mortification and support for limited religious toleration. One analogy for understanding what More was up to in this work is a hall of mirrors at a funfair: by reflecting back reality in a distorted way, they enable the mind to consider it in a new light. It is an intellectual tease or riddle.

The well-intentioned if misguided virtues of Utopia – of an imaginary heathen society unassisted by faith, Church or sacraments – are used as a rebuke to the corruptions of the Catholic Europe of More's day. The most consistent theme of the book is the need to discourage pride, in Catholic teaching a deadly sin in itself and the root of all sin. More's ultimate conclusion is that the best step towards the achievement of an ideal society is individual personal reform. 'Forgive me father, for I have sinned', not 'I blame the system.'

More said his epitaph should be that as a judge he had been 'relentless towards thieves, murderers and heretics'. The first category of criminal clearly shows that he did not seriously propose the abolition of private property; as for heretics, in pursuing them, he was doing his duty to the King in enforcing what was then the civil law at a time when the Lutheran crisis called for a crackdown. In More's 1531 work *A Dialogue Concerning Heresies*, he equates the duty of princes to counter heresy by law with that of defending their realm from invasion by 'infidels', as 'the peril' resulting from failure to do so involves in both cases 'men's souls withdrawn [from] God, and their goods lost, and their bodies; destroyed by common sedition, insurrection and open war'.

He may have had partly in mind the German Peasants' War, the largest ever uprising of the German masses, which lasted from June 1524 to May 1525. Peasants in Germany, many inspired by Luther and others more radical than he, rose up against their landlords. The 'war' was brutally suppressed by the nobility, urged on by Luther. Some 70,000 mostly unarmed people were killed. Clearly, More did not want such scenes in England.

Whatever one thinks of the sixteenth-century treatment of heresy, in the Western Europe of today we are living with the consequences. Any element of certainty has been knocked away. In More's words from the *Dialogue Concerning Heresies*

> What fruit will the Scriptures bring forth if anyone whatever claims such authority for himself that in understanding them he relies on his own interpretation in opposition to that of everyone else, so that he is influenced by no authority at all not to measure the Scripture according to feeling and fancy?

More also pointed out a fundamental flaw in Luther's teaching: what is the reason for accepting the Scriptures as authoritative? The fact that the Church collated and authorized them as the canon of scripture. As a matter of fact, in his view of the location of authority in the Church, More was less of a papalist than Fisher. Although Roper puts into More's mouth the words that the 'supreme government' [of the Church belonged] 'rightfully ... to the see of Rome, a spiritual pre-eminence by the mouth of Our Saviour himself, personally present upon the earth, only to Saint Peter and his successors ... by special prerogative granted', this is the only such statement on record from More. He appealed rather to general councils of the Church ('or else were there in nothing no certainty'), even believing they had power to depose a pope. Roper was not present at the trial and wrote about twenty years later.

In Fisher's words (in controversy with the Swiss theologian John Oecolamopadius) 'For that see [Rome] will never lack divine assistance in handing down to us the certain truth about doubtful matters, especially matters concerning the faith.' But even Fisher acknowledged the corruption of the contemporary papacy: 'Some may say that nowhere else is the life of Christians more contrary to Christ than in Rome', where the Apostles' successors 'neither fast nor pray, but give themselves up to luxury and lust'. (The pope at the time of Fisher and More's execution, Paul III, had been nicknamed 'cardinal petticoat' as his sister had been one of the many mistresses of the Borgia pope Alexander VI; Paul had had a mistress himself, by whom he had four children, and named two of his grandsons cardinals (aged fourteen and sixteen; in fairness, by 1535 he had long renounced the mistress and instigated a programme of reform.)

Nonetheless, Fisher, like Erasmus, More and other Catholic humanists did share some of the Protestants' goals. They believed in vernacular Bibles – though only those with orthodox Catholic commentaries – being made available in England as they had in most other countries, and in that then rare thing, frequent Communion. Ironically, Luther and Tyndale even agreed with Fisher on the interpretation of the Leviticus text claimed by Henry as a justification for invalidating his marriage to Catherine. ('He who marries his brother's wife does an unlawful thing ... they shall be without children' Leviticus 20:21.). Fisher and these Protestant authorities held that Leviticus referred to a living brother, yet Henry's was dead – and anyway, as Catherine maintained, the marriage had never been consummated.

By contrast with More, Fisher was gentler towards heretics. In the year 1511, Archbishop William Warham burned five. Fisher burned none. Perhaps the example of his holiness and humility had persuaded them to repent. Sometime around 1521 (there is some uncertainty about the exact date), Fisher as Chancellor of Cambridge decided he must excommunicate a student who had anonymously dismissed the papal condemnation of Luther's teaching as 'vanities and lying follies'. But when it came to reading out the sentence in the assembled company of all the students, he broke down in tears and could not continue. He ended by appointing a third day for the sentence, by which time, the guilty party would be excommunicated if he did not confess. In his great commentary – in English – on the Seven Penitential Psalms, he had written: 'No matter how often and how grievously we sin, if at any time we will turn to God in repentance, meekly asking forgiveness, it will not be denied us.' In that work, he had also stressed that none 'can express how joyful the sinner is, when he understands himself to be delivered from the great burden and heaviness of sin'.

In 1528, Fisher told the legates judging Catherine's case that trying to dissolve a valid marriage would set a precedent removing legal protection from all other marriages. If they would consider 'the number and ... enormity of the scandals which will likely flow from this ... they would never attempt [it]'. In our world of casual divorce, we can see that these words were prophetic.

Fisher wrote four highly-regarded volumes against Luther. Ironically, Henry VIII claimed that no other kingdom had such a distinguished prelate. The ambassador of Charles V called him 'a paragon of Christian bishops' for learning and holiness. He was the obvious choice as confessor to Catherine of Aragon, then still Henry's Queen. As a result Fisher was one of her advisers in the nullity suit of 1529. He plainly stated that the marriage was valid, shocking his audience in the papal legate's court by the directness of his language. He declared that, like St John the Baptist, he was ready to die in the cause of marriage, and that 'As it was not so holy at that time as it has now become by the shedding of Christ's blood, he could encourage himself more ardently, more effectually, and with greater confidence to dare any great or extreme peril whatsoever.' The King's furious reaction was expressed in a long Latin address to the legates. Fisher's copy still exists, his annotations in the margins showing cool detachment from the princely wrath.

On 21 June 1529, Henry convened a court to finally dissolve his marriage to Catherine. The bishops were gathered in the presence of Cardinal Campeggio, sent from Rome. Catherine had fallen at Henry's feet and pleaded with him to stay faithful to her. She had then left the room. The King now started to remind the bishops that they had all signed and sealed the document of divorce. Speaking for them Warham, the Archbishop of Canterbury said 'That is truth, if it please your highness. I doubt not but all my brethren here present will affirm the same.' But Fisher severely embarrassed Warham by insisting he had not agreed to sign, in spite of his 'hand and seal' apparently being on the document. The King's response seemed reasonable enough; no doubt it masked deep-seated anger:

'Well, well, it shall make no matter; we will not stand with you in argument herein, for you are but one man.'

This phrase 'You are but one man' should ring down the ages in honour of Fisher.

The cause was now referred to Rome, so Fisher's official involvement was finished. But the King never forgave him. In November of that year, the Long Parliament began a series of attacks on the Church's authority. From the Lords, Fisher warned Parliament that such acts could only lead to the end of the Church in England. He advised the King's chief opponent in the Commons, Sir George Throckmorton, not to speak against the encroachments on clerical freedom unless there was a real chance of checking them. Thus, he diverted the King's wrath towards himself, quite possibly saving Throckmorton's life. The Commons complained, through the Speaker, that Fisher had shown disrespect for Parliament. It is likely this complaint was made at the King's instigation. Henry summoned Fisher for an explanation. Fisher gave it and Henry accepted it. He left it to the Commons to declare it insufficient, making himself look magnanimous.

On 25 October 1529, replacing Cardinal Wolsey, who had been sacked for his failure to achieve a divorce, More attained the highest office in the land, becoming Lord Chancellor. It was most unusual for a layman to get the job. In that office, he was famous not only for a rare incorruptibility but also a promptness in dealing with cases that saw a seven-year backlog cleared within two. From now until his resignation in 1532, it was part of his duty to wage legal war on heresy and its dissemination. He did so with a zeal inspired by his own loathing. Later in the Tower he was to write:

> [One should] leave the desire of punishing unto God and unto such other folk as are so grounded in charity, and so fast cleave to God, that no secret ... cruel affection, under the cloak of a just and a virtuous zeal, can creep in and undermine them.

In 1530 continued legal moves against the Church led Fisher, with the Bishops of Bath and Ely, to appeal to Rome. The King at once forbade such appeals and arrested the bishops, but held them only for a few months. In February of 1531 the Convocation of the Clergy met. They were now forced to pay £100,000 – a sum equivalent to over £35 million today – to buy the King's pardon for having recognized Wolsey's authority as papal legate. When they tried to barter, the King insisted they recognize him as 'Supreme Head of the Church in England'. At Fisher's insistence the phrase 'so far as the law of Christ allows' was added to the Act. With this amendment More was persuaded not to resign his chancellorship but to accept the Act. Speaking against the royal supremacy, Fisher said that accepting it would be to 'renounce the unity of the Christian world, and so leap out of Peter's ship, to be drowned in the waves of all heresies, sects, schisms and divisions'. The King's men threatened to drown him and his supporters in the waves of the Thames.

Literally sickened by the weakness of the Church's stand, Fisher became ill. There was an attempt to poison him. It killed two of his servants and some poor people living on his charity. His fasting saved him. Then a would-be assassin fired a light cannon from the home of Anne Boleyn's father across the Thames at Fisher's study in Lambeth; he missed. Fisher went back to Rochester. He was not invited back to Parliament the following spring.

It was then that the King demanded that 'annates', a tax formerly paid to the Pope, should be paid to him. He also declared that henceforth Convocation be summoned only at his pleasure and discuss only matters he approved.

On 10 May 1532 Archbishop Warham, with two other bishops and four abbots, signed the 'Submission of the Clergy'. It was completed on 15 May. Within hours, More returned the great seal of England, the symbol of his office as Chancellor. He knew this was the death in England of the Church's freedom. Fisher was now placed under house arrest at Lambeth. A year later the new Archbishop Cranmer, 'annulled' the marriage to Catherine and 'validated' that to Anne. Henry married the pregnant Anne Boleyn. More boycotted the coronation. Fisher was freed again.

Now in the most controversial act of his life, he appealed to Catherine's nephew, the Emperor Charles V, to overcome Henry by military force, saying such work 'must be as pleasing in the eyes of God as war upon the Turk'. But Charles was too busy with exactly that. Technically, this would make Fisher a traitor to Henry; but just as More told his judges that no Christian king could make a law such as that which had condemned him, so the King had forfeited his right to loyalty by his tyrannous treason against the Church. But for Fisher, the case was worse than that: schism meant the likely damnation of thousands of souls cut off from the Church. Catherine thought differently. She said she would 'consider herself damned eternally were she to consent to anything that might provoke war'. But Charles was far from happy about events in England. He wrote secretly to More suggesting he leave England to become first Minister of Charles's Holy Roman Empire.

Early in 1534, Parliament made itself the judge of marital

disputes. It declared the marriage to Catherine unlawful and said that anyone who maliciously wrote against the 'lawful matrimony' between Henry and Anne Boleyn was a traitor. An oath was required of people to the Act – including rejecting papal authority. 'To great wailing and lamentation' Fisher rode through Rochester. His fellow humanist, Cuthbert Tunstall, Bishop of London (later Durham) had taken the oath. Catherine had chosen Tunstall as an adviser. He had even been excluded from Parliament for leading the York Convocation in a protest against the royal supremacy. He had written to the King the year before reminding him that he had once fought France because Louis XII had 'assisted and nourished schism' – as Henry was now doing. But in 1534 he was threatened by the King, and finally cracked. By 1535, he was one of those who tried to persuade Fisher to take the oath.

In 1534 Parliament also made it treason to 'maliciously wish, will or desire' to deprive the King of any of his titles. This was thought-crime. It was the first time the law had been applied to such intangibles.

In February 1534 More and Fisher were both named in the attainder for treason of the so-called 'Nun of Kent', a young woman called Elizabeth Barton. She had claimed to have seen in divinely-inspired visions that if the King persisted with his divorce, he would lose his kingdom and die a villain's death. Here More used his legal skills to wriggle out of the death-trap. But Fisher had accepted Barton's statements as genuine. Now he was being interrogated about them. Condemned to perpetual imprisonment and loss of property, he was at first only fined, due to poor health.

On 13 April, before a royal commission, More refused the oath required by the Act of Succession. He was imprisoned for a few days. By 17 April he was in the Tower. He was to be kept there for fifteen months. As he well knew, he had effectively signed his own death warrant .

For More, as well as being the final spiritual training for martyrdom, this period was also fruitful for his writing. Among other things, he produced *The Sadness of Christ*, a

Latin meditation on the Gospel accounts of Jesus in the Garden of Gethsemane. He was encouraged to find that 'the very prototype and leader of martyrs ... should be so terrified at the approach of pain, so shaken, so downcast'. In the sleeping disciples he saw the bishops of his own time, saying 'Why do not bishops contemplate in this scene their own somnolence?' The book was never finished, as the warders came to take More to the block just as he was writing about Jesus' arrest.

Many attempts were made to persuade More to bow to the King's will while he was in prison. As a traitor, all his lands and property were forfeit and his family was plunged into poverty. His favourite child, Margaret, pleaded with him to take the oath, saying she had taken it herself. He laughingly compared her to Eve offering Adam the apple.

The King's councillors tried lying to More and Fisher, telling each that the other had taken the oath. More answered he would never pin his soul to any man's back 'not even the best man living, for I know not where he may hap to carry it'. Fisher was not caught by this either. Strictly kept apart, the two old friends managed through their servants to send things to each other's cells. More sent Fisher oranges; Fisher sent More half a custard. Then they started to send messages. Fisher pointed to the term 'maliciously', saying that 'therefore a man who spoke nothing of malice did not offend the statute'. More's down-to-earth reply makes Fisher seem naive: 'it would not be so interpreted'. He advised Fisher to give different answers from his own 'lest the council should suspect confederacy'.

In his cell, Fisher wrote to Cromwell, he was suffering from the cold, as his only clothes were 'shamefully ragged and torn'. He also asked for devotional books and a priest for confession. Both were refused. Bishops were sent to him to try to change his mind. Aged sixty-five but looking twenty years older, he was cold and hungry, ill, humiliated, in solitary confinement and without sacramental consolation.

At the start of 1535, his health broke down. The King ordered that a friend be allowed to give him food and wine.

This was one Antonio Bonvisi; he had persuaded More of the papal primacy, as opposed to that of councils alone. On 7 May, Sir Richard Rich asked Fisher to give his opinion on the Act of Supremacy. He was told this would help the King's conscience. In return he was promised by Henry 'on his honour and the word of a prince' not to harm him. Fisher was taken in. 'I am bound by the law of God' he had written 'to believe the best of every person until the contrary is proved.' So he simply stated that Henry 'was not, and could not be, by the law of God, supreme head of the Church'. Both he and More would have agreed to the succession of Anne Boleyn's issue (Elizabeth I); what they balked at was the supremacy over the Church. Yet the Act required assent to both.

In May 1535 the new pope, Paul III, thinking to save Fisher's life, created him a cardinal. All it did was to hasten his death. Henry forbade the cardinal's hat to be brought to England, saying 'Well, let the pope send him a hat when he will. But I will so provide that, whensoever it cometh, he shall wear it on his shoulders, for head he shall have none to set it on.' He then sent members of the Privy Council to the Tower to try to get Fisher and More to swear to the Act of Supremacy, on pain of execution for treason. He also had sermons preached against them, wrote Chapuys, the imperial ambassador, in 'most of the churches'.

On 17 June Fisher was arraigned for treason in Westminster Hall, for denying the King to be head of the Church. Derived of his bishopric, he was treated as a commoner and tried by jury, rather than by the Lords. He was sentenced to be hanged, drawn and quartered at Tyburn, but this was commuted to beheading on Tower Hill.

As the Commons had insisted on the insertion of the word 'maliciously', Fisher clung to that: 'Perceive plainly that there was no manner of malice in me at all, and so I committed no treason.' As More had predicted, this defence proved futile.

Cromwell accused More of the same 'malice'.

'Not so, Master Secretary . . . I think none harm, I say none harm, I do none harm, and if this be not enough to keep a man alive, in good faith I long not to live.'

On 22 June, five days after his trial, at about five o'clock in the morning, the Lieutenant of the Tower, Sir Edmund Walsingham, came to Fisher's cell to tell him that he would be executed at about ten o'clock. Fisher asked to be allowed some time to sleep, as he had slept poorly due to illness. At nine, Walsingham returned. Fisher was dressing. He asked Walsingham to pass him his fur tippet 'to put about my neck'.

'What need you now be so careful of your health? Your time is short – little more than half an hour.'

'I think none otherwise, but I pray you, yet give me leave to put on my ... tippet, to keep me warm for the while until the very time of execution ... [I will] not hinder my health in the mean time not a minute of an hour.' It is not quite up to More's level of wit, but shows a gentle and laconic sense of humour in the face of impending death.

As does the following incident: a moment before leaving the Tower, the Cardinal's guards halted. Praying for guidance before he opened his New Testament at random, Fisher found: 'Now this is eternal life: that they may know you, the only true God, and Jesus Christ, whom you have sent' (John 17:3).

'Here is even learning enough for me to my life's end.'

Mounting the scaffold unaided in spite of his obvious frailty, Fisher said in a voice 'plain, strong and loud' that he was dying for the faith of Christ's Catholic Church. 'And I pray God save the king and the realm, and hold his holy hand over it.' He asked the people to pray for him, recited the *Te Deum* and a psalm. He then pardoned the axeman.

At sixty-six, but looking much older and often sickly, he had endured ten months' imprisonment in the inhospitable Tower.

For three days afterwards they left his headless body, stripped naked, on the block, burying it at the King's orders without rites or shroud. His head was stuck on a spike on London Bridge alongside those of the Carthusian martyrs who had suffered two months earlier. More had seen them being dragged to execution on hurdles and said to his daughter Margaret 'Do you not see that these blessed fathers be now as cheerfully going to their deaths as bridegrooms to their marriage?' People, it was said, marvelled that Fisher's head stayed 'very fresh and lively'. That was not supposed to happen. Traitors' heads were meant to rot. After a fortnight, it was thrown in the Thames.

On 1 July 1535 More, weakened by imprisonment without warm clothes or bedding and with probable pneumonia, was tried in Westminster Hall. When the Lord Chancellor reminded More that the universities, the bishops and all the most scholarly men in the kingdom had agreed to the Act of Supremacy, he said:

> I nothing doubt but that, though not in this realm, yet in Christendom about, of these well learned Bishops and virtuous men that are yet alive, they be not the fewer part that are of my mind therein. But if I should speak of those that are already dead, of whom many be now Holy Saints in heaven, I am very sure it is the far greater part of them that, all the while they lived, thought in this case that way I think now.

Like Fisher, More was condemned to the usual traitor's death. Henry extended the 'king's mercy' to both, commuting the sentence to beheading, wringing from More the bitter joke 'God forbid the king's mercy should befall any of my friends.' More also said he hoped that he and his judges might 'hereafter in heaven all meet merrily together, to our everlasting salvation'.

He asked in a prayer written after his death sentence 'specially to rejoice in the presence of Thy very blessed body, sweet Saviour Christ, in the holy sacrament of the altar'. Like Fisher, he must have felt the deprivation of the sacrament most keenly. This was a deliberate spiritual torture by the Government to add to the physical privations of the cold Tower cells. Fisher had written that at Mass 'the whole person is enraptured' and an early biographer wrote of him that as he was saying it 'many times the tears would fall from his cheeks'. The day before his execution, More wrote a last letter to his daughter Margaret, in which he said

> [I] would be sorry, if it should be any longer than tomorrow,
> for it is Saint Thomas' even [the vigil of St Thomas a Beckett]
> and the Vtas [octave] of Saint Peter and therefore tomorrow
> long I to go to God, it were a day very meet and convenient
> for me. I never liked your manner better than when you
> kissed me last for I love when daughterly love and dear
> charity hath not leisure to look to worldly courtesy. Fare well
> my dear child and pray for me, and I shall for you and all your
> friends, that we may merrily meet in heaven.

Fisher had said when asked why he had slipped away from
his guests at a Christmas party he was hosting in 1531 or
1532 'I have other things to do than cheer my guests ... for I
tell you in secret, I know I shall not die in my bed.' Here is a
contrast to More's sanguine temperament. One cannot
imagine More ducking out of a Christmas party; but Fisher
had upon his shoulders the weight of apostolic care for
Christ's flock.

On 6 July 1535, in the morning, More was beheaded. To
the Lieutenant of the Tower, while mounting the scaffold he
joked: ' ... see me safe up; and for my coming down let me
shift for myself'. As he pulled his beard away from the block
he said: '*This* hath not offended the king.'

The King had asked him to be succinct on the scaffold. He
obeyed this last command. He asked the people's prayers.
His last words: that he died in and for the faith of the Holy
Catholic Church. 'Afterwards he exhorted them and
earnestly beseeched them to pray God for the king, so that
He would give him good counsel, protesting that he died his
good servant, but God's first.'

More had said in his defence 'If there were no other but
my self upon my side, and the whole Parlement upon the
other, I would be sore afraid', but 'I am not bounden to
change my conscience and conform to the council of our
realm against the general council of Christendom.' It is for
that 'general council', under the pope – as against the
narrow assertion of a national church originating from a

tyrant's dynastic ambition for a male heir and his passion for his mistress, its theology a mish-mash of Luther, Calvin and others, its visible head a secular monarch – that More and Fisher died.

This concept of the 'general council of Christendom' – and part of its geographical reality – was broken by Henry's schism. In losing touch with it, England lost not only the source of its culture and civilization for the previous nine and half centuries (if one dates the establishment of Catholicism from St Augustine's mission in 597) but also its living links with the beautiful unity and hierarchies of European Catholic culture, 'trampling underfoot' in the later martyr St Edmund Campion's words (about Lutherans) 'Church, Councils, Episcopal Sees, Fathers, Martyrs, Potentates, Peoples, Laws, Universities, Histories, all vestiges of Antiquity and Sanctity'.

In dying for this culture unified under the papacy, Fisher and More could, in the broadest sense, be thought of as 'conservatives' in contradistinction to the Protestant 'reformers'. The latter were in fact revolutionaries in their attitude to religion as unlike More's and Fisher's friend Erasmus they were not content with reforming the Church's corruptions, but rejected many of its principles to found completely new institutions.

That great Anglican Tory Dr Johnson called More 'the person of the greatest virtue these islands ever produced' – which may seem a little unfair on Fisher.

It is ironic that More ended by dying for papal supremacy, as in life, perhaps partly from living in an age of notoriously corrupt popes, he had placed much more stress on the authority of general councils of the Church. 'sith all Christendom is one corps [sic], I cannot perceive how any member thereof may without the common assent of the body depart from the common head.' He had even advised the King to tone down his praise of the papacy in his 'Defence of the Seven Sacraments' lest at some future time he might find himself in a quarrel with the Pope. But in the end, Henry's obstinacy had forced the issue.

Entertaining and dramatic as is the well-known film *A Man for All Seasons*, one should be careful not to accept as authentic the lines Robert Bolt gives More: 'What matters to me is not whether the Pope's supremacy is true, but that I believe it to be true, or rather not that I believe it, but that *I* believe it.' That is the opposite of what More, and Fisher, believed. They died for the objective Truth, divinely revealed, living and organic; the Truth unified, interpreted and safeguarded by the one true Church, not for some peculiar assertion of self-righteous egotism. The etymological root of the word 'heretic' is 'one who chooses'; they did not choose those parts of the truth which happened to appeal; they wanted the whole truth, the catholic and, hence, the Catholic Truth.

Chapter 4

Cardinal Reginald Pole

Lucy Beckett

On 7 January 1546 Cardinal Pole, one of the three presiding papal legates, opened the first substantive session of the much delayed Council of the Church at Trent with a remarkable address. He appealed to the assembled cardinals, archbishops and bishops to examine their consciences, to acknowledge their guilt for the condition of the Church, and in penitence to pray for the assistance of the Holy Spirit. He also warned them to place their duty and obedience to God always before their duty and obedience to the princes of the realms from which they came, and begged them to avoid contention among themselves and to deal with others with gentleness and mercy. The address was greeted with stunned silence. Then Cardinal Del Monte, the senior legate, rose to his feet and began the *Veni Creator Spiritus*; everyone stood and joined in.

It was a high point in the complicated, disappointed life of a man who four years later missed being elected pope by a single vote, and who was by many in England thought of for decades as the most suitable husband for Mary Tudor, daughter of Henry VIII and Catherine of Aragon, a marriage which would have made him effectively King of England.

By the time of his address to the Council, Pole had suffered deep and bitter personal experience of all the ills he hoped the Council would deal with and all the hindrances to the healing of the Church which he implored them to avoid. He knew what he was talking about and had thought long and hard about what he knew.

Reginald Pole was born in 1500, the third and much the most gifted son of Sir Richard Pole, a loyal Tudor gentleman working for Henry VII in the Welsh borders, and his wife Margaret Plantagenet, daughter of 'false, fleeting, perjur'd Clarence', murdered brother of Edward IV and Richard III. The adjectives, put by Shakespeare into Clarence's own mouth in *Richard III*, have an anti-Yorkist Tudor flavour which pervades the play and was still politically correct in the reign of Elizabeth, daughter of Henry VIII and Anne Boleyn, when it was written. The few descendants of Richard, Duke of York who survived Henry VII's seizure of the crown in 1485 were the only serious rivals to the Tudors after the family bloodbath among the grandchildren and great-grandchildren of Edward III known as the Wars of the Roses. The Yorkists' claim to the throne was stronger than the Tudors'. Margaret Pole's brother, Edward, Earl of Warwick, imprisoned since he was a child of eight, was killed, aged twenty-four, on the orders of Henry VII in 1499, an innocent victim of dynastic fear. Although after Margaret Pole was widowed in 1505, Henry VII treated her kindly, and Henry VIII allowed her to become the closest English companion of his wife Catherine of Aragon and eventually the governess of his daughter Mary, Edward's murder in the interests of Tudor security on the throne was by no means the last in Margaret Pole's family.

Life began promisingly for the young Reginald, dedicated to the service of God by his devout mother and educated long and well at Henry VIII's expense. Taught as a child at the Charterhouse at Sheen, and probably for a time by Benedictine monks in Canterbury, Pole was at Magdalen College, Oxford, for eight years from the age of thirteen and was tutored in the Latin and Greek of up-to-the-minute classical scholarship by Linacre and William Latimer. This was the brief heyday of the Renaissance in England, learned, pious and full of hope for a civilized future. Thomas More, a family friend, writing his *History of King Richard III* while Pole was at Oxford, looked back to 'the common custom of close and covert dealing' of the dynastic wars now, he thought, safely over. More's *Utopia* and Erasmus's annotated edition of the New Testament, the first Greek text to be printed, were published in the year Pole was sixteen. When he was twenty-one, with the King's approval and generous support, he went to Italy, and spent six years studying in the university at Padua, then at the peak of its fame. He impressed his tutors. Both the famous scholar Leonicus, who taught him philosophy from the Greek texts of Plato and Aristotle, and Pietro Bembo, doyen of Italian Ciceronians, wrote to friends praising Pole's kindness and courtesy as well as his intellectual gifts and diligence. 'Possibly the most virtuous, learned and grave young man in the whole of Italy today', Bembo called him. Padua is twenty miles from Venice where, with a group of fellow-students and mentors, some to be friends for the rest of his life, he spent holidays reading and talking in the city where Giorgione and Giovanni Bellini had recently died, where Titian was approaching his prime, and where the family of the printer Aldus Manutius were turning out the great series of Aldine classical texts for the use of all Christendom. Pole began to collect variant readings for an edition of Cicero's works.

But by the mid-1520s two quite separate clouds, at first small but soon sinister, had appeared in the sunny sky that had so far shone over this fortunate young man. In 1517 Luther had posted on the door of a Wittenberg church the theses that, like pebbles thrown on a mountainside, started the avalanche of the Reformation in a Europe glittering with the largesse of the corrupt Renaissance papacy and with the exhibitionist rivalry of the young rulers Francis I of France, Henry VIII of England and the Habsburg Emperor Charles V. Many of those privileged by birth and education who were born at the turn of the sixteenth century must have looked back across the ravages of the Reformation, as four hundred years later another generation looked back across the First World War, to a childhood or youth golden in its confidence and never to return. Meanwhile in England Henry VIII, Pole's revered cousin and benefactor, had begun to cast about for a reason that would justify replacing Catherine of Aragon, his wife of nearly twenty years whose many pregnancies had failed to produce a living male heir, with the bewitching Anne Boleyn who was refusing to be merely his mistress and would surely give him a legitimate son if he married her. Both the Reformation and Henry VIII's 'great matter' affected the whole of the rest of Pole's life in a number of ways, most of them painful and all of them isolating since he knew no one – and indeed there was no one – similarly exposed to what became the cruel demands of both.

The first demand came from the King. Pole owed Henry everything – the sense among the Yorkists that they were alive in Tudor England only on sufferance soon turned out to be entirely sound – and not long after his return to England from Italy in 1527 he discovered that some repayment was expected. For two years he lived in the house Dean Colet had built in the garden of the Sheen Charterhouse, studying theology and staying as far as he could out of the plots and policy-making at Court. Cardinal Wolsey was governing England for the King, and failing to deliver the divorce that had become Henry's overriding objective. Wolsey's cleverest protégé, Thomas Cromwell, was learning from his master's failure as from his successes the necessity of providing Henry with what he wanted: a training in politics which eventually gave Cromwell power in the land almost equal to the power Wolsey had lost before his death. Pole later wrote of a meeting during this period between himself and Cromwell – the details may be emblematic but the truth revealed is undeniable – in the course of which he discovered Cromwell's project for achieving and keeping power, Wolsey being the model and Machiavelli the theorist: give the King what he wants while maintaining the appearance of virtue; the King's will constitutes the law and it is not to be judged or limited by any law of God or the Church. Pole's allegiance was to actual virtue, to the King's honour as an absolute priority over the King's will. Nearly ten years of bitter experience of the consequences of sticking to his principles as against Cromwell's lay between this meeting, if it really took place, and Pole's account of it, and no doubt sharply clarified the story.

It became impossible for him to steer clear of 'the king's great matter'. Studying in Paris in 1530, Pole was commanded to elicit, with bribes, from the canon lawyers and theologians of the Sorbonne the verdict that Henry's marriage to Catherine was sinful (therefore cursed, Henry now firmly believed, with sonlessness) on account of Catherine's childhood marriage to Henry's elder brother, which the Queen swore to her dying day had never been consummated. Pole did what was asked of him, but when he returned to England he found Henry offering him the Archbishopric of York, held for years by the disgraced and recently dead Wolsey (who had never set foot in the archdiocese). The condition attached to this offer was explicit: public support for the divorce. Instead of agreeing Pole allowed himself to express his disapproval; Henry was so furious that Pole was afraid the King might kill him. A few months later Pole's private letter to the King explaining his reasons for hoping that the King would accede to the Pope's decision against the divorce so impressed Cranmer, still only an academic and an archdeacon, that he recommended it should never be made public. Pole's reasons did not include a warning against breaking the unity of the Church to make the divorce possible: no one had yet thought of this. They soon did.

Within three years of the scene between Pole and the King, Anne Boleyn's pregnancy had prompted Henry to marry her, at first bigamously; Acts of Parliament organized and pushed through by Cromwell had declared the absolute sovereignty of the English crown over the English Church, abrogating papal authority in the realm; and Cranmer, though confirmed as Archbishop of Canterbury by the Pope, had declared in a hole-in-corner court of his own Henry's marriage to Catherine null and void, and had anointed and crowned Anne Boleyn, five months pregnant, as Queen of England. The child for whose legitimacy all this had been done was born in September 1533, and was a girl. By then

Pole, with Henry's permission, had been back in Italy for eighteen months.

He was living abroad – he did not return to England for over twenty years – and was becoming more and more occupied with the study of theology and of the condition of the whole Church, and more and more involved in the work for its reform being prepared by a group of like-minded clerics and scholars, some of whom were becoming his close friends. The pressure from home, however, grew fiercer. Finding there was some opposition to the Acts of Parliament which by 1534 had declared Henry VIII head on earth of the English Church and the Pope a foreign bishop, Cranmer, Cromwell and the King were browbeating with a compulsory oath of submission the very few who clearly understood what was happening. Sir Thomas More, Bishop Fisher and a handful of monks and priests were imprisoned. The new pope, Paul III, intending to encourage the opposition to Henry, made Fisher a cardinal in 1535: Henry's response was the execution of Fisher, More and the Carthusian priors who agreed with their resistance. This bloody assault on the world of learning, monastic peace, loyalty to the Church and to Queen Catherine in which Pole had grown up only stiffened his resolve far away in Rome to hold firm to the orthodox belief in the Church united under the Pope that was stronger in him by the year. Asked by a Padua friend who was now an agent of Cromwell's to write in support of the royal supremacy, Pole instead wrote a treatise, *On the Unity of the Church*, in which his real fear for Henry's soul and for the English Church cut off from papal authority became clearer and clearer as he wrote. And he wrote despite pleas for him to change his mind reaching him from his mother and his elder brother, and in full knowledge that if his appeal to Henry's conscience failed the danger threatening his family, hostages to royal vengeance in England, would greatly increase. (Henry's conscience was by now beyond appeal: in this same year he charged Anne Boleyn with adultery and incest, her evident offence being only her failure to produce a son; he had her executed and replaced her with Jane Seymour eleven days later.)

The Pilgrimage of Grace was a muddled, naive northern revolt against the break with Rome and the despoiling of the English Church by Henry and Cromwell, now appointed 'Vicegerent' to wield the King's absolute authority in religious affairs. The rising produced an unseizable opportunity for Pole to rescue England from apostate tyranny. Despatched by the Pope to assist the rebellion but without an army or money to find one, Pole was given no help by either Francis I or Charles V and had to return to Rome having achieved nothing but the stoking of Henry's rage at what could readily be seen as open treason. Now constantly observed by Cromwell's spies and pursued by assassins – there was a price of 100,000 gold English crowns on his head – he accepted the office of cardinal from Paul III. For Henry this was the last straw. In 1538 Pole's weak younger brother was bullied into providing false evidence against their elder brother, Lord Montague, and cousin, Lord Exeter, easy enough to achieve under the 1534 Treason Act which made mere verbal denial of the King's supremacy punishable by death. Exeter and Montague were executed and Pole's mother, on no evidence at all, was attainted and imprisoned in the Tower. In the same year Henry ordered the destruction of the shrine in Canterbury Cathedral of St Thomas Becket, another exile who had defended the authority of the Church against an English king, and had its greatest treasure, a ruby given by Louis VII of France, made into a thumb ring for himself.

By this time Henry VIII was hated and feared by many of his subjects. Had Pole been more of a politician and more of a man of action he might, in 1537, or 1539 when Charles V and Francis I were briefly at one and England began preparing for an invasion, have swept into the country, displaced the unpopular King and married Mary, the heir to the throne. But he was no Henry Tudor, no Henry Bolingbroke. He failed to persuade either foreign power that an English crusade was worth bothering with and again settled in Italy with his friends to the work of planning the extirpation from the whole Church of the abuses which had made possible the Renaissance papacy, careers such as Wolsey's, and the avalanche of defections which crashed down from Luther's pebbles.

This greater cause concerned England, as yet, scarcely at all: Henry VIII was a schismatic engaged in the destruction of every monastery in his country, but he was not a heretic, and the English Church at the start of the Reformation had been in better order than most. But by the 1530s the greatest crisis in its history was everywhere threatening to tear apart the Latin Church. Honest and intelligent bishops and cardinals had realized for years that a General Council had to be called both to deal with the widespread abuses it had been only too easy for the Lutherans to attack, and to reiterate and consolidate orthodox doctrine so as to define as heresy the theological errors of the Protestants. Over and over again the summoning of the Council was delayed, by imperial politics, by nervous popes, by vested interests in corruption.

Paul III, clever and patient, was in some ways an unregenerate pope – he made two of his teenage grandsons cardinals – but he could nevertheless see the necessity of a Council. He appointed a group of cardinals, including Pole, Pole's admired friend Gasparo Contarini, Venetian patrician and diplomat, and the fierce, austere Giampetro Carafa, to prepare a programme for reform. In 1537 they produced a substantial *Advice on what is to be amended in the Church*, a thorough and sensible, entirely untheological document which so alarmed reactionaries in the Curia that it was shelved rather than published as a papal bull, and was later put on the *Index of Forbidden Books*. Meanwhile theology, the driving force of what was positive rather than negative in the Reformation, was more and more preoccupying Contarini, Pole and a group of Pole's friends gathered round him in Venice and then in the peaceful city of Viterbo, to which in 1541 the Pope appointed him as governor of the Patrimonium Petri.

They took the trouble to find out and to understand what

it was that had struck Luther so forcibly as to transform him from a crotchety late-scholastic monk into a prophet of personal conversion for hundreds of thousands of Christians. They discovered that at the centre of Luther's theology was a grateful realization that it is the goodness of God rather than the goodness of human beings which saves: this realization, orthodox in the writing of St Paul and St Augustine, was flying round Europe under the label 'justification by faith alone' and had become, because of the rest of what Luther had said and done which had destroyed the unity of the Church, regarded by most Catholics as evidently heretical. Pole and his friends found that they could not deny to this belief the truth of experience understood with the help of the New Testament. In 1511, before anyone had heard of Luther, Contarini, nearly twenty years Pole's senior, had undergone a conversion moment of this kind, while Pole, seared in the fire of Henry VIII's hatred, had, without the scholastic training of the universities, studied the Bible and Augustine long and hard in a Venetian and Benedictine spirit and come to the unrevolutionary conclusion that there is indeed nothing we can do to earn the grace of God, freely given to us for our salvation.

In 1541 a theological colloquy between Catholic and Protestant theologians at Regensburg actually agreed on a complicated formula describing justification which satisfied both sides: the papal legate was Contarini. This was the last moment of hope for those, Charles V among them, who believed it possible to reunite the broken Church. But after much further discussion agreement turned out to be impossible on what each side took to be the consequences of grace given by God: two irreconcilable notions of the Church, its sacraments and above all its teaching authority. And then both Paul III, with Carafa beside him in Rome, and Luther rejected the justification formula.

This was a dreadful year for Pole. Henry VIII had Pole's mother, nearly seventy, executed in the Tower. Contarini, loved and revered by Pole for years, reproached him for not supporting the Regensburg formula strongly enough in

Rome and then, in the summer of 1542, died. Vittoria
Colonna, a friend and mother-figure to Pole in Viterbo, and a
great Renaissance lady, said that Contarini's death hit Pole
harder than any other loss. In the same summer two prominent members of his Viterbo circle, Pietro Martire Vermigli
and Bernardino Ochino, defected to Switzerland (and
became famous Protestant preachers), and Cardinal Carafa
set up the Roman Inquisition with the express purpose of
rooting all traces of heresy out of the Catholic Church. One
of the first books he proscribed was the *Beneficio di Cristo*,
a powerful and briefly very popular work on grace by a
Benedictine monk, revised in a near-Calvinist spirit by Pole's
friend, the poet Marcantonio Flaminio. In Viterbo Pole had
pulled Flaminio back from the brink of Protestantism. But
from now until the end of his life Pole was regarded as a
heretic by Carafa and his rigorous, unimaginative party in
the Curia, and as a coward and hypocrite by the Protestant
theologians of Europe.

Pole and the few who thought as he did were certain that
it was possible both to believe in the incapacity of fallible
human beings to earn salvation and to believe in the inde-
fectible teaching authority of the Church and in the efficacy
of its sacraments. The authority of tradition, the orthodox
interpretation of Scripture, was as necessary to the Christian
as Scripture itself. (The Lutherans had in practice soon
found that, having abandoned the authority of the Pope,
they needed the authority of the secular state to hold their
churches together: one man and his Bible can call almost
anything Christianity.) To believe both these things at once
seemed to Contarini and Pole not only possible but central
to Christian life as described by Paul, Augustine, Bernard,
and the whole non-scholastic theological tradition. Pole
called it the *via media*, the middle way, but he and his
friends lived and thought at a moment of rapidly hardening
extremes and soon saw the middle way almost crushed out
of existence by over-simplification.

Erasmus as early as 1523 had written: 'I have said that *all*
of Luther's teaching cannot be suppressed without

suppressing the gospel' and a year later, to Melanchthon, Luther's calmer lieutenant, 'I would have had religion purified without destroying authority.' Had the Council eventually convened at Trent been called twenty years earlier, theological and disciplinary reconciliation might have obviated the lasting division of the Church. When the Council did begin (partly because Charles V had promised Parma and Piacenza as fiefs to Paul III's disreputable son), Pole's Erasmian perception that there was orthodoxy as well as heresy in Luther had missed its moment. The Council as its first major theological achievement produced a decree on justification which had as little rather than as much in common with Protestantism as could be managed. Similarly, a decree recommending the study of Scripture unmediated by patristic commentary was rejected only because the Protestants wanted Christians to read the Bible. Pole left Trent after six months, ill from disappointment, but accepting without criticism and for the rest of his life everything the Council decided. As his friend Cardinal Seripando, Master of the Augustinians, said of Pole at Trent: 'Nothing is more characteristic of him than silence.'

His obedience, and the continuing favour of Charles V, made him a strong candidate for the papacy in the ten-week conclave following Paul III's death in 1549. He missed election by one vote, refused to accept appointment by acclamation, and bore with his usual outward calm the disappearance of his chances with the arrival of the French, led by Cardinal de Guise aged twenty-three. Carafa's suggestion that Pole's orthodoxy was questionable seems not to have affected the outcome.

In England Edward VI, the son Henry VIII had done so much damage to produce, died at the age of fifteen in 1553, having nominally presided for six years over a rapid Protestant reformation organized by Cranmer. He was succeeded, after the nine days' flurry of an attempted coup by Protestant nobles, by his half-sister Mary, now aged thirty-seven. Pole's return home, and the reconciliation of England to the Catholic Church, were delayed for more than a year by Charles V's determination to marry the Queen to his son Philip, King of Spain, in aid of a Habsburg encirclement of France, and by the emperor's knowledge that Mary and very likely her people would prefer her to marry Pole, still not ordained priest. When the cardinal at last arrived in England as papal legate, he and Mary had only four years of life ahead of them: they died on the same day, the feast of St Hugh of Lincoln, in November 1558.

The four years started gently and well. Addressing Mary, Philip and both houses of parliament on 28 November 1554, Pole said: 'I come not to destroy, but to build; I come to reconcile, not to condemn . . . For touching all matters that be past, they shall be as things cast into the sea of forgetfulness.' There was no attempt to retrieve the property of the monasteries from its new owners. A few monasteries, including Westminster Abbey and Pole's beloved Sheen Charterhouse, were restored with communities of former monks. Pole, not ordained and consecrated as Archbishop of Canterbury until immediately after Cranmer's death in March 1556, inaugurated a Catholic programme of reform of the English Church: non-residence and the holding of many benefices by one man to cease; every priest and bishop to set a moral example, to study the Scriptures, to help the poor; every diocese to have a seminary; preaching to be improved; a new (not Protestant) English translation of the Bible to be undertaken; triennial episcopal visitation of every parish. These measures set the pattern for great Catholic leaders of the next generation, notably St Charles Borromeo in Milan and St Philip Neri in Rome. In England there was no time for them to come to fruition.

Meanwhile, as Pole, failing in health, worked for the good of the English Church, the threads of his past life entwined him in a last terrible knot. His personal clemency did not prevail against Mary's persecution of Protestants. Their sophisticated foreign leaders, including Vermigli and Ochino, given academic posts by Cranmer, had escaped abroad, and most of the nearly 300 who were burnt to death for their loyalty to the new faith were simple people. This was an episode in English history seen with reason as not only horribly cruel but Spanish and unjust. The persecution and the burnings were Tudor brutality and the exercise of royal power literally with a vengeance: how hard Pole tried to temper Mary's identification of heresy with treason is not clear. He saved a few from the stake, and even John Foxe, whose 1563 *Acts and Monuments of matters happening in the Church* (usually known as 'Foxe's Book of Martyrs') was a propaganda triumph for Protestantism which lasted for centuries, conceded that Pole 'was none of the bloody and cruel sort of papists'. He did nothing, however, to prevent the most inept of all the burnings, that of Cranmer. The Queen had already spared the Archbishop's life as a traitor convicted for complicity in the plot at Edward's death, but she was determined to see tried for heresy the man who had divorced her parents, proclaimed her illegitimate, and destroyed Catholic life and liturgy in England. Under the pressure of imprisonment and theological persuasion Cranmer, never a strong man, thoroughly renounced his Protestantism. Had his life then been spared Mary and Pole would have achieved a famous victory for Catholic truth and forgiveness; as it was, his dreadful death and last-minute withdrawal of all his recantations had precisely the opposite effect.

If the very few convinced Protestant bishops had been quietly imprisoned and no naive enthusiasts murdered, the return to Roman obedience in 1554–8 might have been as popular as was the return to the Mass and the liturgy, and to the devotions and imagery of Catholicism. Pole himself, with years of experience as a counsellor of souls, knew that most people's religion is a matter of what they do far more definitely than it is a matter of what they are sure or not quite sure that they believe. Neither ceremonies nor Bible-reading, he said, is 'the thing that giveth us the very light', because that is the Spirit of God, but 'they are most apt to receive light that are more obedient to follow ceremonies than to read'. But the teaching and example Pole was so unusually well prepared to give his countrymen was to come to very little in England outside the hidden recusant tradition of Elizabeth's reign and later times. On the other hand, the lessons of counter-productive persecution, and of a foreign marriage which lost England's last foothold in France on account of a Habsburg war, were well taken by the Princess Elizabeth. And even Elizabeth eventually had to order the execution of Mary, Queen of Scots to preserve the Protestant succession to the throne so that the Reformation principle of *cuius regio eius religio* should not lose England back to Rome.

It was the final irony of Pole's life that he, who had spent decades in exile and sacrificed the liberty and lives of his family in loyalty to the authority of the Pope as against the authority of the English crown, had in his last years to depend on the authority of the English monarch to keep him in the country in disobedience to the order of the Pope.

Pole had been in England only six months when Cardinal Carafa, once his friend but now his implacable enemy, was elected Pope Paul IV. The old man, seventy-nine at his election, was unreasoningly hostile to every trace of thought he saw or imagined in the Church that was consonant with anything Luther had ever said, and also, as a Neapolitan, to Habsburg power and influence. He fought a futile war against Spain; Contarini and Pole had long doubted the benefits of the temporal power – territorial control of the Papal States – of the papacy. And he regarded Pole's Viterbo circle as a nest of heretics. He pursued beyond the grave the reputations of Flaminio and Vittoria Colonna, both of whom had been sustained within the Church by Pole, imprisoned on heresy charges Cardinal Morone, a friend of Pole's for many years, and withdrew Pole's legatine commission to 'Habsburg' England, transferring it to an eighty-two-year-old Franciscan friar. He told Pole to return to Rome, to face heresy charges at the Inquisition. Mary refused to let him go and Pole stayed in England.

A little more than a year before his death Pole wrote a long impassioned letter to the Pope, defending, entirely convincingly, his orthodoxy throughout his life, as he had once defended the unity of the Church in a long impassioned letter to Henry VIII, and saying now, as he had then said of the King, that the Pope was simply wrong. He added that he is able to say such a thing to the man for whose office he has suffered so much because cardinals are appointed to advise and warn popes, who can err like anyone else. It is an impressive, sad and moving letter. A draft survives. Pole burnt the copy he wrote to send to Rome. 'Meanwhile', Seripando wrote of this pontificate, 'the reform of the Church froze.' After Paul IV's death, Morone was released and wholly vindicated by Pius IV. He presided over the successful concluding session of the Council of Trent in 1562–3 and survived Pole by more than twenty years.

Pole was buried according to his wish close to the desecrated shrine of St Thomas Becket in Canterbury Cathedral, under a plain stone inscribed with the three words 'Depositum Cardinalis Poli'. The grandeur of the despoiled place and the simplicity of the memorial are appropriate. This scholarly Plantagenet prince, brought up in an atmosphere of comfort, culture and terror, lived through perhaps the most personally testing period in the history of England and of the Church, and found himself, by birth and by calling, at the eye of both storms. He preferred to live out of the world. Every so often in Italy he was able to take a little time out of ecclesiastical politics and live, as he had lived as a student in Padua and Venice, a semi-monastic and very Augustinian life with a few friends, prayer, silence, talk and a lot of books. A study and a garden, he wrote to Vittoria Colonna, would always set him to rights. In Condivi's *Life of Michelangelo*, written while its subject was still alive and with his help, Pole is mentioned first, 'for his rare virtues and singular goodness', among those few friends the artist had 'whose learned and cultivated conversation could be of profit to his mind, and in whom some beams of genius shone forth'.

His friends were loyal to Pole, and he to them, throughout difficult lives. And though several of them suffered from the suspicion of a faction in the Curia incapable of distinguishing heresy from deep consideration of some of the irreducible paradoxes of Christian life, the day of Contarini, Pole and their fellow-Catholics devoted to the healing of the Church would, four centuries later, at last arrive. Pope John XXIII opened the Second Vatican Council in a spirit of openness, forgiveness and collective responsibility that was remarkably close to the spirit in which Pole had opened the first session of the Council of Trent. On the first evening of the reign of Elizabeth I, Pole must have died feeling that everything he had set his hand to had failed. But his pastoral model inspired much that was good in the Church of the next generation and, in any case, as his first biographer wrote, in the times in which he lived it was more than notable to have always been 'cheerful, just, incorruptible, elevated in spirit, unshaken by disaster, and wholly submitted to the will of God'.

Chapter 5

St Robert Southwell, SJ

Clare Asquith

'They boast about the heroes of antiquity, but we have a new torture which it is not possible for a man to bear. And yet I have seen Robert Southwell hanging by it, still as a tree-trunk, and no one able to drag one word from his mouth.' The words are those of Southwell's interrogator and cousin – Robert Cecil, Elizabeth I's Secretary of State. The cold, detached tone, the curious personal circumstances, bring home not only Southwell's heroism, but the bizarre nature of the country and the period into which he was born. One of the missionary priests who ran the gauntlet of Cecil's security network in order to bring the Catholic sacraments back to England in the final years of Elizabeth's reign, he spent six intensely active years in London, the country's Protestant heartland, before being caught, imprisoned and finally executed in 1595. But Southwell was not just an unusually brave man. While on the run he wrote, and the extraordinary nature of his writing meant that by the time of his death, he was one of the country's best-selling authors. The extent of his literary achievement, sidelined for centuries, is only now beginning to be recognized. His latest critics and biographers claim that his epistles and dramatic monologues break new ground as they address the uniquely complex psychological predicament of his fellow countrymen. Southwell's primary goal was to provide comfort and guidance to England's beleaguered Catholics. But before long, concerned at the influence of England's officially regulated printing presses, he widened his appeal, issuing an explicit challenge to his own generation of poets and play-wrights to incorporate spiritual themes into their work, hitherto cautiously secular. They responded; and his impact on one particular writer was to be momentous. Scholars now believe that Southwell's literary mission was a formative influence on some of the most original and innovative aspects of the poems and plays of William Shakespeare.

Southwell and Shakespeare belonged to a generation faced with an unprecedented moral dilemma. During their lifetime it became apparent that the Protestant Reformation, against all the odds, was taking permanent root in England. Imposed from above on an unwilling country, the English monarch's new state religion demanded explicit conformity from hundreds of thousands who viewed it as nothing less than heresy. The result, noted with concern on both sides of the religious divide, was a drift to secularism among a people weary of a doctrinal quarrel which had raged for over half a century. Southwell's own family was typical of the times, enriched yet radically damaged by the events that followed Henry VIII's break with Rome. Through his mother, Bridget Copley, he was connected to a formidable network of wealthy Catholic gentry spread out across the Sussex Downs and along the south coast, their Spanish links and oppositional stance a constant anxiety to a government threatened by foreign invasion. But though he spent much of his childhood with these covertly subversive cousins, he was not native to Sussex. His father's family were East Anglian, and his home was the converted monastic site of Horsham St Faith's in Norfolk, part of the country which had been the first to absorb Reformist ideals from the Low Countries. His father was outwardly a Protestant conformist, while his grandfather, Sir Richard Southwell, embodied the most outrageous aspects of the 'new men' who profited from the country's religious upheavals. As Holbein's portrait of him suggests, dirty work was Sir Richard's speciality. He was one of Cromwell's most dependable henchman, relaying the 'salacious tidbits' that ensured the ruin of the shrine at

Walsingham, depriving the saintly Thomas More of books in prison, furnishing evidence that destroyed his childhood friend, the poet Henry Howard, Earl of Surrey, and finally showing no qualms about burning heretical Protestants, his erstwhile co-religionists, under Mary. He died a rich man, but his wealth turned out to be a poisoned chalice. Most of his children, including Robert's father, were the offspring not of his wife but of his mistress, his wife's cousin, who lived with the Southwells as one of the household. The ensuing lawsuits over the Southwell inheritance were to beggar his descendents, and meant that his grandson was brought up against a background of bitter family litigation.

From the very beginning, Robert Southwell's personal manner and way of life seem to have been intended as an implicit condemnation of the values that had brought his grandfather to such prominence. He later suggests that he was an irritatingly priggish son. 'Even from my earliest infancy you were wont in merriment to call me Father Robert' he wrote in a letter to his father. But fervour for the beleaguered Catholic cause, no doubt deepened during long visits to his Sussex country cousins, was tempered by unusual personal charm. He was not simply an exceptionally good-looking boy – one of the most dramatic moments of his childhood was his abduction by a gypsy woman, apparently entranced by his beauty – but he possessed a rare capacity for tactful, intelligent sympathy. Unlike many other Catholic polemicists, he had a natural lightness of touch which lends humanity to his impassioned spiritual writing, and much of his work demonstrates a nuanced awareness of the difficulties and weaknesses of his fellow-countrymen. One latest biographer characterizes him as a reconciler by nature, ever concerned, in his own words, to change 'a late enraged foe / Into a quiet friend'.

In 1569 when Southwell was nine years old, the country was convulsed by the abortive rising of the Catholic North against the new Protestant regime. In the bloody aftermath of the rebellion, the papacy issued a bull exempting Catholics from loyalty to their excommunicated monarch.

Laws against Catholic were immediately tightened; among the first to take cover were Southwell's aunt and uncle, Catherine and Thomas Copley, who used their influence with the Queen to dodge the full weight of anti-fugitive legislation before leaving their great Sussex house in the ready hands of the Lord Treasurer and travelling abroad to Louvain. A few years later, in 1576, the fifteen-year-old Robert followed them overseas to Douai, in Belgium, in order to complete his education free from government harassment. This was a dangerous course – boys who went abroad to avoid the ban on Catholic education in England ran terrible risks . But the alternative was equally perilous. The net appeared to be closing in on Southwell's family in particular – that same year, Southwell's two brothers were summoned to the Star Chamber and fined £200 for alleged sedition. Having escaped the Queen's security services to reach Douai, however, the 'beautiful English youth', as one contemporary student described Southwell at this period, would have found himself in congenial company. The English College there had been set up by Cardinal William Allen as an Oxford University in miniature – and as at Oxford, the studies often led to priesthood. Many of the tutors were exiles from Oxford, a number of them able men who had left England in the wake of the charismatic Edmund Campion's defection in 1571. Southwell and his fellow-students attended the large Jesuit school at Douai. There, unlike contemporaries at home, they were exposed to the full force of the Catholic Counter-Reformation. Conducted wholly in Latin, and covering a far broader range of subjects than the average English grammar school, Jesuit education was the most advanced and enlightened of its day. The calibre of Jesuit school drama in particular was famous across Europe – the Jesuits considered the theatre a vital teaching tool, along with poetry and the visual arts. It is clear from his writings that the sensuous and dramatic richness of his new environment made a profound and lasting impact on the impressionable young Englishman.

Here, too, he was exposed to the increasingly heady

mixture of indignation and missionary zeal at the English College. For some years now Allen had been sending missionary priests back to England, and the English government had become concerned at their numbers. In 1577 reports arrived of the execution for treason of Father Cuthbert Mayne, a graduate from Douai. Further executions followed. But the authorities miscalculated: the consequence of the crackdown was a stiffening of Catholic resistance, and a steady increase in applications to the priesthood at the new colleges abroad. Southwell and his companions have often been portrayed as naive, idealistic exiles, indoctrinated with an unhealthy thirst for martyrdom by unscrupulous Jesuits. But it is not clear at this early stage whether the young Robert Southwell considered joining the English Mission at all. If he had a vocation when he arrived at Douai, it seems to have been uncertain; the contemplative Carthusian order initially held the greatest appeal for him. But after a prolonged inner struggle he decided on the active, academic Jesuit order, with a view to joining a mission abroad, perhaps to the Indies – not England, a political hornet's nest which the Jesuits at this stage deliberately avoided. He travelled to Rome and was eventually accepted into the Jesuit novitiate at Sant Andrea. He was received on the feast-day of St Faith, suggesting again that Southwell saw his life as a restitution for the misdeeds of his grandfather.

Unquestioning obedience is one of the first conditions of Jesuit life, and over the next eight years Southwell's capacity for patient submission was tested to the limit. The brilliant, well-born scholar with a penchant for high-flown writing was put to work in the kitchens, in hospitals and among the poor on the streets. He underwent the searching discipline of Ignatius' *Spiritual Exercises*, and learned the habit of meticulous self-examination required by his superiors. Later, countering the propaganda that the exiles were 'dissolute young men' he defended in heartfelt terms those who 'abandon our country, friends, and all such comforts as naturally all men seek and find in their native soil: we must relinquish all possibilities of favour, riches and credit; we must limit our minds to the restrained and severe course of the society of Jesus, or the seminaries; where the place is in exile, the rules strict, the government austere, our wills broken, the least fault chastised, and a most absolute virtue exacted'. In Southwell's case, the austere regime proved beneficial; the development of his literary style indicates that he matured rapidly. A rigorous self-discipline replaces his earlier self-indulgence; florid tendencies give way to a clear-headed lucidity; loosely Italianate conceits evolve into dense, taut imagery. Southwell clearly delighted in the characteristically intellectual Jesuit exploitation of startling visual symbolism. He excelled academically. By 1581, when he completed his course of philosophy at Sant Andrea with a 'Public Defence', his friend John Dekkers wrote that 'he was without a rival in philosophy among his fellow students of the Roman College'.

In 1581 he was transferred to the English College in Rome to continue his studies, and also to take up a series of administrative positions, first as tutor and then Prefect of Studies and of the Sodality. He was back among his fellow countrymen, but the experience, judging by his diaries, was traumatic. The atmosphere among the students had changed from the simple Catholic patriotism of his days in Douai. A year earlier, under pressure from the papacy and from desperate English exiles, the General of the Jesuit Order had altered his policy towards England. Edmund Campion and Southwell's own superior, Robert Persons, two leading Jesuit scholars, had sailed in disguise to Dover and made contact with the country's leading Catholics. Their aim was to challenge the Protestant regime to public debate and to rouse wavering English Catholics to a more courageous form of passive resistance. The outcome was brutal and shocking. Campion got his debate, but only after hours on the rack; he was hanged, drawn and quartered in London. Persons managed to elude capture and escape to Rome. The fate of Campion and his fellow victims became an international cause celebre, widely compared to the fate of Christian martyrs under Domitian. The English colleges commissioned lurid frescoes of their deaths, and English novices were hailed in the streets as future saints and martyrs. But among English Catholics there was dissent over a mission which, however heroic, could be seen as gratuitously provocative and suicidal. The English College in Rome, penetrated by the agents of Elizabeth's spymaster, Sir Francis Walsingham, had become bitterly torn as to its purpose. For the impassioned majority, a key function of the College was to offer a training ground for the English Mission; but an opposing faction hotly denied that this was any part of the original foundation of the English College, and urged peaceful negotiation with Elizabeth's government. These 'stirs' as they became known spread rapidly and eventually split the Catholic resistance both at home and abroad. Southwell, now in his early twenties, was at the very eye of the storm, attempting as Prefect of Studies to arbitrate between two factions of men often older and more politically sophisticated than he. For a young novice with scrupulously high standards of personal sanctity, who clearly had a leaning towards the contemplative life, it was an agonizing situation. His diaries reveal that his daily examination of conscience plunged him into deep depression. Holiness in this fevered, poisonous atmosphere seemed impossible. He found life 'cramped, confined and dreary'. The frescoes of martyrdoms taking shape on the walls of the college chapel began to hold a genuine appeal for him. 'To die quickly is a safe thing', he wrote at this period, though 'to live long in pain for Christ is a holy thing'. Encouraged by Parsons, he applied for the English Mission, but at first the Society refused to countenance the loss of a man of his intellectual and administrative ability. As his students continued to risk their lives, some perishing of typhoid and malaria in Rome, others dying in prison or on the scaffold in England, Southwell began to chafe at his thankless staff job as he fended off a barrage of anti-Jesuit charges of cowardice, inhumanity and elitism.

It was probably at this period that he began work on prose and poetry based on his intimate involvement in the harsh realities of the English predicament. This work was eventually to galvanize English literature. It includes a series of interior monologues spoken by anguished figures apparently abandoned by God. One is the long poem 'Saint Peter's Complaint', in which Peter is torn by remorse, having repeatedly betrayed Christ on oath under pressure from a mere serving maid. The moment was of acute relevance to a country where an oath denying the Church's authority was extorted by a female monarch. Another lengthy complaint, this time in the form of a prose-poem, is uttered by the archetype of the repentant sinner, Mary Magdalen, who questions minutely the reasons for Christ's delay in appearing to his stricken, sinful follower after the Resurrection. Her crisis of faith was shared by English Catholics, deprived of priests and the sacraments, living amid 'shadows', 'where the truth once was, and is not'. These explorations of a baffled, guilty psyche poisoned at the very deepest level, arise not only from his close acquaintance with the religious politics of England, but from his own sense of abandonment during his life in the English College in Rome.

At last, in 1586, two years after his ordination and after repeated requests, a wiser and more wary Robert Southwell received permission to go to England. His companion and superior was to be Father Henry Garnet, a practical, cautious mathematician. Their combination of shrewdness and drive, of administrative expertise and literary ability, were precisely what were needed. Their immediate mission was to repair the porous underground network, and to set up a printing press to counter the spread of secularism and Protestant propaganda. It was with great reluctance and foreboding that their superior let them go.

Neither of them was under any illusions. Their chances of survival have been estimated at roughly one in three. Even before they set sail, news of their movements had arrived on Walsingham's desk. Southwell's letter to a friend 'from death's ante-room' on the eve of departure anticipates torture and martyrdom, and though he 'welcomes' the prospect he begs for prayers that his fortitude and faith remain strong: 'The flesh is weak and can do nothing, and even now revolts from what is proposed.'

Southwell's apprehension that 'sea and land are gaping wide for me' was accurate. The pair could not have chosen a worse time to travel. Walsingham was putting the finishing touch to an elaborate sting operation, designed to ensnare as many young Catholic activists as possible in what became known as the Babington Plot. Anthony Babington himself, the unhappy tool of the security services, was closely connected to Southwell's family, and had already been instructed to discover his whereabouts.

But from the moment they landed in early July, alarmingly close to a watching figure above a deserted beach between Dover and Folkestone, Southwell and Garnet appeared to lead a charmed life. They had placed their mission under the patronage of St Luke, and in their vivid newsletters attributed their many narrow escapes to his protection: it may be that something of his grandfather's canniness survived in Robert Southwell. His story of an inept boatman satisfied the curious onlooker, and he and Garnet vanished gratefully into the crowds thronging the roads to a fair at Canterbury. They made separate journeys to London (Southwell having somehow acquired a horse), and received a hero's welcome from the Catholic gentry there. The inspiring impact of their first encounter with English recusants is described in intensely emotional terms by many returning priests. Southwell was overwhelmed by their reception, awed by the determination, courage and bravado of his hosts, humbled by their hunger for the sacramental life they had lost. All the suspicions, fears and doubts of his years in exile gave way to a sense of utter dedication: for such people he was prepared to give everything, to succour them, to become their spokesman – his urgent goal now was survival in order to work, rather than the more self-regarding hunger for martyrdom.

The first month was a whirl of activity, as the pair were hustled covertly from one great household to the next in and around London, saying Mass in hushed and crowded rooms, often escaping government agents by a whisker. Garnet, an excellent musician, records a memorable evening in Hurleyford where he first sang with the great recusant composer, William Byrd, who was to become his close friend. But the exhilaration was short-lived. At the beginning of August the Babington Plot was exposed. A wave of arrests, confiscations, imprisonments and executions followed, among precisely the circle on whom the pair depended. 'We are hemmed in by daily perils' wrote Southwell, 'never safe even for a moment.' Garnet reported that Southwell had in fact been spotted and trailed by an agent as he walked through London, but 'Robert ... liked to walk at a good pace' and had inadvertently escaped by a sudden acceleration and change of direction. On another occasion the house of the Vaux family was raided; Southwell who was saying Mass there only reached his hiding place thanks to the aplomb of the Vaux' small daughter who blocked the stairs, commanding the armed posse to retire 'or else my mother will die for she cannot abide to see a drawn sword'.

This cat and mouse existence could not last long. In such a climate very few people could offer them protection. But again, Southwell played his cards well. In late autumn he received a summons to Arundel House from the wife of the imprisoned figurehead of English Catholics, Sir Philip Arundel. In fact Ann Arundel merely wanted the sacraments; but as Southwell's stay lengthened from one day to two, she realized that he had assumed she wanted a private chaplain. By then he had won her over. She became his devoted patron, and for the next two years sheltered him in a remote room in Arundel House providing him not only with an invaluable London base with outlets onto the river Thames, but the use of a small house somewhere in the suburbs where he could set up a press.

It was a golden opportunity. Ann Arundel became a key protector, patron of other priests and of a number of hazardous ventures. Southwell worked tirelessly over the next few years to build up a workable network of routes and bases around the country for underground priests. The outlook for incoming missionaries was transformed. In the early 1580s, those priests who ventured out of hiding in London were rapidly caught; by the time of Southwell's death, three hundred were safely deployed around the country. The same practicality and dynamism characterized his publishing venture. Dissident printing presses were usually hunted down and dismantled, but the whereabouts of Southwell's and Garnet's printing base still remains unknown.

First off the hidden press were a series of prose works by Southwell himself, addressed to the imprisoned Earl of Arundel and to other leading recusants. Written in direct, refreshing language, *An Epistle of Comfort*, *The Triumphs over Death* and *A Short Rule of Good Life* were designed to provide spiritual guidance and comfort for the entire community of suffering English Catholics. Even today, these neglected guidebooks to the lay religious life are often accessible and attractive, and like Robert Parsons' best-selling *Spiritual Directory* were valued by Protestants as well as Catholics. Images from England's native school of medieval piety merge with the humane, enlightened Counter-Reformation theology which Southwell absorbed from Bellarmine and Allen, all of it leavened with the romantic language of courtly love and homely analogies from a contemporary English life which was still a little unfamiliar to the author. John Gerard, a dashing fellow missionary, has an engaging picture of Southwell asking to be coached in the technical language of falconry as they travelled the country together and fretting anxiously that 'it is 'such an easy thing to trip up in one's terms'.

It is possible that the easy social manners he worked so hard to acquire made Southwell almost undetectable. Assisted by a circle of clever young university men who became his followers, he infiltrated the hunting and hawking milieu where he pursued his mission undetected. Intelligence reports describe someone indistinguishable from the subjects of countless Elizabethan portraits: 'of medium height, auburn hair ... without beard when I knew him ... apparelled in black rash'. He must often have found himself among old family friends and relatives, and he was clearly helped by the fact that he inspired great personal loyalty. Garnet was devoted to him, and Gerard describes him as one who 'excels at the work ... wise, good, gentle, loveable'. Though the net gradually widened in the late 1580s for 'the chief dealer for Papists in England', Southwell and his ventures survived both the crisis that followed the death of Mary Queen of Scots and the widespread terror-executions after the Armada. In November of 1588 Garnet, anxious about his health, sent him away from London for two months to ride round 'a great part of England' at 'the bitterest time of year ... to avoid the Queen's Messengers'. It may be during this period, as he rode through the wild and terrorized Catholic North, that he wrote two of his most original poems. 'A Vale of Tears' strikingly anticipates the Romantics, as it traces the web of affinities between the melancholy state of England and the sublimely melancholy landscape spread out before him, its 'dales with stony ruins strewed'. The other is the poem which has been anthologized ever since, and which Ben Jonson admired so much that he claimed he would have exchanged it for all his own poems. 'A Burning Babe' is a dramatic exploration of the image of a weeping child engulfed in flames which appears in the darkness to one who 'in hoary Winter's night stood shivering in the snow'.

'To close-read a Southwell poem' writes the scholar Anne Sweeney, 'is almost to pray.' It is only now becoming apparent that his series of short poems, published immediately after his death, is an extraordinarily compact and powerful invitation to his Elizabethan readers to turn to meditation, prayer and a change of life. Designed to be read in sequence, they take England's abandoned spiritual state as a starting point. A typical example presents the predicament of Saint Joseph, confronted with his pregnant wife, unvisited as yet by the explanatory angel. His state of mind is that of the English, asked to believe that the cult of the Virgin is a mere superstition and the Church whom she so often represents is corrupt. 'Could such a worm breed in so sweet a wood?' he agonizes; he cannot bear to expose her, and instead chooses exile. Life is meaningless 'cut from my root of joy';

he is 'like herb that grows in cold and barren shade'. Yet he realizes 'change of place' cannot change 'implanted pain'; and to the bewilderment of critics, the poem ends with Joseph paralyzed by indecision, treading 'a maze of doubtful end', gazing helplessly at his fallen bride: 'she wounds, she heals, she doth both mar and mend'. This is not scriptural, or even artistic – but it does faithfully mirror his country's psychology, a condition which Southwell understood better than anyone. The next poem in the sequence provides a ringing response to Joseph who 'in suspense' hangs between faith and despair. It is a straight translation of the *Lauda Sion*, the Church's triumphant Corpus Christi hymn celebrating the doctrine of the Eucharist, written by the Church's 'Angelic Doctor', Saint Thomas Aquinas. Other poems enter into the mentality of those who have profited from the Reformation, those who have been beguiled by Elizabeth's Court and have traded peace of mind for great wealth, fine houses, grand gardens. The solution, according to Southwell, is modest integrity. The final poems extol the joys of a simple life and quiet conscience and hold out hope for the future; the little fish, the hare, the 'tender lark', he assures his readers, can outlive the pike, the merlin, the 'greedy greyhound'.

One of the fascinations of these poems is the insight they give into the mentality of many of Elizabeth's subjects. The proof that Southwell got it right can be seen in his immense influence among his contemporaries. 'You heavenly sparks of wit, show native light', he urged at the beginning of 'Peter's Complaint', and he prefaced his shorter poems with a similar challenge to his fellow writers to 'weave a new web' and turn to things of the spirit. A reciprocal change of heart and direction, at times explicitly linked to Southwell, has been detected in the works of Lodge, Constable, Nashe, Greene, Daniel, Drayton, Marlowe and Shakespeare.

This new, spiritual thread was often necessarily covert: even Southwell's outwardly harmless poems, though they circulated in manuscript, were only published after his death. But there is one piece of Elizabethan resistance writing, printed in England, which is stirringly direct. This is Southwell's *Humble Supplication*, an open letter to Elizabeth herself, informing her of the true situation of English Catholics. It was written in furious response to William Cecil's 'Proclamation', issued in late November 1591, an edict which used unprecedentedly vitriolic language to announce further stringent measures against Catholics, attacking in particular the 'venomous vipers' who came over to infect the realm from Douai and Rome. Southwell's lengthy reply was completed by early December and written on the run in perilous circumstances. He knew his time was almost up. He was by now the object of a nationwide manhunt, led by the Queen's chief agent against Catholics, the psychopathic Richard Topcliffe, who had acquired a licence to torture in his own house and whose sadistic behaviour and jeering manner at the trial and execution of Catholic priests was beginning to scandalize even members of the Privy Council. He claimed a special relationship with the Queen, perhaps one of the reasons why Southwell now chose to address her directly, over the heads of her advisors.

The *Humble Supplicati*on is one of the most brilliant political appeals in the English language; yet, because of historical circumstances, it is also one of the least known. Southwell begins by presenting his case in measured, urbane terms, using arguments likely to appeal to its suspicious target reader. Were the 'General Resurrection' to occur 'in your Majesty's time, a thing not so impossible as uncertain', he suggests, what would be the response to her religious policy of 'all your royal ancestors this fourteen hundred years' who practised the 'ancient faith', among them her father, its famous 'Defender'? He emphasizes the natural submissiveness of Catholics, 'bound to obey the just laws of their Princes'. He makes an elegant case for religious toleration. So-called conspiracies against her life are merely projected plots, designed by 'Master Secretary's subtle and sifting wit' to entrap 'silly fish' like Babington. The Queen is the innocent victim of clever, malicious misinformation about her most loyal subjects. But gradually the restrained, courtly manner falls away. Before long, the letter becomes a passionately indignant and graphic expression of what it felt like to be a Catholic under Elizabeth. Circumstantial accounts of individual tragedies, savage indictments of government cruelty, lucid summaries of resistance arguments, eloquent appeals to principals of justice, the occasional reference to his own imminent fate – all this is caught up in the cumulative sweep of a marvellously sustained rhetorical climax. It is unlikely that the Queen ever read it, but it circulated in manuscript and later found its way into print. There is a record of Francis Bacon commissioning his own copy and expressing guarded admiration for its style.

A few months later, Richard Topcliffe managed to blackmail one of the Bellamy family who were known acquaintances of Southwell. Having arrested and raped one of their daughters, he offered her the protection of marriage to one of his followers in return for information as to Southwell's whereabouts. The ploy succeeded. On 25 June 1592, the Bellamy house at Uxenden was surrounded as Southwell said Mass. He hid; but the game was clearly up. When 'the Goliath of the Papists' finally emerged from the priest's hole and surrendered, Topcliffe had some kind of seizure; foaming at the mouth, he had to be restrained from physically attacking him. He took him to his own house in London, and wrote a gloating note to the Queen about his momentous capture. There Southwell was repeatedly tortured for information, with no result. He was removed to the Gatehouse prison, then to the Tower, but in spite of repeated interrogations, Southwell remained silent. Two and a half years of solitary confinement followed, during which he was permitted only three books – the Bible, his breviary and the works of Saint Bernard. He sent repeated letters to Sir Robert Cecil, begging to be released from his ordeal. 'I am become a suitor for my own execution', he wrote.

Finally, in 1595, he was put on trial. The prosecutor was the Attorney General, Sir Edward Coke, who in his early days had been involved in the Southwell family lawsuits, accepting large annual sums from Southwell's father in order to press his case. Coke had unearthed an issue that highlighted the seditious nature of incoming priests, and which has tarnished the image of English Jesuits ever since. Southwell and Garnet were both presented with the charge of 'equivocation': that is, of teaching that lies were permissible under certain circumstances, in particular when lives were at stake. The unfortunate Anne Bellamy gave evidence, and though Southwell put up a creditable defence the verdict was never in doubt. However, the night before his execution, a visitor came to his cell. It was Lord Mountjoy, a highly-placed courtier sent by the Queen to ascertain for certain whether the 'boy-priest', as Topcliffe dubbed him, had come to England to make an attempt on her life. He earnestly assured Mountjoy that his mission was spiritual, not political. The next day mercy was shown on the scaffold: by the time the noose was cut Southwell was already dead.

An image in the 'Epistle of Comfort' attempts to hearten English Catholics by finding meaning, indeed beauty, in their sufferings. Addressing their persecutors, Southwell recalls the way 'torn and fretted velvet' can be repaired by a seamstress and incorporated into a new pattern more beautiful than the original. 'So God permitteth our flesh by you to be mangled to make it more glorious in the second coming.' This heroic response to hardship was exemplified by Southwell himself, whose life and literary output serve as outstanding models of that quality so admired by the English, grace under pressure. Shakespeare lamented its passing in 'The Phoenix and The Turtle', a cautiously cryptic tribute to the self-sacrifice of the Catholic resistance of his own generation. In a deliberate act of homage, he borrowed the distinctive metre and language from a well-known poem by Southwell himself.

> 'Beauty, truth and rarity,
> Grace in all simplicity
> Here enclosed in cinders lie ...
>
> Truth may seem, but cannot be;
> Beauty brag, but tis not she,
> Truth and beauty buried be.'

Chapter 6

St Edmund Campion

Anthony Symondson, SJ

England in the late sixteenth century is a time remote from
our own but familiar through drama, films, historical recon-
structions and documentaries. For the English it was the
dawn of the modern world. Few can escape being reminded
of this period which moulded the future of the country in
decisive ways that have had lasting consequences. Many
regard it as a golden age. Queen Elizabeth I ascended the
throne in 1558 at the age of twenty-six and she remains one
of the most popular monarchs in English history.
Shakespeare's plays helped forge the English language and
laid the foundations of modern drama. Music, architecture
and learning flourished and the fruits of the Italian
Renaissance were applied at Court and the universities of
Oxford and Cambridge. England as a nation state came into
being. Sir Francis Drake circumnavigated the globe and
helped establish England's prestige as a world power. The
Spanish Armada was defeated.

Roman Catholicism, the historic faith of England, became
a forbidden religion after the unbroken continuity of a thousand years. The Church of England was established by the
Act of Uniformity in 1559 and the Queen assumed governance of the Church in the Act of Supremacy passed in the
same year. The destiny of England was to be a Protestant
country. The Book of Common Prayer was re-issued after
Queen Mary I had briefly restored Catholic worship and had
returned churches to Catholic use after the destruction

under King Henry VIII and her brother King Edward VI. In his eagerness to extirpate heresy, Pope St Pius V excommunicated Queen Elizabeth in 1570 and purported to depose her. This was a mistake and seriously aggravated the position of her Catholic subjects; it also antagonized Spain, France and the Holy Roman Empire.

The consequences for Catholics were severe. A series of penal laws was passed by Parliament to destroy the Catholic religion. The celebration of Mass was forbidden, and all Catholic books and articles of devotion, such as rosary beads and domestic images, were prohibited. Fines of increasing severity were imposed upon all persons who did not attend the services of the Church of England. They were called 'recusants', from the Latin word *recusare*, to refuse. Recusants could not only be fined, but also imprisoned for hearing Mass, and were forbidden to travel more than five miles from home without written licence.

Those who wished to remain Catholics were forced to celebrate Mass secretly, and priests had to train in seminaries abroad, returning to England to minister the sacraments. They were in great danger because the government made any priest ordained abroad guilty of high treason, the punishment of which was death. Anyone who helped a priest was guilty of misprision of treason, also punishable by death. There were many spies and informers who, for money or to gain favour with the authorities, were willing to betray priests and those who helped them. In a climate of fear Catholics had to decide whether to abandon their faith or face the risk of practising it. Many chose to keep their heads down and conform to the new religious order, while others were determined to remain loyal to the faith of their fathers. The state of Catholics betrays the glowing reputation of the period as an era of moderation, adventure and culture. The reign of Queen Elizabeth was a time when torture was most used in England than before or since.

Few suffered more severely under these measures than St Edmund Campion. He was the most conspicuous Catholic martyr of the Elizabethan age. A Jesuit priest, a man of sparkling intellectual brilliance, good natured, polished, attractive, a magnetic public speaker; from boyhood he had been a star. The last seventeen months of a relatively short life of forty-one years – April 1580 to November 1581 – turned him from being a scholar and teacher into one of the bravest, most courageous, men of his generation. This brief, but heroic, time secured his place in English history.

Edmund Campion was born in London on St Paul's day, 25 January 1540, the son of a citizen and bookseller from Sawston in Cambridgeshire; nothing is known about his mother. They were Catholics and had three sons and one daughter. He was a promising boy and the Grocers' Company, of which his father might have been a member, impressed by his 'sharp and pregnant wit', educated him, after a short start at a grammar school, at Christ's Hospital (the Bluecoat School) and St Paul's School. Campion was a brilliant pupil, the winner of many prizes including silver bows and arrows, and pens. On the evening of 3 August 1553, as a Bluecoat boy of thirteen years of age, he made a speech to Queen Mary at St Paul's Cross, on behalf of the London scholars, and his modest grace charmed her as much as his eloquence. This was the first of many oratorical triumphs he was delegated to make in his scholarly life in London and Oxford.

In May 1555 Sir Thomas White, Lord Mayor of London, was given a royal licence to found the college of St John the Baptist at Oxford. The Grocers' Company awarded Campion an exhibition for a scholarship in the new college and this paid for his maintenance. Sir Thomas was a devout Catholic and he wanted St John's to be a stronghold of the old faith. He took an interest in Campion and later William, Cardinal Allen, the founder of the English College at Douai, noted that he was 'very much beloved for his excellent qualities by Sir Thomas White'. There, Campion recorded, 'I studied philosophy for seven years and theology for about six – Aristotle, positive theology and the Fathers'. He took his Bachelor of Arts degree in 1561 and, after graduating Master of Arts in 1564, was with his friend, Gregory Martin, appointed a junior fellow at the age of twenty-four.

The impression Campion made upon his contemporaries was electrifying. He had a magnetic personality and the power of attracting lasting friendships. Intellectually he towered above the majority but he was also handsome, well-spoken, and gracious in manner; so admired for his eloquence that when he became a tutor in the college his students imitated his way of speaking, walk, and style of dress. They became known as 'Campionists'. In 1566 when Queen Elizabeth visited Oxford, Campion welcomed her in the name of the University, and was defender in a Latin disputation held in her presence. The Queen expressed admiration of his eloquence and he won her lasting regard. On her recommendation, he gained the powerful patronage of Robert Dudley, Earl of Leicester, and Sir William Cecil, Secretary of State, her principal councillors.

For a modestly born scholar, however brilliant, with no family connections the prospects of worldly advancement lay either in the University or the newly founded Church of England. Campion was given a further exhibition by the Grocers' Company on condition that he preached in London at St Paul's Cross, for which he was required to be ordained. There was urgent need of sound scholars who were also fluent preachers and one like Campion held the promise of high office. He was ordained deacon by Richard Cheyney, Bishop of Gloucester, a cleric who owed his appointment to Cecil's patronage, and presented to the living of Sherborne in Gloucestershire. They remained friends and correspondents long after Campion's recantation of Protestantism.

Robert Persons, Campion's future Jesuit companion, wrote that

> Campion was always a Catholic at heart, and utterly condemned all the form and substance of the new religion. Yet the sugared words of the great folk, especially the Queen, joined with pregnant hopes of speedy and great preferment, so enticed him that he knew not which way to turn.

He was twenty-nine, an age when young men are susceptible to ambition, and he should not be judged harshly for responding to flattery. But his ordination was followed by 'remorse of conscience and a devastation of mind'. Catholicism remained a burning issue in the University. Some of Campion's closest Oxford contemporaries, including his friend, Martin, were drawn to the Church. Between 1565 and 1580, sixteen fellows and two chaplains of St John's College left Oxford to become Catholic priests at Rheims and Douai in France. All told over 100 fellows and senior members of the University followed during the first decade of Queen Elizabeth's reign, the majority to become priests. Campion's prospects flourished. In 1567 he preached an oration on the death of Sir Thomas White and in the following year he was elected by Convocation to the prestigious post of junior proctor. Interiorly Campion was divided by a crisis of conscience. The glittering prospects offered by Leicester drew him in one direction, his study of the Fathers of the Church in another.

On 19 March 1569 he petitioned the University to be admitted to the degree of Bachelor of Divinity. But a month later he shifted his religious position and did not proceed to the degree in July. Rumours of Campion's Catholic sympathies had reached London. The Grocers' Company wanted proof of his loyalty to the established Church and they asked him to preach at St Paul's Cross but he secured a deferment. It is unlikely that he would have made this move if he felt unable to defend the reformed position. He was offered, but did not take up, a travelling scholarship by St John's and in August he set out for Ireland at the invitation of James Stanyhurst, recorder of Dublin and Speaker of the Irish House of Commons. The intention was to help re-found Trinity College, Dublin, as a place of Protestant learning, an ambition close to Stanyhurst's heart. He only spent a few months in Dublin but during ten weeks he wrote, in association with Stanyhurst, *A History of Ireland*, the substance of which was incorporated in Raphael Holinshed's *Chronicles* in 1587.

Urged by Martin, then tutor to the sons of Thomas Howard, fourth Duke of Norfolk, Campion returned to England disguised as the servant of Melchior Hussey, steward to the Earl of Kildare. He reached London in time to witness the trial and execution of Blessed John Storey, formerly Professor of Civil Law at Oxford, in June 1571. That completed the work of his conversion. Pursuing a treacherous journey he arrived at Cardinal Allen's seminary at Douai later in the month. Here he was reunited with Martin and other friends. News of his departure soon reached Court. 'It is a great pity to see so notable a man leave this country,' said Cecil to Stanyhurst, 'for indeed he was one of the diamonds of England.' Leicester's views are unrecorded.

The college at Douai was founded in 1568 to enable young English Catholics to receive the education they could no longer get at Oxford or Cambridge. It trained men for the priesthood to replace the diminishing number of priests in England and many were subsequently martyred. Douai became a rallying point for exiled English Catholics and political visitors. There Campion resumed his studies, took a degree in divinity in 1572, taught rhetoric, and resumed his role as an orator. But, for reasons unknown, he did not settle. A year later, he set out for Rome as a penniless pilgrim, to seek admission to the Society of Jesus, arriving there barefoot and in rags, much to the amazement of one of his former Oxford acquaintances, whom he met in the street. He tried in vain to persuade Campion to give up his intention but, Persons recorded, he 'made such a speech of the contempt of this world, and the eminent dignity of serving Christ in poverty, as greatly moved the man, and also his acquaintance that remained in Oxford when the report came to our ears'.

Founded in 1543, the Jesuits were still a young Order and had existed for little more than thirty years. They had increased rapidly under their founder, St Ignatius of Loyola, and established a new form of the religious life. When he died in 1556 there were a thousand members at work in nine European countries, as well as India and Brazil. Attracting men from all nationalities and walks of life, they had broken from the choir offices in order to achieve a more apostolic mission. Their spirituality was centred on the *Spiritual Exercises* of St Ignatius which offered a new way of praying. The Jesuit ethos committed members of the Society to a life of external activity with the purpose of helping souls; it also embraced the doctrine of finding God in all things. Bound by a fourth vow of obedience to the Pope, their missionaries broke unexplored frontiers in the New World, India, China, Abyssinia and Japan. Controversial from their foundation, the Society became the spearhead of the Counter-Reformation.

Campion arrived in Rome during a General Congregation of the Society, convened to elect a new Superior General. Everard Mercurian was chosen to succeed St Francis Borgia, the third General. He accepted Campion without obstacles at an auspicious time. The international provincials were present for the congregation and, according to Persons, many cast their eyes upon him, seeking him for their own provinces. No English Province existed at that time and Campion entered the novitiate of the Austrian Province at Prague, in Bohemia, on 26 August 1573. He took first vows and taught rhetoric at the Clementina, the Jesuit College in Prague. In 1578 he was ordained priest by the Archbishop of Prague at the then advanced age of thirty-eight and celebrated his first Mass on 8 September.

Campion remained at the Clementina for six years. It was a happy time; these were the most fruitful years of his life spent since he left Oxford. Not only did he teach, he wrote and directed plays, was Director of the Sodality of the Immaculate Conception, preached and heard confessions in the Prague parishes, visited prisons and hospitals and was in demand for important funeral orations. His life seemed set on an orderly course for the future, and was in some ways much like his old life, but deepened by his faith and vocation. He maintained correspondence with his English friends and pupils but the severance from England was complete and Campion expected to remain in Bohemia for the rest of his life. If he had done so his name would have disappeared from English history.

Cardinal Allen was keen to involve the Jesuits in the English Mission. Allen had left England in 1561 and taken refuge in Flanders, but he returned in the following year and moved among the persecuted Catholics, urging them to be steadfast in their faith. He found that the people were not Protestants by choice; he was convinced that all they needed was an organized body of trained men to look after their spiritual needs, encourage, help and support them, and keep them well-instructed in their religion. Allen wanted the Jesuits for their literary and intellectual talents; 'practised men' he called them.

The General of the Society was less enthusiastic. Mercurian was reluctant to involve the Jesuits in the attempt to influence politics in England because he knew the danger. But he was finally persuaded by Robert Persons to send him and Campion to support the English Catholics with strict instructions to avoid politics and treason. Campion himself was not anxious to return: he received the command in silence, and then said 'God's will be done, not mine'. The charge was not accepted by desire, but under obedience. Campion's contentment in Prague was broken, but the next seventeen months of his life turned him from being a popular and successful teacher into a Jesuit of heroic courage. The peril of the Church in England was known throughout Europe. The night before Campion left, Fr James Gall, from Silesia, wrote over his cell, *P. Edmundus Campianus Martyr.* Another of his Jesuit companions had previously painted the emblem of martyrdom, a garland of roses and a lily, on the wall of Campion's room above the bed where his head rested.

Persons was entirely different from Campion in all but academic achievement. Political by nature, he saw the need for security, secrecy and carefully planned procedures. It was he who had pushed the case for the English Mission, secured Cardinal Allen's approval, and persuaded Mercurian to consent to Jesuit involvement. A yeoman's son and a scholarship student at Oxford, tutor and bursar to Balliol College, he had long equivocated his desire for Catholicism. In 1574 he resigned because of his Catholic leanings, went abroad, and was received into the Church by Fr William Good, SJ. He entered the Society and was ordained priest in 1578. A writer and controversialist, in 1582 he published the devotional *Book of Resolution; or, The Christian Directory* which went into many editions and was widely plagiarized by Puritan opponents.

The missionaries left Rome on foot for England on 14 April 1580 under the leadership of Persons. In the party was Thomas Goldwell, Bishop of St Asaph (who soon fell out due to age and infirmity), thirteen secular priests, Ralph Emerson, a Jesuit lay-brother, and two laymen. Passing through Milan, they were detained for a week by St Charles Borromeo, who made Campion discourse every day to his household on theological topics. From there they travelled on to Geneva where they visited Theodore Beza, the Calvinist theologian, but he refused to discuss religious matters. On 31 May they reached Rheims. There the party broke up and travelled separately by different routes to England. Campion and Persons reached Calais, and made their plans to cross the Channel; in the meanwhile, the other missionaries had scattered along the coast, as it would have been unsafe for them all to embark at the same place.

Persons boarded ship disguised as an army captain, and when they arrived at Dover he presented himself to the port warden without suspicion. It was not so easy for Campion. Assuming the name Patrick, disguised as a jewel merchant, he played the part less well and raised suspicion. The warden accused him of being Cardinal Allen and decided to send him to London, under armed escort. But Campion prayed, 'O Lord, let me work at least one year for my country, and then do with me what Thou wilt.' Immediately, a change came over the official and, to the surprise of all, he said he could go. Campion hurried to London and, through an intermediary, found Persons.

Persons and Campion soon called a meeting of priests

who were hiding in different parts of the country. The reason for the summons was to tell newcomers that stringent orders had been received from their superiors to stand apart from politics. The conversion of Protestants was not included in the purpose of the mission; Catholics and lapsed Catholics, known as Church-Papists, were to be their primary care; recusancy was to be encouraged. They were not allowed to wear clerical dress or religious habits; virtue, piety and prudence were to be their weapons; moderation was to be their watchword, and they were warned against familiar conversation with women, 'even the best of them'.

In an inn at Hoxton, then a small village on the northern outskirts of London, Campion wrote an impassioned manifesto to the Queen's Privy Council which came to be known as Campion's challenge or 'brag'. There he set out succinctly 'the scope of our vocation' in terms of the English mission. Part read:

> And touching our Society, be it known to you that we have made a league – all the Jesuits in the world, whose succession and multitude must overreach all the practices of England – cheerfully to carry the cross you shall lay upon us, and never to despair of your recovery, while we have a man left to enjoy your Tyburn, or to be racked with your torments or consumed with your prisons. The expense is reckoned, the enterprise is begun, it is of God, it cannot be withstood. So the faith was planted, so it must be restored

Copies were printed and circulated in England and translations were widely distributed in France, Germany, Italy and Poland.

If Campion had faults he was, perhaps, too angelic, too rhetorical and he turned a mission into a melodrama. These characteristics emerged in the following months. In August the two Jesuits separated and Campion travelled through Berkshire, Oxfordshire and Northamptonshire, ministering to the Catholic population. The Jesuit General had told them to deal directly with the landed families, not in order to curry favour but because they had the means of giving them shelter and security. They met again at Uxbridge in October 1580. There Campion wrote the *Rationes Decem*, the ten points of the Catholic case which he would have used if Protestants had taken up his 'brag' in a disputation. He concluded with an appeal to the Queen that 'The day will surely come that will show thee clearly which of the two have loved thee, the Society of Jesus or the brood of Luther.' But on 1 December the Privy Council had issued a letter declaring that the Queen intended to 'make some examples of [Jesuits] by punishment, to the terror of others'. Campion then travelled through Nottinghamshire, Derbyshire, Yorkshire and Lancashire. The hunt for him intensified.

Persons had set up a secret press in the attics of Stonor Park, Henley-on-Thames, in Oxfordshire. On 27 June 1581 400 copies of the Latin text of *Rationes Decem* were secretly spread on the benches of St Mary's, the University Church in Oxford, before the convocation at which student supplicants for degrees were required to defend their theses; it caused consternation and uproar.

They immediately left Stonor. Accompanied by Emerson, Campion was due to return north to Lancashire but they broke their journey at Lyford Grange, the Catholic house-hold of Edward Yates, in Berkshire. Persons had urged them not to linger. Here Campion celebrated Mass, heard confessions and preached; but on the resumption of the journey, foolishly, against Emerson's advice, he returned because some importunate visitors, disappointed by his departure, demanded to see him. George Eliot, a Catholic informer, had insinuated himself into the house, and alerted the authorities to Campion's presence. On 17 July 1581 he, two other priests and several laymen, were arrested.

The prisoners were taken to the Tower of London, their hands tied and feet bound beneath their horses' bellies, while Campion bore on his hat the inscription 'CAMPION THE SEDITIOUS JESUIT'. He was confined in a cell in the White Tower known as 'Little Ease', where he could neither stand upright nor stretch out. Campion was taken up river to Leicester House to meet Leicester, his old patron, Sir

Christopher Hatton and Thomas Bromley, the Lord Chancellor, but they could not break his resolve. For three months he was tortured and stretched on the rack and interrogated again and again. A false story was circulated that he had, at last, not only recanted, but had broken the seal of the confessional. Though he named some of those who had harboured him, he did not reveal where he had said Mass, nor did he renounce his faith. His partial collapse under interrogation proved him to be human.

On 31 August, on the Queen's orders, bruised and almost dismembered by the long and repeated rackings, he was led with Ralph Sherwin to the first of four public conferences in the chapel of St Peter ad Vincula in the Tower. These were quite different from the proposal for a conference set out in the brag; the procedure was a one-sided affair, designed to bring discredit rather than illuminate truth. Well-prepared Protestant divines had been appointed by the Bishop of London; Campion had only a few hours' notice to prepare. 'Right opposite upon a stool was set Mr Campion Jesuit, having only his Bible.' The conferences lasted for four hours in the morning and four in the afternoon – the intention being to keep them going for days. During the first, those present saw with horror, as Campion stretched out his arms to emphasize points by gesture, that the nails had been torn from the fingers of both hands. There were no rules of debate but Campion performed well; he was able to deviate, distort, retract and engage in 'bragging and impertinent and insolent speeches' and succeeded in defeating his opponents. The conferences were open to the public, sympathizers attended and Campion made many converts, including St Philip Howard, Earl of Arundel, who subsequently died for his faith on the scaffold.

Six weeks later on 12 November, after a final racking, Campion, with six other priests and laymen, was indicted for trial. They all pleaded 'not guilty' of treason; they were ordered to hold up their hands but the effects of racking prevented Campion from doing so without help. 'How could we be conspirators?' he asked, 'we eight men never met before; and some of us have never seen each other.' On 20 November they were brought to trial in Westminster Hall. Campion defended himself and the others, and criticized the conduct of the trial by 'conjectural surmises, without proof of the crime, sufficient evidence and substantial witness' and he reminded the court that 'Probabilities, aggravations, invectives, are not the balance wherein justice may be weighed, but witnesses, oaths, and apparent guiltiness.' The prosecution was weak and the defence made by Campion unassailable; most expected an acquittal, but to the astonishment of all they were found guilty and condemned to be hanged, drawn and quartered.

When Christopher Wray, the presiding judge, asked the accused if they had anything to say, Campion replied:

> The only thing that we have now to say is that if our religion makes us traitors we are worthy to be condemned, but otherwise we are and have been as true subjects as ever the Queen had. In condemning us, you condemn all your own ancestors, all that was once the glory of England, the Island of Saints, and the most devoted child of the See of St Peter. For what we have taught, however you may qualify it with the odious name of treason, that they did not uniformly teach? To be condemned with these old lights – not of England only but of the whole world – by their degenerate descendants is both glory and gladness to us. God lives; posterity will live, and their judgment is not so liable to corruption as that of those who are now going to condemn us to death.

To the wonderment of the court, when sentence was passed Campion began a canticle of praise, *Te Deum laudamus*, and the other prisoners joined in, followed by the anthem *Haec est dies quam fecit Dominus, exultemus et laetemur in ea* (This is the day which the Lord has made; let us rejoice and exult in it). These songs praising God led to more conversions in the courtroom and news spread of the prisoners' courage.

On 1 December 1581 Campion – the brilliant Oxford scholar, orator, Anglican deacon, convert, Jesuit – with Ralph

Sherwin and Alexander Briant were placed on hurdles and drawn from the Tower to Tyburn. They were dragged at the horses' tails on a wet morning through the gutter and filth, followed by a jeering rabble. One Catholic gentleman wiped his face, spattered with mud and foul matter. Campion was the first to mount the cart beneath the scaffold. When the rope was put round his neck he attempted to address the huge crowd but the sheriffs interrupted him and urged him to confess his treason. To which Campion replied, 'If it be a crime to be a Catholic, I am a traitor.' He maintained his innocence, declined to join in prayer with the ministers, and asked all Catholics to say the Creed on his behalf. His last audible words were for 'Elizabeth, your Queen and my Queen, unto whom I wish a long reign and all prosperity.' The cart was drawn from beneath him and he was left hanging in the air. Before he died he was cut down and disembowelled; his head was then cut off and body quartered. His heart was torn out and the executioner, holding it high in his hand, cried out, 'Behold the heart of a traitor!' and flung it into the fire. The martyrdoms of Sherwin and Briant followed. Thereafter, as a warning, their heads and quarters were displayed in various prominent places.

During the course of time since the martyrs' arrest and trial it was estimated that 4,000 people had been won back to the Faith. Some became priests and religious, others simply remained faithful. One was St Henry Walpole, a young law student of Gray's Inn. His clothes were bespattered by Campion's blood; he became a Jesuit and was himself martyred at York in 1595. For the rest of his life, Robert Persons wore the rope that had bound Campion's hands to the hurdle tightly round his waist as an act of mortification; it is now one of the most sacred relics kept at Stonyhust College, in Lancashire.

What can be made of St Edmund Campion's bravery, witness and death in a post-Christian age? The Church was granted freedom by the Catholic Emancipation Act in 1829 and has grown into a virile body. There is no Government-sponsored persecution of Catholics in Britain today.

Anti-religious sentiments are common, ridicule is occasionally employed, legislation sometimes compromises Catholic teaching, but the main response to religious conviction is indifference. None are called to shed their blood for the Papacy, the Church and the freedom to celebrate Mass and the sacraments.

Some would see Campion as a fool for throwing away a brilliant future that would have brought him honour and riches. Faith still demands loyalty, courage, and grit. Following Christ, accepting the Gospel and the teaching of the Church, being men and women for others and signs of contradiction in a secularized world is a tough, but fulfilling, option that draws us into the life of Christ Himself. St Edmund Campion's and the English Martyrs' sacrifice kept the flame burning and strengthened the resolution of their contemporaries. Few were fanatics; they put truth first and won us the freedom to do likewise.

Chapter 7

Richard Challoner

William Sheils

When Richard Challoner was born on 29 September 1691 the future for English Catholics did not look bright. Between 1678 and 1681 the community had been subjected to a wave of anti-Catholic persecution which led to the execution of a number of priests and some prominent Catholic laymen in the wake of the so-called Popish Plot, an entirely fabricated story of an attempt to assassinate Charles II and replace him with his Catholic brother and heir, James Duke of York. It was of course James' likely succession to the throne which provided the background to the febrile political atmosphere which characterized the 1680s, at both a popular extra-parliamentary level and within the institutions of state themselves. Constitutional attempts to exclude James from the succession were defeated, but when Charles died at the beginning of 1685 the country found itself governed by a Catholic monarch.

The new king was confronted by a rebellion in the west which was easily put down, and he then proceeded to introduce legislation to ease the situation of his co-religionists who, under the Test Act, were subject to a series of civil restrictions on their participation in the state. In ecclesiastical terms he assisted the establishment of the vicars apostolic, dividing the Catholic community into four regions governed by superintendents who exercised quasi-episcopal jurisdiction over the clergy and people. This was a system which was to endure until the restoration of the hierarchy in 1851, but James' other innovations were less helpful, and indeed harmful to his Catholic subjects. The ecclesiastical commission was re-established in order to discipline Anglican clergy who took an aggressively anti-Catholic stance, and James used his prerogative powers to dispense with the Test Act and permit some Catholics to hold office. Parliament objected to this infringement of its right, and MPs refused to pass legislation removing the civil and religious restrictions on Catholics. Faced with opposition James issued a Declaration of Indulgence in April 1687 suspending all civil restrictions on Catholics, an action which revived the link which many English Protestants, looking over the channel to France, made between Catholicism and royal absolutism. Furthermore events in Ireland, always likely to make Protestant opinion nervous, were not re-assuring, for sweeping changes had taken place in the administration of the country following James' accession, with Catholics replacing Protestants in senior positions in government, both central and local, the army and the professions. In 1687 James embarked on a purge of local office-holders, both rural and urban, in England in an attempt to pack Parliament with Catholics or those sympathetic to them, so that many of his most loyal Anglican supporters, those who held a high view of the divine origins of royal authority, began to have doubts. The birth of a prince in June 1688 provoked a crisis which led to the invitation to James' sister Mary and her husband William of Orange to share the throne. Lacking much support James fled to France, the Protestant succession was secured and Catholics excluded from the subsequent Act of Toleration, which gave freedom of worship to nonconformists.

All this would have been welcomed by Challoner's father, a dissenting artisan living not far from Lewes in Sussex, a town noted for its festive anti-popery based around popular celebrations of 5 November. The family's circumstances changed dramatically following the death of Richard's father while Richard was still an infant. His widowed mother, still in her early twenties, went into service, taking her young son with her, joining the household of Sir John Gage at nearby Firle Park. The Gages were a prominent Catholic family who retained Jacobite sympathies, and it is likely that Richard's mother, who had many Catholic relatives, was brought to their attention through these contacts and, perhaps, her own Catholic loyalty.

That Catholicism was strengthened and confirmed during her years at Firle Park and in 1704 she moved to Warkworth manor in Northamptonshire, as housekeeper to Lady Anastasia Holman. This brought the young Richard Challoner into the very heart of English gentry Catholicism: Lady Holman was the daughter of Viscount Stafford, who had been executed during the so-called Popish Plot, and oversaw a devout household which reached beyond its own estate to encourage co-religionists elsewhere. A key figure in this was Lady Holman's chaplain, John Gother.

Gother, himself a convert, had been trained as a priest at Lisbon, a college noted for its policies of accommodation with the English state, through the writings of its former President, Thomas White (alias Blacklo), and the activities of another alumnus, John Sergeant, who acted as secretary of the chapter, the governing body of the English Secular clergy, from 1646 until 1667. Gother himself was committed to an essentially pastoral rather than polemical ministry, beginning his work in England in 1681 as a catechist among the London poor. He is most famous for his series of devotional books, written after the failures of James II, which became the staple instructional manuals for priests in the field and for the laity themselves, at all levels of society. These cheap and accessible books offered guidance to the laity in understanding the Mass and advocated the model of piety embraced by Francis de Sales, that of the devout life lived in the world, disciplined and sober in which the priest served as teacher and confessor to his flock. Gother died in 1704 soon after Richard's arrival at Warkworth, but it was chiefly through his influence that the thirteen-year-old was sent to train for the priesthood at Douai College in 1705.

Douai was under suspicion of Jansenism at this time, chiefly as a result of the perceived opinions of Edward Hawarden, professor of theology until 1707. Challoner spent fifteen years at Douai, was ordained in 1716 and took his licentiate in theology three years later, defending the proposition 'that no Thomist could deny the Pope to be infallible'. In the context of the time this was a controversial thesis to defend in the wake of the papal constitution against the Jansenists, *Unigenitus*, which had been issued by Pope Clement XI in 1713. Challoner had subscribed to this, along with his colleagues, in 1714, but the constitution still remained a matter of controversy within the French Church. The Bishop of Arras did not accept *Unigenitus* until 1721, and even then in a qualified form, and regarded Challoner's defence of infallibility as 'imprudent'. Challoner was appointed professor of theology and vice-president of the college in the following year but, perhaps in consequence of these divisions within the French Church, was unsuccessful in his attempt to secure a chair at the University of Douai in 1721. The university did award him a doctorate in divinity in 1727, by which time he had published his first work, a defence of *Unigenitus* published in Latin. In 1728 he published the first of what became a regular stream of pastoral and controversial works in the vernacular, *Think Well on 't, or, Reflections on the great truths of the Christian religion for every day in the month*. The pastoral purposes of this work stress both Challoner's strengths and also the impact of the Jansenist controversy on the college, resulting in an intellectual conservatism among staff and students. By this date his time at the college was drawing to a close and, in his fortieth year, he set out for the mission in the autumn of 1730.

Challoner followed the example of his earliest mentor, John Gother, in ministering in London. As the capital London contained the largest and most varied concentration of Catholics in the kingdom. Numbering some 20,000 they covered all social categories, from families of labourers, weavers and warehouseman in the eastern parishes, through craftsmen, professionals and shopkeepers around Covent Garden, to the households of gentry located around the embassy chapels in the Northern and Western districts. These embassies brought a cosmopolitan flavour to the capital's Catholic experience, which was also evident at the lower end of the social scale through the substantial numbers of Irish among the labouring population. For all the splendour and exoticism, in English eyes, of the baroque settings of the embassy chapels, the London Mission was very much a mission to the poor, living in crowded conditions and attending services in lofts, pubs and cockpits.

The structures in place for ministering to these disparate congregations were far from adequate; the Bishop, Bonaventure Gifford, was in his eighties, and his aristocratic co-adjutor, Benjamin Petre, ineffectual. Furthermore, many of the clergy acted more or less independently of these structures: the embassy chaplains, about thirty in number, were in effect employees of the embassies; many of the clergy who served the aristocratic and gentry houses during the season operated as domestic chaplains; and even some of those who worked among the middle-class and poor residents were paid out of specific charitable funds, providing them with a degree of independence. In addition all categories comprised a mixture of regular and secular clergy, with separate chains of command. It was among the poor residents of the capital that Challoner's ministry began, preaching, giving the sacraments, and dispensing charity among them in their 'cellars, garrets, hospitals, work-houses and prisons', around Clerkenwell and Holborn. The work was hard but satisfying, distress was relieved and his baptismal register grew, so that in later life he regarded these years as among the most rewarding ones of his ministry, longing to be 'left in a lower station to preach to the poor'.

The work of preaching also involved the production of texts with which to persuade hearers or which might assist other priests in their work. Challoner took on this ministry with energy, producing a number of controversial works in the vernacular during the 1730s in defence of the Catholic Church. The first of these, *The Unerring Authority of the Catholick Church* published in 1732, reveals both his purpose and style. It was not an original text, being grounded firmly in the tradition he had imbibed at Douai, and was organized around eight propositions drawn from both scripture and tradition, as evidenced in the Fathers and the history of the

Church. They were directed specifically to English experience, as for example in the discussion of proposition five, 'The religion to which our forefathers the English Saxons were first converted from heathenism . . . was no other than the Roman Catholick', and Challoner deliberately chose to meet his opponents on their own ground. When quoting scripture he used the King James Bible rather than the Douai version, and he supported his argument with quotes from authorities such as Luther and Calvin, or English Protestant sources such as the works of Bishops Jewel and Tillotson, whenever possible. The congruence of such authorities with Roman Catholic belief did not indicate, however, that the Anglican Church formed part of the one true church. Challoner denied High Church claims to Apostolic Succession, and viewed the liberal stress on the Bible and conscience among other Protestants as fundamentally subversive to the concept of the Church, writing in 1734 in *The Touchstone of the New Religion*, 'Protestants maintain . . . that many different Sects, divided from each other in Faith and Communion, may nevertheless belong to the Church of Christ.' This was not an ecumenical age, and what lay at the heart of Challoner's argument was the question as to what constituted the one true church, and in his view the answer was unequivocal, it was to be found in Rome and only there. These were the foundations of Challoner's controversial writings throughout the 1730s and early 1740s, and their appeal can be judged from the fact that a number were regularly reprinted. His argument, designed to help co-religionists and to appeal to conservative Anglican opinion, did not develop much until the emergence of Methodism, with its emphasis on the senses and on enthusiasm, through its hymn-singing, and its theological break with the stricter versions of Calvinism. Some Anglicans chose to see in these features a parallel between Methodism and popery, which they sought to exploit for polemical purposes, and Challoner chose to respond, indirectly through revising Abraham Woodhead's *Life of St Teresa of Avila* in 1757, and more directly in his *A Caveat against the Methodists* in 1760, in which he differentiated the true religious sensibility of Catholicism from the false enthusiasm of

Wesley's followers, calling Wesley and Whitfield 'wolves in sheeps cloathing' who had 'intruded themselves into the ministry of their own head'. The subsequent controversy generated more heat than light, demonstrating the less creative side of Challoner's intellect.

In 1737 Challoner acquired administrative responsibilities to add to his pastoral and literary work when he was appointed Vicar General of the London circuit by its aristocratic Vicar Apostolic, Benjamin Petre. The London district incorporated the Home Counties and extended south and west to include Hampshire and the Isle of Wight, comprising a Catholic population, estimated at 25,000 in 1746, which was served by about ninety priests, two-thirds of whom were seculars, and the rest regulars, mostly either Jesuit or Franciscan. In addition to the congregations mentioned earlier there were rural missions based in aristocratic households, like that of the Vicar Apostolic's family at Ingatestone Hall in Essex, or the Norfolk's at Arundel Castle, as well as those of more modest landowning families like the Southcotes at Witham. Some of these communities were vulnerable, and when the Southcotes sold their estate at Merstham the chapel soon closed and within a few years there were only two Catholics left in the area. Other congregations, however, witnessed growth at this time; that at Isleworth to the west of London increased from 100 in 1747 to 150 eight years later. In 1737 these congregations as well as those in the capital had become part of Challoner's responsibility, but Petre almost lost his assistant in 1738 when Challoner was appointed principal of Douai. In an uncharacteristic display of vigour the Vicar Apostolic intervened to prevent the removal of such an energetic deputy.

That energy was revealed in his visitation of the district in 1741–2, in which he conducted confirmations throughout the region. Now aged fifty, Challoner's routine settled in to the pattern it was to sustain for the remaining forty years of his long life. His daily routine began at six with prayers and meditation, followed by Mass, usually at eight, or later if for a congregation. Thereafter the morning was spent on correspondence and on his writing until he returned to his breviary at one o'clock, followed by lunch with his chaplains. The afternoon was spent visiting friends or on pastoral visits, often incorporating a walk in Holborn Fields when at home. The early evening was occupied with attending to business, receiving the many visitors someone in his position had to deal with, and hearing confessions. Before supper at nine he said his Office and claimed such time as he could for meditation and reading, retiring to bed soon after. It was a routine and discipline which he rarely altered, and one which many bishops, past and present, would instantly recognize. It was also a discipline which Challoner sought to extend to the clergy in his charge, some of whom, comfortable in the relative independence from ecclesiastical authority which their patrons or posts provided, had slipped into an amiable mediocrity. In order to reinvigorate his priests he set up weekly conferences through which they could strengthen their sense of collegial responsibility, sustain their theological reading, and share the pastoral problems they faced, especially difficult cases of conscience. Daily prayer, annual retreats, regular preaching and catechising of the young were the mainstays of this discipline, reflecting the *devot* tradition of St Francis de Sales.

That tradition informed his most lasting literary and devotional work, *The Garden of the Soul*, first published in 1740. The book went through many editions and revisions, but became the 'devotional backbone' of English Catholicism until the mid-nineteenth-century revival under Newman. It was designed to assist the individual to spend the day in the presence of God, through a pattern of prayer. Its thrust therefore was individual and meditative, rather than collective and communal, but its ability to link its instructional purposes to the sacraments and the liturgy established the individual's place within the wider worshipping community.

The book was self-consciously non polemical: opening with a brief section on belief, it then moved to an exposition of the Ten Commandments, followed by a series of 'Gospel lessons to be pondered at leisure by every Christian soul', reminding the reader of the choices to be made between the worldly and the Christian life, and the demands of Christian love. As such it was activist rather than contemplative, designed for those who 'living in the World, aspire to Devotion' as its subtitle read. Much of that devotion took place in a domestic setting around the ritual of family prayers and especially evening prayer, as later editions of *The Garden* recognized, and prayer was the hallmark of Challoner's spiritual formation. Even in those sections devoted to the Mass the emphasis was on providing devotions to assist the individual attender rather than congregational participation; printing prayers for private devotion instead of the ordinary or proper of the Mass. In this way the liturgy became an extension of the round of prayer which characterized a Catholic life. Whilst this may have reflected the experience of a community whose public worship remained prohibited it also drew on the experience of nonconformity, where the life of regular prayer would be transmitted by the individual into the performance of those worldly obligations which Christians owed each other: charity, fellowship and mutual support.

There was nothing original in *The Garden of the Soul*, much of its teaching being drawn from the *Manual of Devout Prayers* of John Gother, Challoner's mentor, but its popularity both touched a need within mid-eighteenth-century Catholicism and also created a mind set among its adherents such that the phrase 'Garden of the Soul Catholic' came to be used to describe those English Catholics cautious of the Romanizing tendencies which many later associated with the 'Second Spring'.

In addition to this devotional writing Challoner devoted much energy to providing his co-religionists with a sense of their own heritage, and the heroic efforts of their priests in bringing the community to the relatively stable position it currently enjoyed within English life. In his *Memoirs of Missionary Priests*, first published in 1741–2, he set out the example of those priests martyred for the faith, using eye witness and contemporary accounts wherever possible, providing an alternative to the Protestant martyrologies of Foxe, and in his later *Memorial of British Piety* (1761) he traced a national past for his co-religionists. The construction of this national identity was fostered not only in contemplating the English Catholic past, but also in his work of translation, which included a rather staid version of the Bible in English to bring the Douai version up to date, and also in translations of European devotional classics, such as those of Thomas a Kempis and Francis de Sales.

It remains to ask for whom this effort was expended? What kind of Church and community did Challoner serve, and in what circumstances did its members live? The English Catholic community in the early eighteenth century was no longer persecuted and Challoner and his fellow priests could preach publicly in well known centres such as the Ship tavern without too much fear of harassment. Occasionally the shadow of Jacobitism disturbed the community, especially in the aftermath of the '45 when outbreaks of anti-Catholic rioting were recorded in the capital and some provincial towns, but in general Catholics coped with the financial and legal restrictions imposed upon them by the state and lived in harmony with their Protestant neighbours, many of whom assisted their Catholic friends to circumvent the financial penalties of their recusancy by acting as trustees for Catholic property.

In cultural terms the decorative and liturgical grandeur of the embassy chapels, and especially the Sicilian chapel which served as Challoner's de facto cathedral, gave the community in London a certain Counter-Reformation chic which was reinforced among the provincial landowning classes by their experience of the Grand Tour. Politics intervened as ever, and matters were not always straightforward. The annual round of popular national commemorations such as November 5, which not only marked deliverance from the Gunpowder Plot but also the arrival of William of Orange in 1688, served as regular reminders to the general public of their Protestant legacy. At a more local level Catholics were sometimes excluded from the benefits of parochial support by their neighbours at times of economic stress, and in the rapidly growing industrializing communities of the North and Midlands cultural tensions were increased from mid-century in the light of the influx of Irish migrants and seasonal workers. Among the propertied classes individual conversions to Catholicism were accompanied by fears for the social and economic impact on the family and wider community. The late 1760s were difficult years for Catholics, with increasing prosecutions of priests, one of whom was sentenced to life imprisonment, and schoolmasters and, in 1767, the authorities undertook a national census of Catholics. Challoner, already an old man, was also prosecuted soon after this, but charges were dropped following the refusal of the Lord Mayor of London to act and the intervention of the Lord Chief Justice, Lord Mansfield. The actions of these authorities at this time suggest that during Challoner's vicariate, and in no small measure in consequence of his leadership, English Catholics came to be seen, and to see themselves, as occupying a legitimate, if restricted, place within British society. This circumstance received statutory recognition in 1778 by the passing of a Relief Act, which granted freedom of worship to Catholics on the same terms as other dissenters.

Challoner himself was uncertain about the terms of the Act, which stipulated that the monarch should be prayed for in the canon of the Mass, but was content to allow the laity to take the lead on this issue. The passing of the Act provoked violent response among some protestants and on 2 June 1780 a large gathering, some 60,000 strong, assembled in Southwark to demand its repeal. Sections of the crowd broke away and ransacked two of the embassy chapels, provoking a week of anti-Catholic rioting, known as the Gordon riots from the name of its leader, in which chapels, houses and business premises belonging to Catholics were destroyed, as indeed were some owned by Anglican politicians known to be sympathetic to the Catholic cause, such as Lord Mansfield. The Act was the catalyst as much as the cause of the rioting, in which 285 people died, and after which twenty-five of the rioters were executed. Challoner did not escape the riots, being forced to make a hurried departure from his house in Queen Square and seeking refuge at Finchley in the house of William Mawhood, a Catholic merchant. He returned home, but was badly shaken by the events of the summer and suffered a stroke on 10 January 1781, dying twelve days later. He was buried in the family vault at Milton in Berkshire, with both Anglican and Roman Catholic rites.

The religious violence which cast a shadow over Challenor's last days recalled the aggressively anti-catholic atmosphere during his infancy ninety years earlier, but the circumstances in which English Catholics lived and worshipped had changed significantly over the course of his lifetime. By 1780 Catholics could worship freely, if unostentatiously, and for the most part enjoyed civil, and sometimes close, relations with their Protestant neighbours. The organization of the community had been transformed from that of a mission, dependent upon lay support both economically and socially, to that of a church, administered by bishops who governed clerically led settled congregations mostly centred on towns and increasingly independent of gentry leadership. Challoner had done much to effect that change: his devotional writings had provided both laity and clergy with a model of lasting value, and his historical work gave the community a secure sense of its own past; his pastoral work among the clergy created institutions which provided them with collegial purpose and mutual edification, and his work among the laity, informed by acts of charity and the reconciling of consciences through confession, sustained the varied communities of the capital, and especially the poor.

His was not a heroic life in the conventional sense, and his writing contained nothing that was original. In Monsignor Ronald Knox's view Challoner was 'an adapter, an abridger, a continuator, rather than an original genius', but a long and disciplined life of service to his church and to his people produced a community confident in both its Catholicism and its Englishness. This had not seemed possible in his early years, but was to prove to be his enduring legacy until the 1840s, when this quietist devotional pattern became submerged by Irish immigration following the famine and the Ultramontane piety of a later generation of English Catholics, many of them converts themselves.

Chapter 8

Robert 9th Lord Petre

James Stourton

Cardinal Manning once observed that he knew that the Church was built on the foundations of St Peter but he had discovered that it was also built on those of Lord Petre. He was referring to Robert 9th Lord Petre, a pivotal figure in the history of Catholic emancipation. Although his actions as a leading member of the English laity in the early Catholic relief acts from 1778 onwards point towards the future, Lord Petre was increasingly a figure from the past. He represents the end of an era of aristocratic control of the English Catholic Church, the watershed between the recusant period and the growth of a confident Ultramontane Church with strong Irish and middle-class elements. The achievements of Lord Petre were considerable but overshadowed by a certain hauteur which caused rifts with his co-religionists from both the laity and clergy. A man of great charity and personal devotion he was the epitome of the Cisalpine wing of the late eighteenth-century Church with all its strengths and weaknesses.

The term 'Cisalpine' or this side of the Alps came to denote those who wished to keep the Church essentially English in character with a simple form of worship that was discreet and non-confrontational. It came to be contrasted with the 'Ultramontane' (beyond the mountains) wing who took their cue from the other side of the Alps and preferred a grander liturgy and greater control from Rome. It was the 'Ultramontane' form of worship that was to win eventually the day and appeal to the nineteenth-century converts.

The accession of George III in 1760 may be seen as the end of the Jacobite years and the beginning of the Cisalpine brand of English Catholicism, with a strong allegiance to the Crown and its institutions. The surviving Catholic gentry were keen to play their part once more as active and loyal subjects of the Crown. The papal refusal to recognize Charles Edward as Charles III had lowered tension and the young English King 'who gloried in the very name of England' was virtuous and respectful of his Catholic subjects. He was a friend to the Weld family of Lulworth and when they asked him whether they could build a place of worship, he tactfully recommended them to fit up a family mausoleum instead. As is often pointed out we can observe the increasing social freedom and confidence of the Catholic nobility in the new reign through their country-house building. James Paine was their preferred architect whose masterpiece, Wardour Castle in Wiltshire, for Lord Arundell happily still stands.

The eighteenth-century English Catholic Church was run from the country houses of the gentry. The four Vicars Apostolic representing London, the Midland, Northern and Western districts came for the most part from aristocratic recusant families like the Stonors, Giffards and Petres. The greatest of them, however, was Richard Challoner who came from a very different background. Born in 1691 at Lewes he was the son of a wine cooper. He and his mother were converts under the influence of the Gage family at Firle. The boy was sent in 1705 to train overseas for the priesthood at Douai College where he was regarded as the outstanding candidate of his time. He returned to England in 1730 and spent the next fifty years in missionary work in London which he represented as Vicar Apostolic from 1757. His writings, much influenced by Francis de Sales, were simple, direct and very influential themselves. Later in life he longed to be 'absolutely released from all kinds of superiority and left in a lower station to preach to the poor'.

It is estimated that there were 70,000 Catholics in mid

eighteenth-century London from all walks of life. The most visible manifestation of Catholicism in the metropolis were the Embassy chapels, the Sardinian in Duke Street 'the cathedral of London Catholicism', the Imperial in Hanover Square, the Portuguese in Golden Square, the French in Greek Street, the Venetian in Suffolk Street and the Spanish in Ormond Street. These were places of curiosity to the rest of the capital with their fine music and ritual and for the most part were accepted tolerantly. At the other end of the scale Irish labourers would gather in ale houses and cockpits but the most striking aspect of the period is a largely over-looked Catholic professional middle class.

Bishop James Talbot, the brother of the 14th Earl of Shrewsbury, succeeded Challoner as the Vicar Apostolic of the London district in 1781 and remained as such until 1790 and it was he who would have to deal with Lord Petre's self-appointed Catholic Committee. This committee in its various formations was to be the stage for Lord Petre's public life. Bishop Talbot saw at once the usefulness of the committee and at first defended it against a suspicious clergy whose opposition turned into open hostility at the end of the decade.

The Petre family came to prominence at the beginning of sixteenth century as the largest landowners in Essex. Despite their staunch Catholicism, they managed to hold on to their wealth which made them amongst the very richest of all Catholic families. Robert Petre's father died of smallpox when the boy was only a few months old and his mother, who was the daughter of the Jacobite, Earl of Derwentwater (executed for his part in the 1715 rising), died when he was eighteen. Lord Petre had several country houses in Essex: Thorndon Park, Ingatestone Hall, Writtle Park and Crondon Park (leased out of the family) as well as a grand house in London's Park Lane. His main seat was Thorndon Park, an Elizabethan house, which Lord Petre's father had begun to alter using the Italian architect Leoni. Robert abandoned this project and appointed James Paine to create a magnificent mansion on a new site in the Palladian style. Its main features were an enormous rectangular columnar hall and a grand chapel in one of the wings. The house stands today as a parody of its former self rebuilt after a disastrous fire in 1878. Here he kept several priests and chaplains as well as giving houseroom to scholars, some of whom did him little credit.

By virtue of his wealth and position Lord Petre emerged as the leader of the Catholic community. The Duke of Norfolk at the time was a recluse who shut himself away in the library at Greystoke Castle and his successor, the Prince Regent's friend, Charles Howard was a Protestant. What kind of a man was Lord Petre? There are virtually no private papers from which to form a view. A story has arisen that he burnt his correspondence at the end of his life to cover his acrimonious disputes with the clergy but while the fact may be true the reason may not. It is clear that he took his responsibilities very seriously and used his enormous fortune to support Catholic causes. The present Lord Petre believes – perhaps too harshly – that his ancestor 'was no great intellect' and characterized him as representing 'common sense, virtue, religion and loyalty'. Rather surprisingly Lord Petre became a Freemason. Unable to attend the House of Lords, Lord Petre no doubt sought influence through other means. He rose rapidly in the Order and was made Grand Master in 1772 at a time when it was unusual but not unknown for Catholics to join. Lord Petre married twice, firstly in 1762 Anne Howard, niece of the 9th Duke of Norfolk who died in 1787. The following year he remarried, Juliana Howard of the same family.

By the second half of the eighteenth century penal fines had abated but legislation remained that granted informers a reward of £100 for the conviction of a priest. Judges and in particular Chief Justice Lord Mansfield increasingly threw out such cases. Although one might have expected the Whigs to have been the more consistent supporters of Relief Acts, it was the Tories who actually passed much of the legislation. Interestingly most of the Catholic nobility appear to have imperceptibly moved at the end of the century from being Tory to Whig. The first stirrings of change came with Lord North's government anxious to secure the enlistment of Catholic Highlanders for the American wars. There had already been a movement towards freedom of worship in America, as well as the conciliation of Ireland in the light of the American wars. In 1774 the Quebec Act had given rights of worship to parts of Canada. It was four years later that Sir George Savile introduced a bill to the British Parliament after discussions with Lord Petre and his Committee.

The first Catholic Committee was formed in 1778 when Lord Petre invited a small group of lawyers to discuss the means of bringing Relief Acts before Parliament. They elected him chairman. The committee decided that they needed to canvas a larger group of peers and gentlemen and shortly afterwards held a meeting at the Thatched House Tavern where it was agreed that the first step should be to petition the King. The following day Lord Petre had an interview with the Prime Minister who gave the suggestion his blessing. The petition signed by the Catholic peers and gentlemen was presented to the King at the end of the same week. They suggested an oath of loyalty denouncing Stuart claims to the throne and denying papal jurisdiction in England. William Sheldon, who was the first secretary of the committee rejected 'any application to the clergy in temporal matters, the English Roman Catholic gentlemen being quite able to judge and act for themselves in these affairs'. Even so Lord Petre took the trouble to consult Bishop Challoner over the text who cautiously gave it his *nihil obstat.*

The laity had provided the financial support as well as the places of worship that kept the English Catholic Church alive throughout the recusant era. There is no doubt that the Age of Enlightenment had mellowed the antagonisms of the seventeenth century and the Catholic gentry weary of exclusions and penalties sought accommodation with the State and saw the clergy as the principal bar to the adaptations necessary before legislation could be passed. The first Relief Act was passed in 1778 and those who took the oath were able to buy and inherit land. By that year there were only 8 surviving Catholic peers, 19 baronets and 150 landed gentlemen. The bill fell far short of emancipation; it did not even legalize worship but prevented prosecution. Informers against priests could no longer be rewarded. The backlash was not long in coming. Lord George Gordon representing the Protestant Association presented a counter petition for the repeal of the Act and rioting broke out – the so-called Gordon Riots – which lasted for five days and caused damage on an unprecedented scale. 285 people died, many Catholic chapels and Newgate Gaol were burnt as well as Lord Petre's house in Park Lane. He refused the compensation offered to him by the Government for fear of making Catholics even more unpopular.

Despite the subsequent riots, 1778 turned out to be something of an *annus mirabilis* for Lord Petre. That autumn George III was to visit Warley Barracks and Lord Petre proposed that the King might honour him with a visit to Thorndon Park. It was the highpoint of his life and a significant benchmark in the fortunes of English Catholics and their acceptance by their peers. Mark Bence-Jones opens his pioneering book *English Catholic Families* with a description of this famous visit. Fortunately, a couple of diary accounts of this event have survived written by Lord Petre and one of his chaplains which give us a vivid sense of its importance.

> It was supposed that the King would come on October 2nd ... Lord Petre sent for his London upholsterer who arrived the next morning. The great drawing-room, state bedchamber, and two dressing rooms must be newly furnished. Three days later no less than one hundred men and women, upholsterers, gilders, japanners, cabinet-makers and painters are hard at work, and the house steward is ordering gold plate etc from London. On the 30th, two coaches dash up to the Hall beinging [sic] nine French cooks with their implements. More cooks and confectioners appear next day. At last on the afternoon of the 2nd, Lord Amherst sends an express with the information that his Majesty has fixed 19th October for his

visit. So cooks and confectioners are posted back to London, as many orders as possible are countermanded, and a whole new set of eatables is bespoken for a fortnight later. Meantime, his Lordship's neighbours had no cause to regret the mistake. For the next few days there was a succession of dinner parties to eat the dishes which would not keep … Their Majesties were served on gold plate … and Lord Petre added to his family silver all the plate he could hire in London and borrow from the Duke of Norfolk, Earl Waldegrave, Lord Mildmay and other friends.

At this point we have the voice of Lord Petre himself:

The honour of such a visit must be highly esteemed by a subject. It was so by me, and I shall always hold it the most flattering circumstance of my life that his Majesty gave me the opportunity of showing him in the ordinary course of life that respect, loyalty and affection which the laws of my country prevent me from doing on more formal occasions. That same zeal that animated me to search into the most insignificant trifles that could please or show attention to my King, if ever wanted and called for, would exert itself in his service.

Against his Majesty's arrival on the first day about three o'clock, I had assembled all the country, some on horseback and some on foot. The horse advanced to meet his Majesty a little beyond Brentwood, and returned with him through the town (which I had caused to be ornamented with boughs and flags), the bells ringing and bon-fires blazing without number round the country so as to be either seen or heard from all the windows of my house. The army arranged on each side of my avenue, the park of artillery giving constant fire, his Majesty advancing in the midst with all his suite, accompanied with innumerable horsemen, was, I think, the finest sight I ever beheld.

Despite the promising developments of 1778, the historian, Archbishop David Mathew believed that the ensuing decade, the 1780s, represents the lowest ebb for English Catholicism, perhaps a case of the darkest hour of night being the hour before dawn. It was very much the decade of

Lord Petre and his leadership of the laity. He re-formed his committee in 1782 for a five-year term to attempt to complete the work of bringing toleration for Catholics. The first meeting was at Gray's Inn and the five participants elected Lord Petre as their Chairman although there is no doubt that the intellectually most compelling figure was a young lawyer, Charles Butler, who became the first Catholic barrister in England. Their aim was 'the application for a further repeal of some of the penal laws against them, one of the causes urged against their obtaining such relief is the absolute and unlimited dependence of their Superior Clergy upon the Court of Rome ...'. It was the need to refer to Rome over the appointments of bishops that was particularly at issue and for this reason Lord Petre wanted to control the membership of the committee to exclude the diehard Ultramontanes who included Thomas Weld of Lulworth. It is interesting to note that Weld, Lord Arundell and Lord Clifford were all Jesuit educated and had clear ideas about papal obedience. They were to be a thorn in the side of Lord Petre and his committee. They could not countenance a national church or what Archbishop Mathew rather provocatively called 'a closed corporation of the polite unenthusiastic Catholicism of the Thames Valley'.

The committee's work was made more difficult by the transient administrations of the British Parliament until after the 1784 election when William Pitt gained a clear majority and also by the curious business of the marriage of Mrs Fitzherbert to the Prince of Wales. At the end of the five years in 1787 the committee was re-formed once more to include three peers, Petre, Stourton and Clifford and several gentlemen. It was soon evident that the split between the Ultramontanes and the Cisalpines was as strong as ever. When Thomas Weld was invited to join he refused. The 1787 committee has generally received bad press from Catholic historians and there is no doubt that the members behaved in a high-handed fashion towards the clergy. They were mostly concerned with the appointment of diocesan bishops in place of Vicars Apostolic as well as the establishment of a good school this side of the Channel. Their meetings coincided with an initiative by Lord Stanhope to bring a Bill before Parliament for the relief of non-conformists. Stanhope regarded Catholics as a more difficult case and suggested that they should sign a 'Protestation' to recant certain tenets falsely imputed to them. He sent a suggested text to Lord Petre who passed it on to the four Vicars Apostolic. These senior clergymen felt that the 1778 oath was quite sufficient and objected strongly to the idea. Lord Petre's committee, ever pragmatic, attempted to convince them without success.

The 'Protestation' was the final straw for the Vicars Apostolic who met at Hammersmith, denounced the new oath, and demanded the right to inspect all future proposals. The impasse was at last overcome by the suggestion of Bishop Douglas (who replaced Talbot in the London district) to accept the Oath taken by the Irish. In the meantime the public debate continued in Parliament which brought forth the 1791 Relief Acts that gave legal existence to registered Catholic places of worship. Catholics were also finally admitted to professions. This was as far as matters would go in Lord Petre's lifetime. We have a glimpse of this momentous change from the clandestine worship in the homes of the gentry in a letter written in the same year by Lord Petre to Bishop Sharrock:

> I received your proposal relative to the building of a chapel at Monmouth. The collecting of Catholics into towns in place of struggling missions has always been a measure much recommended by me. On those, now legal establishments, the Catholic religion must ultimately depend. The middling classes will find themselves more independent, and the Gentlemen will feel themselves at liberty to consult their own convenience in the expense attending chaplains. I shall therefore willingly subscribe fifty pounds.

In 1792 Lord Petre and other members of the Catholic committee formed themselves into what they called the Cisapline Club. This time they made no claim to represent the body of English Catholicism and the Club gradually devolved into a dining club for people of similar outlook. It had little or no effect on events. The process started by Lord Petre a decade earlier now had a momentum driven by wider circumstances and it was the politics of Ireland and the passing of the Act of Union in 1800 that would dictate the future. Full emancipation (bar certain restrictions such as the Royal Marriage Act) came in 1829 when the doors of English public life were finally opened to Catholics and in the same year Lord Surrey became their first English MP.

At the end of his life, Lord Petre evidently regretted his high-handed behaviour towards the clergy. When he died in 1801 at the age of fifty-nine his passing was mourned by all. His sincerity was never in doubt and nor was his exceptional generosity. He never refused a request such as when Bishop Talbot needed money for 'the provision of spiritual consolations to Catholic prisoners'. He usually subscribed £50 but more for new churches and it would be true to say that he considerably reduced his family fortune through his support for Catholic causes. He went out of his way to help the French refugee nuns from Montargis driven to England by the Revolution and successfully prevented legislation going through Parliament that would have effected the status of émigré convents. But it was his chairmanship of the various committees for which he will always be best remembered. Despite his reputation for being sometimes insensitive to those who did not agree with him, Bishop Douglas, with whom he crossed swords, described Lord Petre chairing a meeting as 'candid in all the different times he spoke' but 'willing to sacrifice his opinion to the sense of the meeting'. In any event he remained the unchallenged leader of the Catholic community and must be credited in large measure for drawing it back into the mainstream of English life.

Chapter 9

John Lingard

Peter Phillips

Though not widely known today, John Lingard, Catholic priest and historian, has well been described as the father of modern historical writing in England. He lived at a time of significant transition for the Catholic community in Britain, a transition in which Lingard himself played a major part. He was born in Winchester on 5 February 1771 before the first Penal Laws had been struck from the Statute Book, and during a summer break from Douai, where he was educated, had joined his father in signing the required Oath of Allegiance to George III in 1791. He was a few years short of sixty before the process was complete and he could write to congratulate Charles Butler on the part he had played in bringing about Catholic emancipation in 1829. By the time of his death in 1851, he had witnessed the dramatic expansion of the Catholic community in towns and cities across Britain as well as the restoration of a Catholic hierarchy in England and Wales.

While recognizing the considerable contribution Lingard made to the Catholic community in England, it is important also to acknowledge the part he played in the transformation of historical scholarship in the first half of the nineteenth century. By an assiduous attention to primary sources newly rediscovered in archives at home and abroad, and often overlooked by his contemporaries, he sought to challenge the Protestant interpretation of England's past. Lingard's *History of England* (8 volumes, 1819–1830) is a political history, but offers one of the earliest in a series of revisionist accounts of England's past which has flowered in the historical scholarship of the late twentieth century. Lingard had a far broader readership in mind than other Catholic historians of the time, seeking to avoid extremes and to produce a *History of England* which would be read with enthusiasm by Protestant England, and challenge the anti-Catholicism which had significantly contributed to creating a sense of Protestant national identity in the century following the Act of Union of 1707. Little by little he sought to restore a rather less aggressive, and less defensive Catholicism to the heart of national consciousness. Although he refused to let apologetic intent compromise his historical integrity, Lingard nonetheless saw himself as an apologist for the Catholic cause, stating forthrightly in a letter to his friend, John Kirk: 'Whatever I have said, or purposely omitted, has been through a motive of serving religion.' Lingard's ongoing attempt to undermine the conclusions of David Hume's popular *History of England* (6 volumes, 1754–1761) offers a good example of this. Yet so powerful were the vested interests of a historical tradition founded on the 'Glorious Revolution', that even in the mid-nineteenth century Macaulay and other popular historians were able to brush aside Lingard's more profound analysis of events.

John Lingard entered the English College, Douai, as a schoolboy of eleven, to escape for home in 1793 amidst the turmoil of the French Revolution and war between France and England. Douai was one of the last cities in the northern provinces of France to join the Revolution but tension in the town was high. One of the first victims of the mob was the College printer, Charles Derbaix, a leading Douai printer and bookseller who had only recently completed the printing of the poster for Lingard's public philosophy examination. Together with another tradesman, accused of illicit dealings in corn, he was taken by the mob and hanged on the nearest lamp-post on suspicion of distributing royalist propaganda. Lingard seems to have been caught up in the fringes of this event and later tells of how he had to run for his life. It is tempting to accept this account of student bravado, but the episode was much more dangerous that Lingard's playful and humorous tone suggests. Like Lingard, many students managed to make good their escape to England, but some were imprisoned in a nearby fortress, returning home only later.

For a short time Lingard acted as tutor to William Stourton who had travelled back to England in his care, but Bishop Gibson called him to join other students from Douai who had made a temporary home at the little Catholic school at Tudhoe, a village just outside Durham. He became a key figure in the gathering of the northern exiles from Douai and in the difficult journey towards the setting up of a new English seminary at Crook Hall, near Consett in County Durham which in turn moved a few miles away to a permanent residence at Ushaw, in 1808, where it still provides theological education for an increasingly diverse group of students, clerical and lay. It was at Crook that he was ordained deacon, but he travelled down to the Bar Convent in York for ordination as priest in April 1795.

Lingard wrote his first book while on the staff at Crook, *The Antiquities of the Anglo-Saxon Church* (1806), as well as entering into a pamphlet controversy fired by the anti-Catholic propaganda of the 1807 election campaign following the fall of the generally pro-Catholic Ministry of All the Talents. Lingard's work brings to the fore the importance of accepting the legitimate authority of the state and acknowledging a tolerant respect for the individual conscience. He took pains to show how Christianity brings culture and civilization together with its promise of salvation, and was as keen, quietly and subtly, to undermine an aggressive approach to the English Church on the part of Rome as he was to indicate England's long-standing links with the See of Peter.

These same concerns are revealed in Lingard's controversy with the staunchly anti-Catholic Bishop Barrington of Durham who republished his 1806 visitation address to the clergy of his diocese during the parliamentary crisis which preceded the

election campaign. Barrington's riposte to Lingard's concilia-
tory response was to reissue his *Charge* for a national readership. The bishop was supported by a host of *Replies, Answers,
Letters* and *Defences* from various Anglican clergy and there
was a controversy in the pages of the *Newcastle Courant*.
Curiously, it was Henry Phillpotts, one of Barrington's most
vociferous supporters in the Durham controversy, whose
correspondence with Wellington paved the way for the emancipation of Catholics in 1829.

With the sudden death of Ushaw's first President, Thomas
Eyre, in 1810, Lingard became acting President of the
College. The work was not to his taste and relations with
Bishop Gibson became increasingly difficult. After seeing
John Gillow comfortably settled in as Ushaw's second
President, Lingard left in the early autumn of 1811 for the
quiet mission of Hornby in the Lune valley. Here he
remained for the rest of his long life. Lingard always
preferred to work in the wings than to strut in the limelight.
He found a home and good neighbours in Hornby and did
his most important work here. Lingard built the Catholic
Chapel at Hornby out of the profits of the early volumes of
his *History*: 'Harry the Eighth's chapel', he joked, because
his study of that King had paid the bills. He shared
generously what he had earned. The quiet daily round of
service to his flock and the life of scholarship he found
congenial: for this he turned down bishoprics and academic
appointments.

Lingard was a valued advisor to the bishops as well as to
laity, a forthright controversialist, and a warm friend. A visit
to Rome in 1817 meant that he was at hand to play a part in
the reopening of the English College there after the ravages
of the French occupation of the city. If he had been
prepared to give up Hornby for Rome in 1826, there is little
doubt that Leo XII would have made him a cardinal.
Whether he became a cardinal *in petto* (unannounced and
remaining a secret kept in the Pope's breast), remains
unknown; he certainly enjoyed sharing the tale in the more
expansive mood of old age. Leo's predecessor, Pius VII, had

conferred on him the triple degrees of Doctor of Divinity and of Civil and Canon Law in 1821 and gradually he achieved European acclaim, his *History of England* being published in French, German and Italian editions. He became an associate of the Royal Society of Literature and in 1839 was elected a corresponding member of the French Academy. Such notoriety turned him into something of a local landmark: the stagecoach would slow down outside his house to allow its passengers to look in on him. To avoid such unwarranted disturbance, Lingard would place his dog on a chair in the window, complete with spectacles and coat, allowing the travellers to catch a glimpse of what they took to be the rather wizened historian hard at work.

The first decades of the nineteenth century bear witness to a growing confidence in the Catholic community in Britain. Less compromising than the generation which had gone before, Catholics nonetheless wished to identify themselves with the mainstream of British life. English history from the Reformation onwards has tended to be isolationist, setting England over against the countries of the European mainland. Lingard's attempt to restore the thread of Catholicism to the skein of English history served also to reintegrate England into the pattern of European history. Lingard made clear that he sought in his *History* to refute the accepted Protestant reading of the history of England. The early volumes were to set the scene, but the chief test of his work would be how he handled the Reformation. Lingard's motive for composing his *History* might lie in religious conviction, but he refused to allow apologetic intent to compromise his integrity as an historian. The five editions of the *History* published during his lifetime allowed Lingard to include new collections of materials as they were brought to his notice, and gradually set out a more explicit statement of Catholic revisionism than he felt appropriate as the task was beginning.

Lingard's historical achievement is considerable. He is the first English historian to make serious use of rare printed material and manuscript sources in the Vatican and other

Italian libraries. He early appreciated the significance of the detailed reports from the Venetian Ambassadors, asking Gradwell in Rome to look out such material in the Barberini Library, which Lingard himself had visited during a trip to Rome in 1817: Leopold von Ranke was, of course, later to come to a similar appreciation of this outstanding collection. Lingard sought out French despatches, as well as material from the state papers of Ferdinand and Isabella and of Philip II of Spain preserved almost inaccessibly in the Spanish castle of Simancas. The pioneering use of such material enabled Lingard to move away from a tendency towards parochialism in English political history by placing it firmly in its European context.

Lingard is one of the first modern historians to highlight the importance of the Henrician Reformation. His sketches of Archbishop Cranmer and of Anne Boleyn provided a strong assault on two of the heroes of the English Reformation: Lingard marshals his evidence to damning effect and it might well be true to claim that the reputation of neither of these figures has fully recovered from his attack. Following Cardinal Pole, he also recognized the importance of Thomas Cromwell and his consummate skill in establishing the machinery of Tudor government. Lingard, in an astute piece of political analysis, showed how the Tudor monarchy had destroyed the ancient balance of the English constitution: the ancient families of the land had been much reduced, their place being filled by new men, favourites and dependants of the Court, owing situation and wealth to the whim of the King, and in no position to resist the encroachments of the sovereign. The bishops found themselves even more subservient: passive obedience had become the orthodoxy of the day. Lingard was critical of both religious parties, highlighting the tragedy inherent in the fact that, with the exception of figures like More and Fisher, the two sides of the religious divide merely 'flattered [the King's] vanity, submitted to his caprice, and became the obsequious slaves of his pleasure'. Catholic and Protestant died together for their belief, the former hanged and quartered as traitors, the latter consumed in the flames as heretics.

An account of the reign of Mary Tudor must offer the most serious test of Lingard's skill. The reign of Mary poses a problem for any Catholic apologist: her reputation was felt to cast a dark shadow on the interpretation of England's history. Hume had used the despatches of the French ambassador, Antoine de Noailles, whose intrigues with disaffected parties in England produced a highly prejudicial account of Mary's policy. Taking his cue from the French Jesuit Henri Griffet's critique of Hume's account of Mary, Lingard, with the assistance of contacts in Paris, traced the remainder of the despatches from the Imperial ambassador, Simon Renard, to the library at Besançon and had them transcribed. Renard had a very different agenda from Noailles, and his reports to Charles V offered a significantly different assessment of the opening months of Mary's reign to that of the French ambassador. Robert Gradwell was also in a position to check references from the *relazioni* of the Venetian ambassador in the Barberini Library in Rome.

Lingard, so often taking an opposite position to Bishop Milner, agreed with him in refusing to exonerate Mary for her part in the executions of the Reformers, arguing that they represented 'the foulest blot on the character of the queen'. At the same time he did all within his power to provide a foil to set the executions in the context of a positive evaluation of that sad monarch. Mary lived in an age where it was expected that the monarch should extirpate heresy: she only practised what others taught, 'it [being] her misfortune, rather than her fault, that she was not more enlightened than the wisest of her contemporaries'. He stresses Mary's virtues: her decency; her preparedness to accept advice. He reflects movingly on her increasing mental sufferings: her popularity dwindling, and with little chance of parenting an heir, she faced the tragic inevitability of her vision for the restoration of Catholic England dying with her.

Whenever he found opportunity, Lingard emphasized Mary's compassion, pointing to the disinclination of

Gardiner and Bonner to participate in heresy trials, and, suggesting that Philip, too, did not support persecution, argued that responsibility invariably lay not with the Queen herself, but her Council. Lingard maintains that the number of executions for heresy was rather less than often accepted and that though his deductions 'will take but little from the infamy of the measure ... in the space of four years almost two hundred persons perished in the flames for religious opinion'. He is incorrect here, considerably underestimating the total: the best contemporary list of executions, preserved amongst the Cecil papers and published by Strype, includes 282 people of whom Foxe recorded 275; it is known that a few more victims died whose names are unrecorded. Lingard emphasizes the provocation given by the Reformers; the internecine squabbles that broke out among the exiles; the plots at home, invariably exacerbated by the duplicity of the French monarch and his ambassador Noailles; and the role of Elizabeth as a focus for dissension, protected only by Philip, who saw her as the only way of preventing England falling under the sway of France, Spain's enemy, on Mary's death. Lingard's account of Mary's reign is indeed a case of special pleading, but Lingard uses his facts well and was able to boast with some justice to his publisher that 'the whole of this part of the volume may be pronounced new to English readers, and an important addition to our history'.

Rather curiously it is the Reformation volumes of Lingard's *History*, united with Bishop John Milner's writings, which furnish William Cobbett with the material for the trenchant social polemic of *A History of the Protestant 'Reformation' in England and Ireland* published between 1824 and 1826. This, as the subtitle proclaims, was intended to demonstrate 'how that event has impoverished and degraded the main body of the people in those countries'. Cobbett took from Bishop John Milner his defence of the monasteries and from Lingard his attack on Cranmer and Anne Boleyn to create a vivid account of the social damage wrought by the Reformation, the most numerous victims being the poor and homeless who had seldom been turned away from monastery doors: as a result of the Dissolution they became friendless. Cobbett abandons the historical objectivity cherished by Lingard to produce a series of verbal sketches paralleled in the later engravings of Pugin's *Contrasts* (1836). There is no doubt that Cobbett took Lingard to places he would not have ventured by himself, but Cobbett's use of Lingard's work serves to demonstrate just how far Lingard had turned away from the historical approach of his Catholic predecessors.

Lingard had a sound instinct for searching out archive material, but this was an instinct allied with remarkable good fortune. A noteworthy example of this is his publication of the Secret Treaty of Dover: writing to Lord Stourton for information which might enable him to present a more favourable picture of Charles II, Lingard intimated that he thought 'the Clifford family may be in possession of some documents respecting him' and asked Stourton to approach them in the hope that they might 'entrust material to the mail'. What came in the post turned out to be a batch of papers relating to Charles II's reign, and including the final protocol of the Secret Treaty ratified at Dover in 1670. Lingard published the Treaty in volume seven of his *History* (1829). It was something of a coup. The documents had been passed on by the King for safe keeping to the first Lord Clifford, one of the signatories to the Treaty, and knowledge of its existence was preserved only within the Clifford family circle. As Lingard comments of the Treaty: 'though much was afterwards said, little was certainly known'. By publishing the document, Lingard offered proof that Charles II's alliance with Louis XIV was political rather than religious in motivation, and he was able to discredit the view, popularized by Whig historians, that it formed the final piece in a Catholic conspiracy to undermine the Protestant cause. It was no such thing.

Lingard's correspondence was not only a matter of historical enquires. In later years he corresponded sometimes more than twice weekly with his friend John Walker, missioner in Scarborough, and with others. These letters provide a delightfully unbuttoned commentary on Catholic life during the first half of the nineteenth century. It is interesting to compare his support for the convert Mary Sanders in her difficulties with her family with his letters to Hannah Joyce, a Liverpool Unitarian: there is no attempt to convert Miss Joyce, though there is a little gentle teasing of her as a heretic. Though he did not bear fools gladly, he approached others always with a delicate respect, numbering non-Catholics among friends and correspondents. Lingard was an indefatigable letter writer and many of these letters have been preserved in archives and private collections. Rarely away from Hornby for long, Lingard relied on a variety of correspondents for the information he needed for his historical studies and parcels of books and manuscripts were regularly sent to his door, as well as notes of research done for him in the British Museum and other collections.

Friends also were swift to beat a path to his door; he was a good host, though he did not encourage visitors. Both Henry Brougham, who became Lord Chancellor in the Whig administration which saw the Reform Bill through Parliament, and the Tory, James Scarlett, Lord Chief Baron of the Exchequer, looked forward to the chance of sharing Lingard's table when they were travelling North. Lingard liked nothing more than a quiet evening with the Anglican priest across the road, who on his death bequeathed his pets into Lingard's care. Hornby has one of the few Anglican churches where there is a monument to the local Catholic priest and it attests his ecumenical sensitivity.

Lingard had been missioner in the little Lancashire parish of Hornby, eight miles inland from Lancaster, for forty years and, to the end, he had reflected on Catholic life in this country with a gentle and probing irony. In the months before his final illness, he witnessed the restoration of the hierarchy, and his pupil Nicholas Wiseman (now a Cardinal and Archbishop of Westminster) with wry humour: 'I always thought it ridiculous myself because Westminster was a bishopric created by Henry VIII, and to make it an archbishopric for Catholics would be strange.' Westminster and its See is now a familiar part of Catholic, and not only Catholic, life in the country: a result, in some ways, of Lingard's contribution to the redefinition of what it means to be English and a Catholic.

John Lingard walked for the last time in his garden on Easter Sunday 1851, examining the saplings he had planted out from acorns provided by his oak, itself once an acorn picked up by Lingard on the shores of Lake Trasimeno during a tour of Italy. The following day he took to his bed. His last years had been dogged by illness which brought considerable pain, and cataracts which made reading in anything but the brightest light more and more difficult. These ailments were met with a characteristic lack of self-pity and a humour marked with what we might now consider an overly brash and Georgian delight in the vagaries of our internal systems. There were days when he became increasingly incoherent, failing to recognize even the closest of friends. Difficulty in breathing made it more convenient to spend those last days and nights propped up on the sofa in his library and there, amidst his books, he died just before midnight on 17 July 1851.

By the time of his death many Catholics regarded him as a representative of the old school, cold and Gallican, and lacking the new-found fervour of nineteenth-century Catholicism. This has led many to underestimate the significance of his *History* and of the role he played in giving shape to the Catholic community. It was an opinion echoed in *The Tablet* obituary, and by many scholars since. This was certainly true of his approach to liturgy: he preferred liturgy to be intelligible and attractive both to the Catholic community and to Protestant visitors, disliking repetitious litanies and the flowery metaphors of the new devotions being introduced from the Continent. He wanted his congregation to understand and follow the celebration of Mass, a fact well illustrated in the *Manual of Prayers on Sundays and During the* Mass (1833), which Lingard compiled for the use of the congregation which attended his chapel in Hornby.

There is little doubt that he would have approved the liturgical changes of Vatican II. He sought simplicity, disdaining both the medievalism of Pugin's Gothic Revival and the unwarranted pomp that often accompanied the opening of churches: the church being 'turned into an opera house' and 'the bishop performing as the first dancer in the ballet', as he remarked of the celebrations which were held at the opening of one church in his neighbourhood. It is to him we owe one of the most beloved of English Catholic hymns, his translation of the *Ave Maris Stella, Hail Queen of Heaven*, which has survived into our modern repertory of hymns, while many a Victorian contribution has been quietly laid to rest.

A public controversialist, an historian who sought to include, rather than exclude, the Catholic in the pattern of our English history, an ironic observer of all types and conditions of people, Lingard was the most unclerical of clerics. As this essay hopes to have demonstrated, this unassuming priest contributed significantly to a sense of burgeoning confidence on the part of the English Catholic community in the early nineteenth century and laid the foundations for a renewal of historical studies reaching far into the future. His inspiration provided a foundation for the late twentieth-century work of scholars as varied as Eamon Duffy, Christopher Haigh, Conrad Russell and Jack Scarisbrick. They owe much to the pioneering industry and careful balance of John Lingard.

10

Augustus Welby Northmore Pugin

Roderick O'Donnell

In Pugin's frontispiece to his book *An Apology for the Revival of Christian Architecture* (1843) the architect illustrates five cathedrals, fifteen parish churches, a monastery, a hospital, a private chapel and a gatehouse which he had designed and built in England and Ireland in less half a decade of frenetic architectural and artistic activity. Through his buildings and his publications he transformed the architectural setting of Catholicism in England from that of a fugitive remnant to that of a national church, and one moreover prepared to challenge the Anglican claim to that role. For ten years from 1838 he can be seen as almost the impresario of the entire Catholic Revival – and his work extended very much to Ireland too. His contribution was recognized by the future Cardinals Wiseman and Newman, by Dickens and Disraeli, by the *Tablet* and *Punch*. His fame even gave rise to an ' –ism': 'Puginism' was the hostile phrase of his religious and architectural critics. Hosts of architects – especially under the influence of the (Anglican) Ecclesiological Society – plagiarized his buildings and his ideas, and were dubbed 'the Anglican' or 'the Irish Pugin' etc. Architect, artist, writer and convert, he was one of the great lay heroes of the nineteenth-century Catholic Revival.

Augustus Welby Northmore in was born in 1812 to a French father and an English mother. He had a pampered early boyhood and an erratically managed education which, architecturally, took place in the extraordinary drawing

The Present Revival of Christian Architecture: frontispiece to *An Apology for the Revival of Christian Architecture* (1843). Thirty-five of his church commissions are shown.

office established by his architectural illustrator father, one of the powerhouses of research and publication on the buildings of the English Middle Ages. Pugin was a brilliant draughtsman – he has been called 'a Mozart of drawing' – and he was involved in the later architectural publications of his father's circle – amongst whom the Catholic architect E. J. Willson was an early influence. The young Pugin was also pulled into the more raffish worlds of the Regency decorating 'trade' – he set up firstly in designing and manufacturing furniture, an enterprise which bankrupted him in 1831 – and of the theatre as a set carpenter; his life and much of his art was to be eminently theatrical. During the next two years, the loss of his wife in childbirth, then of both his parents, a second marriage and birth of his son took place. He was to bury his second wife in 1843, and care for his six motherless children until his happy third marriage in 1848, which produced two more children. He began to look more seriously at architectural practice, which, in his anti-quarian-filled mind, he associated with medieval Catholicism, writing that 'the roman Catholick church is the only true one ... A very good chapel is building in the north and when it is compleat I certainly think I shall recant', a step he took in 1835.

Pugin taught himself his Catholicism (as he did architectural practice); he said 'I gained my knowledge of the ancient faith beneath the vaults of a Lincoln [Cathedral] or a Westminster [Abbey].' But the phrase 'a very good chapel is building in the north' shows that had made an assessment of the Catholic building world. He also knew of Catholicism through his French aunts, and many visits to France. He now set off on a series of tours and meetings in 1836–7 with Catholic lay leaders, including the Earl of Shrewsbury, to whom he dedicated *An Apology*, and the Hardman family in Birmingham. He also presented himself to the bishops and religious Orders; amazingly he converted them all, except the Jesuits, to his cause, that is to the Gothic Revival, and to the necessity for ambitious churches to be filled with every possible liturgical and devotional aid for the revival of the liturgy. From his reading and from his study of the surviving medieval churches, he had firmly in mind the Sarum rite, that of England just before the Reformation, whereas that actually required by the rubrics of the contemporary Church was the Tridentine rite. Pugin preferred to speak of an 'English' rather than a 'Roman' Catholicism, and critics, such as Newman, in identifying 'Puginism' as something inimical to their 'Romanism', tarred his party – that of Lord Shrewsbury – with Cisalpinism or Gallicanism: a belief in the defence of the rights of the local church in relation to those exercised by Rome.

Until his death aged forty in 1852 he was a figure of notoriety in these chosen fields; forthright in his new faith and its practice, though open to debate with sympathetic Anglicans (he was one of the first Catholics to make contact with the Oxford Movement). But given the sharp sectarian divisions of the time, as a Catholic he necessarily cut himself off from the even greater architectural opportunities that Anglican church building and restoration would have offered. Pugin made himself expert in the design of churches – Catholics at the time called their places of worship *chapels* – on a scale for which they had had no previous expectation. He achieved this by monopolizing all of Lord Shrewsbury's patronage. Shrewsbury refused money to churches which did not appoint his preferred architect, a fact that allowed Pugin to take over the cathedral projects in Birmingham and London. Other architects were displaced – he seized from one the completion of the Oscott seminary, and orchestrated the liturgy of its consecration, when he was remembered by Bishop Ullathorne with 'his dark eyes flashing through his tears, calling it the first day for England since the Reformation'. In 1839 he was congratulated by Wiseman on 'achieving the transition from chapel to church-architecture amongst us'. The Blessed Sacrament chapel at Giles's Cheadle (1840–6), his masterpiece, brought even the sceptical Newman to his knees, exclaiming *'Porta coeli'*: Gate of heaven. Another cleric dubbed him 'Archbishop Pugens', while a bishop dismissed him as 'a tradesman'. The story was told of him replying to a bishop who asked for a church '*very* large – the neighbourhood was *very* populous ... it must be *very* cheap – they were very poor; in fact had only £—' with 'My Lord, Say *thirty shillings* more and have a *tower and spire* at once'! Building committees he also treated with contempt, and he refused to take his hat off in the presence of a peer who kept his own on during an interview. In 1842 he published as if a *fait accompli* his bird's-eye view of a rebuilt priory at Downside – of which in the event not a single stone was ever to be laid – to which the shocked correspondent exclaimed to the Prior, 'why he has swept away everything you have done already'. Many of his most ambitious schemes remained on paper, or half finished.

One which came very close to completion was St Chad's Cathedral Birmingham (1839–41). It also demonstrates how he reshaped such church commissions to his own liking. A project to rebuild under lay management a modest existing chapel was transformed by Pugin, in alliance with the bishop, Lord Shrewsbury and the Hardmans into the first Catholic cathedral to be built since the Reformation. He wrote of its 'foreign style of pointed architecture ... totally different from any *protestant* erection. Any person would be aware this was a Catholic church at first sight'. Architecturally too the building was revolutionary: it avoided all the tricks of the neoclassical style – stucco imitating stone, roofs hidden behind parapets – for a frankly expressed use of local red brick with steep slate roofs; Pugin could rightly claim that the design was 'both cheap and effective'.

Internally the Cathedral had all the panoply of fittings and shrines of a late medieval church; indeed much of the furniture was medieval: the pulpit was fifteenth-century Flemish, as was the superb brass lectern; Pugin himself gave the fifteenth-century German wooden statue of the Virgin and Child – and this at a time when most Catholic churches had no statues at all. These were the models or 'authorities' which Pugin constantly cited and this statue was to be the basis of those later made by George Myers. The most notable design of his own was the rood screen which was paid for by the Hardmans, and which incorporated further medieval woodwork, such as the statues on the mullions. It was to be ejected in the re-ordering of 1967. And where medieval fittings were not available or adapted, Pugin made designs inspired by them and revived the lost techniques for their manufacture: encaustic tiled floors, stained glass, wood-carving and metal-working, wall paintings and vestments, chalices, missals and other service books. And the bishop even had a small but serviceable palace opposite.

It was typical of Pugin's priorities that a school was omitted, and the old chapel had to be fitted up for that purpose. It was the liturgy which obsessed him: the Catholic Church in England would be revived through the exact performance of the liturgy in such Gothic churches. Ruskin guyed Pugin as one 'blown into a change of religion by the whine of the organ pipe: stitched into a new creed by the gold threads on priests' petticoats'. But for some it worked just like that: as a seventeen-year-old schoolboy, the future Professor St George Mivart, was received into the Church after attending his first High Mass in St Chad's Cathedral one Sunday in 1844. Pugin had an understanding of the meaning of the liturgy shared with only a handful of priests at the time, and here he anticipated much that would be explored by the later liturgical movement: he had a deep understanding of the Mass and the office, Gregorian chant, the importance of lecterns, and of side chapels (rather than tabernacles on high altars) for the Blessed Sacrament, full 'Gothic' vestments and surplices; he deplored popular and extra-liturgical devotions such as Benediction, the music of Mozart and Haydn, 'Roman'-cut vestments and French lace, all called by him examples of 'that mass of vitiated taste, the modern French school', which he witheringly ascribed to the influence in church of 'societies of ladies'. Pugin complained in 1840 that 'the churches I build do little or no good for want of men who know how to use them' and he was to explain the use and meaning of his churches in books such as *The Present State of Ecclesiastical Architecture in*

St Chad's Cathedral, Birmingham: Pugin's rood screen (1840–1),
re-arranged in this form in 1854, was demolished and disposed of
in 1967.

England and the sumptuous but expensive *Glossary of Ecclesiastical Ornament and Costume*. (1844). Through his collaboration with John Hardman Junior as 'medieval metal-workers' and later for stained glass at Hardman & Co. he achieved a truly remarkable reform of what would later be called 'liturgical arts'.

Pugin's publications reached a wider audience than his buildings. He had a flair for self-publicity and lived in an age of pamphleteering and of journalism, and through these mediums he found a wider audience than the few antiquarians and architects he had known as he began to move into architectural practice, and amongst Catholics. He first threw himself into architectural and religious politics with the book *Contrasts; or, A Parallel between the Noble Edifices of the fourteenth and fifteenth centuries and similar buildings of the present day, showing the present decay of taste* (1836) which was so inflammatory that it had to be privately printed. He electrified his readers by denouncing the prevalent neoclassical or 'Pagan' style in architecture, which he attributed to the Protestant Reformation. Historically, he drew on techniques of seventeenth-century writers such as Dugdale, and of the more recent antiquarians such as John Carter and the Catholic Bishop John Milner, who used architectural evidence to challenge the Reformation or to promote the claims of the Catholic Church. With its iconoclastic tone and brilliant line drawings he contrasted medieval buildings drawn in rich detail with half-starved caricatures of contemporary buildings, contrasting even the diets of the Middle Ages with that of the nineteenth century.

The Present State of Ecclesiastical Architecture in England (1843) proclaimed his success as a church-builder, with over thirty-five churches to his name. In this book he presented some of his most coherent thought on how Catholic churches should be designed, furnished and used. (Seven years later he again summed up his practice in a highly self-critical retrospect in *Some Remarks on articles which have recently appeared in the 'Rambler' relative to ecclesiastical architecture and decoration*, 1850.) His most

Contrasted Residences for the Poor: Modern Poor House, Antient
Poor Hoyse. *Contrasts* (1841).

important architectural theoretical treatise, *The True Principles of Pointed or Christian Architecture* (1841) marks him out as an architectural reformer and, as such, one of the begetters of the Modern Movement in architecture; drawing on French architectural rationalism and English picturesque thought in architecture, he revalidated the Gothic as a style suitable, because of its rational or 'natural' construction, as well as on national and religious grounds, for the reform of not just its architecture but of society as a whole, groaning under the dislocation and poverty of urbanization and industrialization, so starkly felt in the 'hungry forties', as the 1840s were to remembered. For Pugin a populace that lived and prayed in Gothic buildings would function better as a society. His answers to the 'question of England' debate were romantic, religious, mystical and Tory – although Lord Shrewsbury himself was a Whig. He had much in common with programme of the 'Young England' Tories who appear very thinly disguised in Disraeli's *Coningsby* (1845) along with Pugin's architecture and patrons. His buildings embody a sort of Merry Englandism – he wrote 'Catholic England was Merry England' – but the economic basis on which many of his projects were based was weak; many convents and churches faced ruin when the Shrewsbury title fell into Protestant hands in 1856.

Pugin built much, and designed yet more in the applied arts. Much of his decorative and applied arts work survives at the Palace of Westminster and it is here that his legacy as a designer is most readily appreciated. The Houses of Parliament comprise one of the most iconic buildings in the world. It was rebuilt, after the fire of 1834, by the architect Sir Charles Barry, who had Pugin's help as a draughtsman with his successful competition entry drawings (1834), in the 'estimate' drawings of 1835, and then continuously from 1844 in the decoration of the interior. Whilst Pugin's role was underestimated in the nineteenth century, it is now popularly over-estimated: he did not design the building, but he was certainly the genius behind the design, fitting-out and furnishing of the interiors. From 1844 he had an official title and a salary as Superintendent of Wood-Carving, but he did much more than simply provide drawings and casts for the woodworkers, important and highly successful as this was.

Dismissing architecture as 'the Trade', he saw himself instead as devoted to a patron or to the Church or perhaps to one great building – as the Palace of Westminster turned out to be. He had a horror of architectural office practice, and refused work which involved preparing for competitive tender or full specifications. He saw himself instead as the medieval master-mason of the Romantic imagination, signing his early drawings not as *'architectus'* but *'commentarius'*: mason or master of the works. But he got no publicity from his work at the Palace, and indeed Barry's masking of Pugin's contribution remains controversial. Pugin's relationship with Barry was a personal, not an official one: he defined himself as 'your agent entirely [having] nothing to do with any other person'. He had a similar attitude, though one not of subordination but direction, to John Hardman and George Myers, and one of collaboration with Herbert Minton, John Crace, and their workshops, saying that he would not work 'with men I have not schooled'. Thus he produced endless drawings for Barry and for his own 'men': designs of wallpaper, fabrics, stained glass, floor tiles, brass work, iron work, 'state' and working furniture. His purpose was that his designs be executed accurately and that therefore the 'real thing' – an authentic Gothic Revival, not decorators' tricks – would thus be propagated. (He was to take the same attitude at the 1851 Great Exhibition.)

The poverty that dogged much of Pugin's commissioned work for Catholic church architecture means that he and his collaborators were seldom to be given their head; it was thanks to Barry's insistence that they were in the new House of Lords, which opened in 1847. It was as lavish as the country houses and castles from which the peers came – indeed Alton Towers, where Pugin had worked for Lord Shrewsbury, was cited as a model to be copied, and

Shrewsbury sat on one of the committees. Pugin's setting was ideal for an Indian summer of great aristocratic power: the Victorian era, even with its broadening franchise, still saw prime ministers leading the Government from the Lords well into the 1890s. This extraordinary 'Catholic' decorative *tour de force* was foisted on a Parliament that had been dedicated to denying Catholics any voice at all in constitutional arrangements until 1829, a mere fifteen years beforehand, and which was still subject to periodic and vociferous anti-Catholic outbursts such as the 'Papal aggression' reaction to the Restoration of the Hierarchy in 1850.

The tenor of the interior, particularly the House of Lords chamber, is Pugin's, and, although no Catholic bishop sits here, the interior is brimming with the iconography – statues, coats of arms, Latin inscriptions – of the Catholic Middle Ages exactly as Pugin had imagined them in *Contrasts.* Examples of Pugin's genius as decorator can be seen everywhere, especially in the flat pattern decoration inspired by heraldry, for which he provided original and endlessly decorative sources throughout. His control of colour, of line and of shape, inspired by heraldry, manuscript illustrations and other 'authorities', is masterly. He applied it also in wallpaper, fabric, curtain and carpet designs. Pugin's economy of style and ability to simplify distinguishes him from the formless welter of realism which characterized so much mid-Victorian decoration, as the Great Exhibition of 1851 was to show. Although little of his stained glass now survives, there is much in his style by his son-in-law J. H. Powell; but a wealth of metalwork can be seen, from the fantastic brass lamp standards in the House of Lords, and the magnificent brass doors to Peers' Lobby, to the sturdily wrought and structured architectural brass and ironwork such as window and door furniture. Over such small works, he complained 'I could make church as easy as grate' [a church design as easily as a fire-grate]. But the results are superb. His woodwork designs and the quality of the carving achieved are particularly high in the intricate

The chamber and bar of the House of Lords, Joseph Nash, c.1853.

panelling and figure carving in the Lords' chamber – often copied from casts of medieval examples. The chair and table furniture reflect his ideals of constructed joinery, as illustrated in his publications.

Pugin's leading role in the evolution of the professional middle-class house has been underestimated by historians, beginning with Pevsner. At the Grange, Ramsgate, constructed (1843–4) for himself and for his family and for the artistic colony he was gathering together, he designed an astonishingly original house. Its clarity was obscured by Edward Pugin's later alterations which the recent restoration of the house to an 'ideal' state by the Landmark Trust has reversed. The house is now at its most striking, brilliantly, indeed shockingly, decorated inside in dense overall patterns and very strong colours. It is a design of an architect with a manifesto to create in his own house and living arrangements, as we might say, a *'lifestyle'*, for the middling sort' as he put it. Here, and in the adjacent church, Pugin was as he said 'both paymaster and architect'. He once again built in local brick, and allowed the functions of the house to be expressed in its plan and on its elevations.

The key is the stairs-hall, a two-storey space inspired by the Hall of the medieval house, from which the ground- and first-floor family rooms branch off; kitchen, servants and children are tightly packed into in a separate wing and up a stairs tower, but still intimately related to the rest of the house, not regulated behind a green-baize door or by class and age. Here, refusing to set up an office or hire clerks, Pugin 'worked from home', so that from morning prayers with the family in the chapel, to the singing at bedtime of the *Salve Regina* in front of the statue in the hall, he could be surrounded by his large family as he worked, interrupted only by meals and play, even if it was like 'living in a pig market' when the children overran him. From here, armed with his myriad of letters and drawings, he travelled by train, boat and carriage to his many building sites. 'I am like a locomotive, always flying about', as he said, and, like modern man, he worked dangerously long hours, and was absent for

weeks on end. Next to the Grange he built his 'trophy' building, the church of St Augustine (1845–1850), telling his son
'Watch this church; not a single True Principle will be
broken'. Pugin built it as a thank offering to God for his
professional success, paid for entirely by him and given to
the diocese on his death, and from 1862 forming the church
of the adjacent Benedictine Abbey, another of Pugin's
wishes.

Pugin was much interested in the seminaries, hoping that
the students would develop an interest in the church
history, liturgy and art of the Middle Ages, as his title
'Professor of Ecclesiastical Antiquities' at the Oscott
Seminary shows. There, to complement existing collections
of relics, vestments, and chalices, he made up a study collection of architectural and sculptural fragments for the
students to draw or model from, just like his own education
in his father's office; and indeed two students at St
Edmund's College, Ware, did just that, decorating the ceiling
of the sanctuary in 1853. Pugin altered and lavishly furnished
the seminary chapel at Oscott (1838), built a complete
chapel at Ushaw (1844–8), designed and built St Patrick's
College Maynooth (from 1845). At St Edmund's, a mighty
brick church was built (1844–53) with a great hall-like T-plan
church with a 'west end' ante-chapel and cloister. Massive
Decorated-style windows form the only decorative elements
against the plain buttressed brick walls rising sheer, somewhat reminiscent of his unexecuted design for the chapel at
Maynooth.

Pugin's main interest, as always, was in furnishing and
decorating the interior. The project was held up by lack of
funds: he designed a tomb and other furniture in memory of
Bishop Griffiths in 1848, which was very slowly imple-
mented. His high altar, which survives intact, was complete
by 1853. His great work was the rood screen, actually a deep
jubé, like a small internal porch with two altars either side of
the central passage and a platform and organ gallery above;
here is the wooden cross, which was shown minus the
crucifixus figure and statues of Our Lady and St John at the

1851 Exhibition. There had been a furious reaction to his proposal to show these carved figures at the exhibition. Accusations of the building of a 'Roman Catholic chapel' were made and the storm reached both the Prime Minister, Lord John Russell, the instigator of the 'Papal aggression' outbreak, and even Prince Albert. Pugin successfully defended his 'Popish chapel' but the statues had to be omitted from the exhibition, demonstrating the difficult context in which he still had to work. Such reactions came not only from Protestants: the stark realism and painted flesh tones of his Rood groups offended cautious Catholics too who preferred that their religious emotions be mitigated through the idealization of classical and Italianate art: a correspondent in the *Rambler,* a Catholic periodical reflecting the position of the Oxford Movement converts, called 'the rood and figures most unsightly' and those at St George's Southwark 'coloured in the coarsest possible way – repulsive'; the statue of the Blessed Virgin – another of those descended from Pugin's gift to St Chad's – was said to be 'coarse, fat, stiff and deformed'. (Such reactions also greeted the first works of the Pre-Raphaelites.) The opening of St George's in 1848, and in particular its rood screen, was to be met with a chorus of disapproval in the *Rambler.*

Pugin insisted that Rood screens dividing the laity from the clergy, the nave from the sanctuary, were required in the Catholic liturgy, and he wrote *A Treatise on Chancel Screens And Rood Lofts, Their Antiquity, Use, and Symbolic Signification* (1851) to prove his controversial point. By now his omnipresence on the Catholic scene provoked a counter-reaction, especially amongst recent converts such as W. G. Ward (whose appointment at St Edmund's caused Pugin to exclaim 'that man should not be allowed to live near so fine a screen'). This group, supporters of Newman's Oratory, took Pugin very seriously as an opponent, and whispered about 'delating' – the technical term for denouncing – his views at Rome, rather as both liberal and conservative Catholics do today. Following the Restoration of the Hierarchy, in one of his very last writings, *An Earnest*

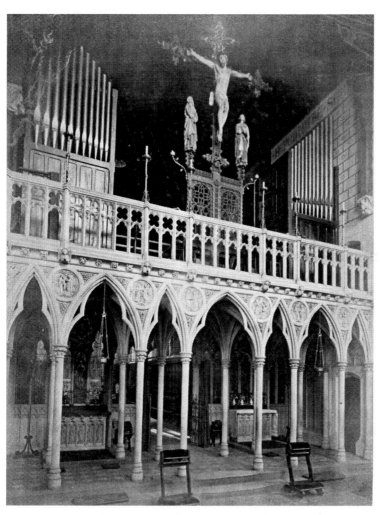

Rood screen, St Edmund's College, Ware.

address on the subject of the Re-establishment of the Hierarchy, (1851) he suggested how the new bishops should be financed – just the sort of unsolicited advice that the bishops did not want to hear. Now Lord Shrewsbury's and Pugin's views were to be sidelined just like those of Lord Petre. From now on, the middle- and upper-class laity were expected merely to 'pay and pray' in the newly clericalized, centralized ultramontane Church, which drew strength instead from the 'pennies of the poor' for the churches needed by large urban congregations.

Pugin died aged only forty, many of his views rejected by the Church, a disappointed man. The Pugin family left for Birmingham, and only returned to Ramsgate in 1862. And it is extraordinary to think how Victorian architecture might have developed had he lived: recent commentators have analyzed in his late works the beginnings of the High Victorian style. His first legacy was his buildings. However, so many of his churches have been altered or re-ordered that only one or two can be seen as he intended them, notably at St Giles Cheadle. The next legacy was his family of sons and sons-in-law. His decorative style was continued by his son-in-law J. H. Powell at Hardman & Co. in stained glass and metalwork, in particular at the Palace of Westminster and in many churches. His son Edward was to be the leading Catholic church architect until his death in 1875, and it was his adaptation of his father's style and church plans to better accord with the Tridentine liturgy which critics hailed as 'as a complete revolution in church building'. But his failure to authorize a biography was a major set back to his father's reputation; instead Benjamin Ferrey's *Recollection of ANW Pugin* (1862) – he even got Pugin's initials wrong – had to do, until the publication of Rosemary Hill's brilliant but tantalizing *God's Architect, Pugin and the building of Romantic Britain* (2007).

At first, leading Catholics turned their backs on Pugin – notably in the *Rambler* and in the *Tablet*, where his publications and buildings were attacked. This debate, known as the 'Rood Screen Controversy' was intended to banish the

Gothic from Catholic church-building, but it was not to succeed. Despite some notable exceptions such as the Italianate Brompton Oratory (1878–84) and the 'Italo-Byzantine' Westminster Cathedral (1895–1903), most Catholic church-building remained Gothic well into the twentieth century.

Outside England, the Gothic Revival was never tarred with the brush of 'Puginism', and in Belgium especially the style was the badge of the Ultramontane party led by the architect Count Jean-Baptist Bethune; the same is true in Catholic Germany; the Gothic was also the badge of Catholic self-assertion in Ireland, and in the English-speaking world, especially Australia. By the 1870s, some Catholic artists and architects, following the Belgian model, formed the Guild of SS Gregory and Luke, taking up his teachings again. The best example of their work was the restoration and fitting out of the church of St Etheldreda, Ely Place, London, (1877–9), But only one of them, J. F. Bentley – who despairingly characterized most Catholic churches and their decoration as 'gaudy claptrap' – designed and built with Pugin's intensity. Typically, other Catholic architects were much busier and more prolix, such as Dunn and Hansom at Our Lady and the English Martyrs Cambridge (1885–1890) and F. A. Walters at Sacred Heart Wimbledon (1886–1901) and especially the Pugin & Pugin firm with the youngest son Peter Paul, until his death in 1904.

More thoughtful Anglican architects, starting with Bodley, began to re-assess and indeed imitate Pugin; in 1892 Richard Norman Shaw, visiting St Augustine's, exclaimed 'we have not advanced very much. Such work makes one feel … very small'. It is a comment on the scale and amplitude of the surviving artistic and architectural production of Pugin that no-one has yet succeeded in writing the critical art-historical monograph that is so much required of him.

Chapter 11

Cardinal John Henry Newman

James Tolhurst

When he came to write the history of his religious opinions, *Apologia pro Vita Sua* (which was something unusual for those times) Newman said, 'I must give the true key to my whole life; I must show what I am that it may be seen what I am not.' For almost a hundred years, people seemed to concentrate on what Newman wasn't. At long last it seems that they are beginning to realize the greatness of what he was.

Newman was born in London on 21 February 1801, the eldest of six children. His father, John, was a banker in the City. His mother, Jemima Fourdrinier was the daughter of a prosperous paper manufacturer. They created a lively, musical and happy family. At seven, Newman went to the same school in Ealing as the authors Thackeray and Captain Marryat. He went up to Trinity, 'a most gentleman-like college' (said his headmaster) in 1816, and did not leave Oxford until 1845.

He was to say to Dr Ullathorne, the Bishop of Birmingham, when he was an old man, that he was 'inside all his life' while Ullathorne 'battled for the Church in the world'. In a sense it was true. If we want to learn something of John Henry Newman we must read his works. Apart from the *Apologia* he wrote so many letters that it has taken over thirty bulky volumes to publish them all. He admitted freely that he was a literary man who loved the classics. He also was fond of novels and devoured Walter Scott and Anthony

Trollope. He would write two *Tales*, as Newman called them, *Loss and Gain (The Story of a Convert)* and *Callista,* set in a third-century North African town during the time of Roman persecution. But in a sense he does himself an injustice because although he lived an intellectual life, he made continual forays into the larger world.

For half of his life, Newman was a member of the Church of England and for twenty years a curate, and then vicar of St Mary's Oxford. It was largely from that pulpit that he preached what we now know as *Parochial and Plain Sermons*. We need to remember that sermons not long ago occupied a good forty minutes (this also applied to the main High Mass in Catholic churches). Newman preached not simply a literary piece but very much from the heart. He also had a definite poetic touch. 'Christ', he said, will acknowledge Himself – his image in us – as though we reflected him, and he, on looking round about discerned at once who were his; those, namely, who gave back to him his image.' On another occasion, 'One alone is constant; one alone is true to us; one alone can be true; one alone can be all things to us; one alone can give meaning to our complex and intricate nature; one alone can form and possess us.'

Yet even as he was writing his sermons and visiting his parishioners, dealing with their problems and at their bedsides when they were dying, he was involved with all the financial and managerial demands of his College. He still was able to produce an analysis of the doctrine of justification and a mastery work on the Church in the fourth century, confronted with the Arian crisis. It was his contact with the Fathers of the Church, especially St Anthanasius, St John Chrysostom, St Basil and St Augustine which began the investigation into the exact nature and structure of the Christian Church. Those who are born Catholics find it hard to appreciate the great soul-searching which goes on in the hearts of converts. In Newman's case his search was particularly painful because he was at the centre of things. There were no theological colleges in his day – all the bishops came from Oxford and Cambridge – a former Archbishop of

Canterbury had been vicar of St Mary's; in his congregation were future royal chaplains and prime ministers (Gladstone among them). The life of an Oxford don was – and is – extremely stimulating. The conversation in the common room of a high quality (Newman's colleagues included Keble, Pusey, Whately, Hawkins, Froude and Blanco White, the ex-priest), and the interaction with undergraduates a real challenge. He had also introduced daily communion at St Mary's and built a chapel at Littlemore on the outskirts of Oxford.

Although it was Keble who preached the sermon at St Mary's on National Apostasy which marked the beginning of the Tractarian Movement, Newman was very much the guiding hand behind the Tracts. He also wrote the most. Tracts were not normally associated with the high ideals of apostolic succession, separation of the Church and State and the writings of the Fathers on the sacraments. Newman was quite candid about their impact, 'The Tracts give offence, I know, but they also do good.' Newman could not content himself with a perception of the treasures of Christianity without a desire to share them, which would bring him ulti-mately into conflict with the authorities of the Church. In the same way he could not be a Tutor without trying to have an impact on his undergraduates – which would bring him into conflict with Hawkins, the Oriel Provost, who succeeded Dr Whately.

The paths of conversion are many and varied. Some – like W. G. Ward – decide in a rush of enthusiasm. Newman argued himself into the Church. He was to say in his early days that he never sinned against the light. He endeavoured to be scrupulous, fair and honest. Fair to the Church of England and honest to the Church of Rome. His familiarity with the Fathers – whose teachings many clergymen despised – led him eventually to consider the possibility of Anglicanism being the *Via Media*, between Protestantism and Roman Catholicism. It was a courageous position to take as it seemed to belittle the contribution of the Smithfield martyrs. Newman merely intended to evaluate the Catholic contribution to Anglicanism but thus became a symbol of Catholicism to Protestants. This was especially so when he provided a Catholic interpretation to the Thirty-Nine Articles.

The public rejection of Newman's arguments by the bishops was a bitter blow. Gladstone maintained that Newman was treated 'worse than a dog'. It did however force him to consider whether there was such a thing as a development of doctrine, since other avenues had been closed. He began with the text 'Mary kept all these things, reflecting on them in her heart' (Luke 2:19). Eventually this became one of the most important books of theology, *An Essay on the Development of Christian Doctrine*. Newman left the book at the end of a sentence (and later wrote thirty letters of explanation to friends) when he learnt that Fr Dominic Barberi, the Passionist, was coming to Littlemore to receive Richard Stanton and Frederick Bowles into the Church. He asked to be received also. It was 8 October 1845.

Although Newman's conversion caused great joy to the Catholics (and dismay among his former colleagues) it was for Newman a great wrench. He had been a figure of stature, but as a Catholic he had to submit to being catechized by an Italian priest, and having to line up with young seminarians to go to Confession to Dr Wiseman, the Bishop at Oscott College.

Eventually Newman was sent to Rome for ordination and when he was there decided that his choice for the priesthood was the Congregation of the Oratory (founded by St Philip Neri in 1548) for it was 'like a college with barely any rule'. Newman, the former fellow of Oriel started his Oratory in a former gin palace near the present bus station in Birmingham. As a large and growing industrial town, it attracted a large number of Irish immigrants. Newman was not at all dismayed. He commented that 'boys and girls flow in for instruction like herrings in season'. At his first night he had between 500 and 600. He provided English Compline, with the quaint translation of Psalm 91:6: 'The business that walketh in darkness.' When there was no one else, he played the organ. He also noted that the confessors were often bitten by bugs in the confessional and the passageways smelt like the 'For Gentlemen' on railway stations.

Newman, the literary man went with Fr Ambrose St John to Bilston in 1849 where there was a cholera outbreak. His parishioners cried when they went and pressed on them bottles of ale. Soon Alcester Street was abandoned for Edgbaston and Newman set about buying the roof of a factory to form an economical church.

No sooner established than he was accused of having torture chambers in the cellars. (Maria Monk's salacious 'history' was on everyone's lips). Newman invited MPs to come and look. He gave lectures in King William Street (the home of the London Oratory) in which he had to hide his laughter behind the manuscript as he provided a contemporary version of the parable of the Pharisee and the Tax Collector, 'A lazy, filthy beggar woman 'not over scrupulous of truth' who believed in God and tried to fulfil her duties of him, had a better chance of heaven than the 'state's pattern man' who relied on himself.' He was speaking from experience.

Critics were to say that Newman threw away his life and stunted his mind when he became a Catholic. Those who look dispassionately can see a development. The Catholic Church provided even more scope for thought since it was not held captive by Protestant theology. But this didn't mean that Newman found it plain sailing. His essay in *The Rambler* on *Consulting the Faithful in Matters of Doctrine* was delated to Rome by Dr Brown, the Bishop of Newport. In this as in other theological matters Newman always exonerated.

A more serious assault on his good name occurred in the Achilli trial. Newman had in the course of lectures at the Birmingham Corn Exchange in 1851 mentioned the case of Fr Achilli, a Dominican who had been dismissed for gross immorality,'a profligate under a cowl'. He had left the Church and become a Protestant. He sued Newman for libel and his case was taken up by the Protestant Alliance.

Evidence of Achilli's misdeeds could not be obtained in time and when the case came to trial the judge found him guilty and took the occasion to point out that this was only the consequence of his desertion of his friends in the Church of England. He was fined a hundred pounds, but the costs of the case amounted to twice Newman's total resources. A public appeal in England and USA successfully raised more than the amount required.

During the Achilli debacle Newman was asked to become Rector of the new University of Dublin. He was invited to give a series of talks on the idea of a university, find a building and appoint staff. Over the years Newman built the University Church (the surplus from the Achilli appeal provided the basis), wrote the statutes, lectured, issued a magazine *The Atlantis*, and appointed lecturers, while all the time acting as Superior of his community at Edgbaston. He was in the end destined for a disappointment (although his medical faculty survived), as the bishops in Ireland could not agree on funding or overall management.

It was the same with the invitation to provide a new translation of the Scriptures. Newman fitted up a Scriptorium at the Oratory and had decided on the typeface. The Archbishop of Baltimore had even suggested that they would propose a trans-Atlantic edition. Fr Faber virtually admitted to Newman in his last illness that the London Oratory fathers had been promised the task, but nobody had possessed the courage to inform Newman, and the whole project eventually collapsed.

There was also the question of an Oratory in Oxford – for which Newman bought five acres of land. Although Bishop Ullathorne gave his approval, the hierarchy hummed and hawed and thought – and delayed on the grounds that Newman in Oxford would be too controversial.

Newman was of course controversial. He refused to believe that thought could be put into a straitjacket. He also would not consider his former Anglican friends were dishonest in their beliefs. He considered that a man may be true even if his ideas were not and, 'that individuals in the

English Church are invisibly knit into that True Body of which they are not outwardly members' (cf. Vatican II, *Decree on Ecumenism* n. 3).

Newman was passionate about truth. It stung him deeply when Charles Kingsley, the author of *The Water Babies* and Regius Professor of Modern History at Cambridge, wrote 'Truth for its own sake has never been a virtue with the Roman clergy. Fr Newman informs us that it need not be, and on the whole ought not to be.' The response was the *Apologia pro Vita Sua* (*Apologia* = defence or justification of one's beliefs). It was a complete vindication of Newman's *standpoint*. It is in fact the theory of development applied to the history of one's mind. It received praise from many of his former clergymen whom he praised for their kindness and their help. It has remained in print ever since.

Newman went on to write *A Grammar of Assent* which shows that we can be certain of things that do not admit of mathematical proof or direct experience. He was consulted during the first Vatican Council and forcefully maintained that the temporal power was not essential to an infallible pope. However, when his friend Gladstone sought to show how the Vatican decrees could command Catholics to act contrary to their civil allegiance, Newman went into print in *A Letter to the Duke of Norfolk* – the Duke being the premier Catholic layman. He explained the nature of civil and religious authority and the real meaning and extent of papal infallibility. He also emphasized that 'Conscience is the messenger of him, who both in nature and in grace, speaks to us behind a veil, and teaches and rules us by his representative. Conscience is the aboriginal Vicar of Christ.'* Gladstone's response to Newman was 'I had to fold my mantle and to die.'

Pius IX's successor, Leo XIII would create Newman a cardinal in 1879. In doing so he said, 'I always had a cult for him. I am proud that I was allowed to honour such a man.'

---

*Newman's words can be found in the *Catechism of the Catholic Church*, n. 1778.

Pope Leo was only saying that he had always admired Newman – he was at the Nunciature in Belgium when he met Fr Dominic Barberi, en route to England, and was told about his expectations of conversion among the members of the Oxford Movement. However Newman's outstanding virtues have been recognized by Rome, which is a stage on the road to canonization.

Lord Coleridge, Lord Chief Justice, and son of the judge who found Newman guilty at the Achilli trial was only one of those who considered Newman saintly. He said, 'The fascination of the man, personally, is far the greatest I ever felt. He never talks controversy, hardly alludes to difference, and you feel all the while that you are talking to a great and holy Christian.' Part of that impression comes from the fact that Newman exemplified the ideal of a priest after the mind of Christ. He was full of faith from beginning to end: 'God has never failed me. He has at all times been to me a faithful God.' He said in one of his sermons, 'There is no one who has loved the world so well, as he who made it. None has so understood the human heart.' In a sense, it was Newman's own understanding of the human heart that made him so exceptional as a priest. Pusey would say of him, 'He has won more souls to Christ than any beside.' Anyone looking through the letters to and from Newman can grasp the great affection for him and the influence he exercised in all walks of society. He was continually answering doubts, offering suggestions, giving spiritual advice. Cardinal Manning, when he had lost his wife, and Newman had written to console him, replied, 'I hardly knew what has drawn me so closely, and in one way suddenly to your sympathy, but I feel something in the way you deal with my sorrows, particularly soothing and refreshing.' Meriol Trevor, the author of a two-volume biography of Newman, makes the point that love comes to those who give it and from the beginning Newman loved people and delighted in being loved. He combined that with great intellectual gifts of clear logical reasoning. Normally one would cancel out the other but, in Newman's case, his priesthood seems to have been the means that he could allow both faculties to develop together. This has mystified many of his critics and has puzzled many of his biographers. They see in his affection, sentimentality and in his reasoning, cold calculation. They forget the man who loved to play Beethoven and Haydn violin sonatas and was responsible for *The Dream of Gerontius.*

But if we allow the facts to speak for themselves we see someone of great integrity. Bishop Ullathorne – the rough-spoken Yorkshireman, who dropped his 'aitches' – was to say, 'There was no honester man on earth.' As a member of the Church of England he faithfully observed the ritual and teaching. His research into the Fathers was occasioned by an invitation from Lyall and Rose, the editors of the new Theological Library, to write a volume on the Councils of the Church. When it was found to be too favourable to Tradition it was declined and Newman found another publisher. His championing of *The Tracts for the Times* was part of his aim to re-invigorate the Church he loved by reminding it of the rock from which it was hewn. Whately accused the Tractarians of deceit but in fact *The Tracts* were born out of a desire for greater truth.

As Catholics we should esteem the value Newman put on the search for truth which led him to consider the doctrine of the Incarnation as it was developed by the Fathers. The Incarnation leads on to the economy of the sacraments and the Church. But if the Church is to represent Christ, then it must be authoritative. Hence it must be the Roman Catholic Church. Once he had reached that point, there was no room for delay. Nor was there ever any further doubt.

Yes, Newman did believe in theological debate. He was friends with Dr Dollinger (who found it impossible to accept the doctrine of Infallibility) and he was acquainted with those who doubted because they included Blanco White and his brother Francis a Lecturer at University College London, whose *Phases of Faith* maintained that 'Religion is created by the inward instincts of the soul: it has afterwards to be pruned and chastened by skeptical understanding.' His other brother, Charles died a convinced atheist. Newman always had an abiding sense of God's presence which was deepened when he became a Catholic by the doctrine of the Eucharist, and his reverence for the priesthood he exercized. This allowed him avoid fundamentalism which is the death of true research, and liberalism which teaches that 'One creed is as good as another.' He wanted a Catholicism which was faithful and inquiring. He bemoaned the fact that 'Instead of being a world-wide power, we are shrinking into ourselves, narrowing the lines of communication, trembling at freedom of thought, and using the language of dismay and despair at the prospect before us, instead of, with the high spirit of the warrior, going out conquering and to conquer.' This argued in favour of a great respect for conscience.

In November 1889, aged eighty-eight, he heard that Catholic girls in the Cadbury's factory in Bourneville were being forced to attend prayers and a commentary before work. The girls objected, supported by their parish priest, and their employers thought that they were being difficult and their parish priest was simply being awkward. They were quite sure that Cardinal Newman would agree with their position. When Cardinal Newman heard the news, he sent for his carriage and walked the last part of the way through the snow to inform them that as good Quakers they might consider the Catholic girls badly informed in matters of worship but they should not violate their conscientious scruples and allow them to say prayers in another room. The employers agreed and Newman went home pleased, telling Fr Neville, 'If I can but do work such as that, I am happy and content to live on.'

John Henry Newman lived through a time of great discovery and exploration. He saw the railways, electricity, photography and the motor car. He was alive at the time of Trafalgar and read of the sources of the Nile and the Indian mutiny and of the meeting between Livingstone and Stanley. He had a nugget from the California Gold Rush. We tend to regard as heroes, men like the cavaliers. But the term 'cavalier' was derived from the Spanish *caballero* and was a derogatory insult directed towards the allegiance of Charles' court for Spanish Catholic ways. Heroes are made of different stuff and Newman, his Eminence, the Father provides a lesson in all that is best in a gentleman and a priest. He lived his life with dignity right to the end. On the Saturday evening (he would die on Monday 11 August 1890) Fr Neville tells us that Newman came into his room 'unbent, erect, to the full height of his best days in the fifties, without support of any kind. His whole carriage was, it may be said, soldier like, yet so dignified: and his countenance was so attractive to look at; even great age seemed to have gone from his face, and with it all careworn signs; his very look conveyed the cheerfulness and gratitude of his mind; and his voice was quite fresh and strong: his whole effect was that of power combined with complete calm. One might add with readiness to die.

For his memorial tablet in the cloister (for Fathers of the Oratory have a simple cross over their grave with their name) he chose *Ex Umbris et Imaginibus in Veritatem* (from shadows and appearances to the truth). He had always born witness to the truth throughout his life and through his writings tried to bring others to recognize its power. Long ago he had written :

> Still is the might of Truth as it has been
> Lodged in the few, obeyd and yet unseen.

If we are to learn anything from the life of this distinguished and noble man it is his obedience to the voice of God prompting, even urging. Such obedience does not lead to a shrivelled existence devoid of friendship or affection. Newman was not afraid – any more than Teresa of Avila – to accept friendship, particularly when it came to gifts for the community. He wrote to Mrs Bowden for the community gift of a dozen bottles of port and thanked Lord Arundel on one occasion for his sumptuous easy chair, commenting humorously, 'What a Purgatory I shall have.'

When told that Elizabeth Moore regarded him a saint, he replied, 'Saints are not literary men, they do not love the classics, they do not write Tales. It is enough for me to black the saint's shoes – if St Philip uses blacking – in heaven.'

Chapter 12

Cardinal Henry Manning

Robert Gray

When, on 6 April 1851, Passion Sunday, Henry Manning and his friend James Hope were received into the one, true fold at the Jesuit church in Farm Street, they were told – so the triumphant Lady Georgiana Fullerton reported – 'that they could bring to the Church nothing, and were to receive from her everything'. On one view this was simply an unexceptionable Catholic sentiment, of obvious appeal to an enthusiast such as Lady Georgiana, who had herself converted but five years before. With hindsight, however, her exultation might also be seen as the opening salvo in a long campaign by the grander variety of English Catholic to keep Manning firmly in his place. In the short term, it was a campaign that totally failed. In 1865, a mere fourteen years after his conversion, Manning became Archbishop of Westminster; when he died in 1892 hundreds of thousands of Londoners lined the streets to pay their respects as his coffin was borne to Kensal Green cemetery. It was one of the most spontaneously impressive expressions of popular grief in the Victorian age. Yet the 'Upper Ten Thousand' (as Manning had called them) of English Catholics maintained their reserve, and subsequently demonstrated no concern to protect his reputation. Even when Manning became the victim of Edmund Purcell's malicious biography, published in 1895 and later copiously mined by Lytton Strachey for *Eminent Victorians* (1918), hardly a single English Catholic voice was raised in the Cardinal's defence. It was left to

Hilaire Belloc, French on his father's side, radical on his mother's, to announce defiantly that Manning had been 'much the greatest Englishman of his time'.

What, then, had Manning achieved, and why did the Upper Ten Thousand remains unimpressed? The root of the problem, perhaps, was that he had not treated English Catholics as his central concern. From the moment Manning became Archbishop of Westminster in 1865, he was quite clear that his first priority was to work for the Irish immigrant community in London. More than that, he possessed the sympathy and the insight to realize that the despised Irish represented the best hope for the maintenance and growth of the Catholic faith in England.

By 1865 three centuries of persecution had reduced the native Catholics to an insignificant minority. The penal laws had been unevenly enforced, and somewhat relaxed in 1791; they had, nevertheless, been effective enough to ensure that by 1800 there were only some 60,000 Catholics in England, or one per cent of the population. In general the highest worldly ambition of the Catholic gentry was to merge unprovocatively into local life. As if to cast off any implication of disloyalty, they tended to be more John Bullish than John Bull, involved with agriculture, dedicated to sport (Catholics played an important part in the development of cricket) and scornful of any intellectual pretension. Mindful that in 1570 Pope Pius V had exposed them to persecution by the excommunication of Queen Elizabeth, they showed scant enthusiasm for extreme papal claims. If they needed guidance, they were as likely to consult 'the prelates of the squirearchy' as the Bishop of Rome. 'My father is the head of the Protestant church,' remarked the Prince Regent, 'and Lord Petre is is the head of the Catholic Church.' The spirit of the Council of Trent had never really taken root among English Catholics. Among them, Exposition of the Blessed Sacrament was exceptional; disciplines, hair shirts and rosaries were scarcely known; invocations to the saints aroused suspicion, and ostentatious devotions to the Virgin Mary risked being dismissed as 'continental'.

If, by 1851, there were suddenly close on 700,000 Catholics in England and Wales, or nearly four per cent of the population, that was certainly not due to any religious revival, nor to the trickle of converts from the Oxford Movement. It was simply and solely the consequence of Irish immigration, which English Catholics were inclined to regard as a decidedly mixed blessing.

At the London Oratory, for example, Father Faber bemoaned the 'immovable *belts* of stink' which the Irish brought into the church, and which risked driving away worshippers from the washing classes. This is not to say that the better-off English Catholics were all unconscious of their duties towards the newcomers; on the contrary, some of them gave generously towards the construction of new schools and churches. They could hardly conceive, however, that supporting the Irish might be the first principle of Catholic social policy. Indeed, many English Catholics would have been stunned by the notion that the Church should have any social policy at all.

Manning, by contrast, imported into his new religion the moral fervour of the Protestant Evangelical movement. Born in 1808, the youngest of eight children, he had been raised in a family keenly conscious of its duties to society. The philanthropic pattern was evident in the first marriage of his father, William Manning, a prominent West Indian merchant in the City, to Elizabeth Abel Smith, a banker's daughter and a first cousin of William Wilberforce. William Manning's second wife, née Mary Hunter, the future Cardinal's mother, also had Evangelical connections, and never allowed her children to forget their duty towards the poor.

Yet there was another, more worldly, strain in Manning's background. The upper-class Evangelicals retained a keen sense of what Wilberforce called 'useful' people – namely those who were best placed to forward their schemes of charitable improvement. Like many of their descendants among today's secular moralists, they kept one eye on the ills of the world, and the other on the main chance. 'Mr Wilberforce's humanity will go to all lengths that it can with safety and discretion,' observed William Hazlitt, 'but it is not to supposed that it should lose him his seat for Yorkshire, the smile of Majesty, or the countenance of the loyal and pious.' Manning, of course, would show by his conversion that he possessed the courage to separate himself from the English establishment; having taken the plunge, however, he was instinctively aware that a pope may be as useful as a prime minister.

In youth he had dreamt of purely worldly power. His father had chosen a future prime minister, Henry Addington (Viscount Sidmouth from 1805), as his godfather; and Manning, after a dandyish phase at Harrow, began at Balliol to concentrate his formidable ambition upon ascending the political ladder. Already he was very sure of his own opinions, wise in the ways of the world, wholly self-reliant, and not much given to disinterested friendship. At the Oxford Union he spoke with such fluency and authority that contemporaries began to think of him as a potential prime minister, perhaps with the still more earnest young William Gladstone as Archbishop of Canterbury. Certainly Manning's willpower excluded the possibility of failure. 'I do not expect so much as to falter in Schools,' he declared. 'This is a moral and not an intellectual principle.' He duly achieved his first-class degree.

At this stage, however, William Manning's business collapsed into bankruptcy, consigning to oblivion his youngest son's hopes of political glory. Nevertheless Manning struggled for while against this most obvious fact, and his eventual decision to take Anglican Orders cost him much agony of mind. 'If ever I made a choice in my life in which my superior will controlled my inferior will,' he would reflect in his old age, 'it was when I gave up all the desires, hopes, aspirations after public life at the dictate of my reason and conscience.' At the dictate, too, of his bank balance. Yet once he had committed himself to an ecclesiastical career, he did not look back.

Providence duly rewarded him. In January 1833, thanks to his Wilberforce connections, he took up a curacy in Sussex;

by Easter that year he was engaged to Caroline Sargent, one of the rector's four daughters; in May, after the unexpected death of his prospective father-in-law, he succeeded as Rector of Lavington. That November he married Caroline. Of the other Sargent girls, Emily was already the wife of Samuel Wilberforce, son of the Great Emancipator, and later known as 'Soapy Sam'; Mary would marry Henry Wilberforce, Sam's brother; and Sophia, George Ryder, son of the Bishop of Lichfield. Yet despite the strongly Evangelical tone at Lavington, all the son-in-laws of John Sargent, with the strong exception of Samuel, would convert to Catholicism. As Gladstone phrased the matter: 'The Evangelical movement filled men so full with the wine of spiritual, life that larger and better vessels were required to hold it.'

By what right, Manning began to wonder, did he presume to hector his parishioners on their religious duties? 'If I was not a messenger sent from God,' he concluded, 'I was an intruder and impertinent.' What he required, in fact, was a theology which justified his authoritarian temperament. At Oxford Newman was providing just such a system, contending that the Church of England, albeit in origin an Erastian compromise designed to keep religious peace in England, was a divinely appointed instrument for the administration of revealed religion. This was a far cry from the Evangelical position, that the Holy Ghost acted directly upon each individual soul without necessity of priestly or sacramental intermediary. On Manning, whose mind naturally tended towards extremes, Newman's heightened conception of the Church and its mission immediately exercised an irresistible appeal. It was one thing to be a minister, very much more uplifting to be a member of God's officer class.

He began to correspond with Newman, under whose influence he read the Fathers of the Church; and soon he was alarming the Evangelicals with lectures upon the Apostolic Succession. The death of his wife in 1837, while plunging him into deepest grief, intensified his conviction that he had been called to 'toil for Christ's Church in warfare here on earth'.

In 1840 Manning was appointed Archdeacon of Chichester, which gave him a wider platform in Sussex, while in London the growing frequency of his appearances in influential circles began to attract golden opinions. His ascetic features suggested rigorous mortification, and though he never descended into frivolity, the flow of his conversation conveyed a gentlemanly ease. Saints who know how to behave at dinner may reasonably hope for promotion. There were three men to whom the country looked, declared Bishop Phillpotts of Exeter: 'Manning in the Church, Gladstone in the state, and Hope in the Law.' Yet the High views which Manning had adopted blighted his chances of a bishopric, unless Gladstone, with whom he was now in continuous correspondence, should become Prime Minister.

In any case, the rackety and rickety Anglican Church hardly appeared fitted to sustain the apostolic role which Manning now cast for it. In 1834 the Prime Minister, Lord Melbourne had told the Archbishop of Canterbury over dinner that he was 'all for a *rich* and *lazy* Church, against a *poor* and *active* one'. As Manning proceeded in his work, he found himself increasingly troubled by the implications of Erastianism. In 1838 he wrote:

> Men cannot long believe that they may have fellowship with God through a Church and Priesthood of their own appointing. This is beyond even the credulity of unbelief. They must seek out some Church with divine credentials, or let go the faith at last.

The dilemma was practical as well as theological. While Manning had rejected the Evangelical notion of grace acting directly on each individual soul, he had never lost his strong compulsion to combat injustice. Was it feasible, though, to envisage the Church of England as an engine of social reform? Might such an organization really, as Manning urged in his pleas for universal education, find within itself the energy and the funds to run the country's school system? The same questions were raised when Manning urged the abolition of private pews, campaigned for more holidays for labourers, or sought better treatment for convicts. Could he truly hope for enthusiastic support in such matters from a Church in which the best prevailing tone was rather gentlemanly than self-sacrificial?

Men of great energy and practical ability do not care to find themselves reduced to practical impotence. Though Manning strove to brush off the news of Newman's conversion in 1845, he found, as he noted in July 1846, that 'Something keeps rising and saying "You will end in the Roman Catholic Church."' A visit to Rome in 1847–48, and in particular the sight of the Pope (with whom he had an audience) confirmed this instinct. 'It is impossible not to love Pius IX,' he concluded, 'his is the most truly English countenance I have seen in Italy.' Manning always had his Jingo side. Already, though, he was finding deep satisfaction in attending the Mass, and in the Adoration of the Blessed Sacrament.

After much internal debate, copiously annotated, Manning finally abandoned all hope in Anglicanism in 1850, when the predominately secular Judicial Committee of the Privy Council presumed to make a judgement on the doctrine of baptismal regeneration. In that same year, as it happened, the establishment of twelve Roman Catholic dioceses in England, a measure necessitated by Irish immigration, set off the last really ferocious bout of anti-papal rioting among his fellow countrymen. No one could accuse Manning of converting to a popular cause, or imagine that it was easy for him to break all ties with an English Establishment that was so dear to him. 'Now my career is finished,' he told James Hope on the day before his reception. In fact his essential career was just beginning. For the first time in 300 years the Catholic Church was obliged to witness within its ranks the formidable spectacle of a Balliol man on the make. In Rome Manning made the best possible impression upon the Pope; at Westminster Cardinal Wiseman found him indispensable. In 1857 the convert was appointed both Superior of the Oblates of St Charles in Bayswater and Provost of the Chapter at Westminster. Already the old English Catholics were fuming at the convert's advance, and the success of the Oblates did nothing to soothe them. 'I hate that man; he is such a forward piece,' declared the President of Ushaw seminary. Manning, however, was armed with a killing seriousness of purpose, supreme administrative skill, and a total absence of humour. The loathing – the word is not too strong – of the Westminster chapter for their 'parsonical' Provost might have destroyed a weaker man; Manning merely became, as Herbert Vaughan (who would succeed him as Archbishop of Westminster) teased him, 'coldly reserved and ominously civil'. If he had doubts, it sufficed to remind himself that he enjoyed the confidence of both Cardinal Wiseman and the Pope. Truly the God-ordained ways of Rome were a decided improvement upon the muddle of Anglicanism.

Yet far from being an ecclesiastical Machiavelli meticulously planning every step in his own advance, Manning actually attempted to get Bishop Ullathorne adopted as Wiseman's successor at Westminster. For once, however, he proved unpersuasive at Rome. When, after Wiseman's death in 1865, the moment came to appoint a new archbishop, Pius IX was favoured with an internal voice: '*Mettetelo lì, Mettetelo lì*' – 'Put him there, put him there.' And the Pope had no doubts at all about the identity of 'him'. In retreat before taking up the appointment Manning ruthlessly analyzed his failings. 'By nature I am very irascible, and till the Grace of God converted me, I was proud, cold and repulsive. Since then, I hope less so, but I have always been cold and distant except to those whom I personally loved.' He would, he promised himself, fight against these faults, but he could not betray his calling.

> When I was in a system of compromise I tried to mediate, reconcile and unite together those who differed. When I entered a system which, being divine, is definite and uncompromising, I threw myself with my whole soul and strength into its mind, will and action. So it must be to the end. Less definite, positive, uncompromising, aggressive, I can never be. God forbid.

Within a few months, Father Morris, a member of the formerly hostile Westminster chapter, was worrying lest Manning should kill himself with overwork:

> The amount of good he does is wonderful. I have never seen the least sign of weariness about him, and however pressed he may be, his readiness to listen to everyone, and to take part in every good work, I never saw in anyone in my life.

Manning's first imperative was to provide for the thousands of Irish children who were in danger of being lost to the Church for want of proper Catholic education. To that end he set aside plans to build a new cathedral in London, and challenged the richer members of his flock to abandon their 'feasting and profusion of luxury' in order to contribute to a diocesan education fund. The invitation might perhaps have been more winningly phrased; nevertheless the response was generous to an extent that should have laid the new Archbishop's heart more open to the virtues of his English flock. Within two years twenty new Catholic schools had been opened in the Westminster diocese, and Manning kept up the impetus over the succeeding decades. By his death more than 10,000 extra places had been provided in parish elementary schools. He also succeeded, with Gladstone's help, in extricating thousands of Catholic children from Protestant workhouses, so that by 1884 not a single one was left therein. At the same time he developed orphanages, reformatories and 'industrial schools' in which neglected children could be boarded. 'The national character was chiefly formed in its Christian schools,' Manning wrote in 1886; 'what character will be formed in schools without Christianity?' He aimed to postpone the answer to that question for as long as possible, even if this entailed entering into compacts with the heretic state.

When the Education Act of 1870 established the principle of universal primary education, Manning, again using his old friendship with Gladstone, helped to ensure that Catholic schools would continue to receive grants from the Privy

Council. Subsequently, in sharp distinction to other denominations, he managed to raise funds to prevent Catholic schools from falling under the sway of the godless local Boards of education. His aim was that denominational schools should receive support from taxation on the same basis as the Board schools; and although baulked in his lifetime he did much to establish this principle, which would be recognized in the Education Act of 1902.

Such labours being ungrateful to the literary spirit, Manning has never received widespread recognition for his work in education. Nor were the Upper Ten Thousand notably impressed by his ceaseless charitable labours, which made him the first leading Catholic since the Reformation to play a prominent part in the wider circle of English philanthropy.

> All the great works of charity in England [Manning did not hesitate to admit] have had their beginning out of the Church ... What are our people doing? Oh, I forgot; they have no time. They are examining their consciences or praying (with dear Mrs Craven) for success in finding a really satisfactory maid.

Manning, by contrast, did not hesitate to follow his compassionate instincts wheresoever they led. He served on Mansion House relief committees; campaigned against the vivisection of animals; argued for less stressful working hours; helped to promote emigration to the colonies, and supported the doubtful W. T. Stead in his campaign against the prostitution of young girls. In 1884 he was appointed to the Royal Commission on the Housing of the Working Classes, and in 1887 he was co-opted onto the Committee on Distress in London. 'If there had been a dozen Mannings,' reckoned an official who worked with him, 'England would have been in some danger of being converted to Christianity.'

Conscious of the havoc caused by drink among his Irish flock, Manning eagerly joined forces with Protestant nonconformists in their temperance campaigns. In 1872 he himself took the pledge, and next year founded the Catholic League of the Cross, membership of which demanded total abstention from alcohol. This crusade earned him particular scorn: 'There is not one gentleman,' he complained, 'who will give up one glass of sherry to help me in the battle.' Even some of the English bishops opposed him on the issue; nevertheless the Cardinal (for such he had become in 1875) remained ferociously unrepentant. When Vaughan, by this time Bishop of Salford, attended a Licensed Victuallers' dinner, he was removed as executor of Manning's will. 'It was a mistake,' Vaughan later reflected. 'If I had been his executor, his private papers would never have fallen into the hands of Mr Purcell.'

Manning, however, always professed the virtue of being regarded as a fool for Christ's sake. Critics have rather too gleefully exposed conflicts and limitations in his social thought; he was always consistent, however, in stipulating that the law of charity should be the ultimate guide in social action. Above all, he reprobated 'the heartless and headless' remedies for distress proposed by laissez-faire economists who would never themselves be called upon to suffer the consequences of their own prescriptions. It was no use telling Manning that the right to private property was a sacred principle. He would have agreed – and added that 'labour and skill are as true capital as land or money'. For that reason he showed himself sympathetically disposed towards trade unions, and it was the widespread knowledge of this fact that enabled him to find a solution to the London Dock Strike in 1889. 'The more I think, the more I am on the side of Labour,' he wrote after the dispute had been settled. Support for the working man, he came to believe, not only lessened the possibility of violent social breakdown, a spectre which haunted him. It also offered the best hope of recovering the lost masses of England for the Church. 'Their will has been lost by the sins and miseries of the past,' he believed. 'But their will has been changing and may be won by finding sympathy and care in the bishops and priests of the Church.' If it would be too much to claim that Manning was responsible for *Rerum Novarum* (1891), Leo XIII's encyclical on Catholic social action, he certainly shared common ground with the Pope in this field.

The more radical that Manning's views on the condition of England became, the more fiercely he committed himself to extreme conservative and ultramontane doctrines on the authority of the Church. At the Vatican Council of 1870 he had played a vital part in securing the definition of the Pope's infallibility. Having joined the Church to gain the religious certainty which would afford an uncluttered basis for action, he felt a compulsion to reinforce the boon. As he argued, 'If the Church were not infallible, obedience to it might be the worst of bondage.' No matter that the secular modern world recoiled in horror from the definition; Manning gloried in throwing up barriers against the forces of godless indifferentism. In a two-hour Latin speech before the General Congregation of Bishops, he argued for an extreme measure; and on the *Deputatio de Fide* he urged his case with such intemperance that he received a rebuke from the chairman. Pius IX, however, had given him privileged access to his apartments by private passage; and Princes of the Church, awaiting an appointment, were surprised to discover, as Manning left the Pope, that it was the English convert who had kept them waiting.

This favoured position, combined with his intransigent zeal, brought Manning many enemies. Emile Ollivier, the Protestant Prime Minister of France, was struck by the blend of of asceticism and power lust in Manning's appearance at the Council.

> The love of domination emanates from every pore, and when his thin lips allow a smile, one feels it is from pure condescension. Certainly he is pious, sincere, utterly wrapped up in God; nevertheless, do not mistake him for the emaciated monks he resembles. Underneath his seraphic air of content there lurks a politician as insinuating and energetic as any of the kind.

In the end the Council adopted a definition of papal infallibility which fell decidedly short of Manning's wishes; and so, back in Westminster, he endeavoured to foist on it the strongest possible interpretation. Eventually, in 1874, he provoked a diatribe from Mr Gladstone, which in turn elicited a reply from Newman.

> There are those among us, as must be confessed who for years past have conducted themselves as if no responsibility attached to wild words and overbearing deeds ... who have ... stretched principles till they were close upon snapping; and who at length, having done their best to set the house on fire, leave to others the task of putting out the flame.

Mr Gladstone, too, did not miss the opportunity to score off his former Anglican ally. 'If we had Dr Newman for Pope,' he observed to Manning, 'we should be tolerably safe, so merciful and genial would be his rule!' Manning refused to be provoked; indeed, he wrote to Rome to advise the Prefect of Propaganda not to censure Newman. Undeniably, though, relations between the two great converts had been in decline since the late 1850s. Newman held that the ultramontane excesses of Pius IX's pontificate were a departure from the true spirit of the Church, and came to see Manning as the ringleader of those who had poisoned his reputation in Rome. It is true that Manning had cast a wary eye on Newman's editorship of the liberal Catholic journal the *Rambler*, as well as upon plans to establish an Oratory in Oxford and to allow Catholics to attend a Protestant university. So, however, had most of the other English bishops. Newman's fundamental objection was against what he perceived to be Manning's underhand methods. There was something in this, since, even while professing friendship towards his former intellectual master, Manning was capable of writing to Rome in very different terms:

> [Dr Newman] has become the centre of those who hold low views about the Holy See, are anti-Roman, cold and silent, to say no more, about the Temporal Power, national, English, critical of Catholic devotions, and always on the lower side

... I see much danger in an English Catholicism of which
Newman is the highest type ... It is a worldly Catholicism,
and it will have the worldly on its side, and will deceive many.

That was Manning at his least attractive. His critics, however,
sometimes write as though the leading preoccupation of his
life was to foil Newman, whereas in fact his dealings with the
Oratorian took up the tiniest fraction of his time. Like their
great master, the Newmanites have never been slow to
perceive a slight. It has been claimed, for instance, that
Manning deliberately attempted to thwart Newman's
appointment as cardinal; had this really been his conscious
aim, however, he could certainly have acted to far greater
effect. In the last analysis, there is really no call to make
invidious comparisons between the two men. Manning
outstripped Newman in practical achievement as conclu-
sively as Newman outstripped him as a Catholic thinker.
Manning had his failures, of course. His attempts to found 'a
true Tridentine seminary' at Hammersmith, and a Catholic
university at Kensington, both ended in ignominious disaster, largely due to his failure to enlist the sympathies of
influential English Catholics. In the political arena, his
support for Ireland succeeded only in irritating both
Gladstone and Disraeli, while his adoption of Home Rule
was compromised by his determination to retain an Irish,
and Catholic, representation at Westminster.

Yet Manning never betrayed his vow: "Less definite, positive, uncompromising, aggressive, I can never be. God
forbid." In line with this determination, he maintained the
highest view of the priesthood, writing a book, *The Eternal
Priesthood* (1883), which became widely used in seminaries.
It infuriated him that the religious Orders should be
regarded as representing a superior form of Christianity to
that of the regular clergy; that there should be Franciscans
who wore gold watches (what would he have made of Pope
Benedict XVI's penchant for Prada shoes and Gucci
sunglasses?); and that the Jesuits should presume to inter-
fere in diocesan education. He took the last issue to Rome,

and in 1881 a papal bull, *Romanos Pontifices*, established that the educational work of the Orders should be set under episcopal control.

On and on Manning worked, increasingly closeted in his cavernous and gloomy mansion in Victoria. Vaughan piously recorded that the approach to his door became worn with the footsteps of the poor, the forlorn the tempted and the disgraced, but no one who has visited the National Portrait Gallery and seen G. F. Watts's terrifying portrait, painted in 1883, of the Cardinal – 'death's head in a skullcap' as the sitter described himself – can doubt that it would have taken the greatest courage to approach him. His immense charitable achievements were certainly not accomplished through charm: before him, as G. W. E. Russell observed, 'the most Protestant knee instinctively bent.'

With a few selected guests his eye might lighten in welcome. John Ruskin, for example, recorded in 1880 that 'my darling Cardinal ... told me delicious stories all through lunch', which was also delicious. For the most part, however, Manning was an isolated and daunting old man who turned from his labours only to leaf through his journals and compare his work for 'the Irish occupation in England' with the achievements of admired contemporaries such as Gladstone and Shaftesbury. Had he been guilty of ambition? Yes, he acknowledged, 'if it be ambition to desire to see work done that ought to be done, and to be done as it ought to be done, and when ill done to be done better'.

He never lost his mental energy; nevertheless, as he aged, curious thoughts flitted through his brain. The philosopher William Hurrell Mallock was surprised to be informed by Manning that at seances the Devil assumed corporeal forms – sometimes that of a man, sometimes that of a beautiful and seductive woman – 'the results being frequent births, in the world around us, of terrible hybrid creatures half-diabolic in nature, though wholly human in form'. Yet the next time Mallock met Manning, he encountered the cool Balliol intellectual with whom he had an interesting discussion on the difficulties which prevented the modern mind from accepting Catholicism. Incongruously, there remained within the fanatical old Cardinal traces of the Regency man of the world, given to crisp, laconic judgements. 'An English gentleman should know his Aristotle and ride to hounds,' was the kind of apophthegm that he liked deliver. Although he piqued himself on having lived outside society since 1851, he still enjoyed being in the know. One of his converts was Mrs Crawford, whose scandalous testimony in the most sensational divorce case of the era had ruined the radical politician Charles Wentworth Dilke. Mrs Crawford knew exactly how to handle the Cardinal. When she told him about a visit to Paris, 'He tried to be stern but couldn't help being amused by my lively descriptions.'

G. W. Russell, while clear that Manning's 'every conscious thought was for the furtherance of his religion', considered him 'essentially a man of the world', and discovered a 'beautifully mannered, well-informed, sagacious old gentleman, who, but for his dress, might have passed for a Cabinet minister, an eminent judge, or a great county magnate'. In line with this opinion, Manning liked to drop in at the Athenaeum, where he would sit with his hat pulled down over his eyes, apparently leafing through a magazine, but always on the lookout for an acquaintance from his Anglican years. His convert zeal never attached itself to the more theatrical exhibitions of Catholicism. When a visitor came upon him fully robed, Manning passed the matter off in phrasing that recalled the Harrow schoolboy: 'Forgive these togs, but it's the Immaculate Conception, and I have to go to Farm Street.' Indeed, Manning's faith was so secure that, exceptionally for a Catholic of that time, he could even afford generous views of other denominations. 'The Church has a doctrine of intention of the heart,' he told a Protestant woman who had dedicated her life to charity, 'God bless you. God bless you.' 'When the world is drifting to chaos and suicide, I have no will for controversies,' he informed an Anglican confidant. The English, he insisted, were not heretics; they had never rejected the Catholic religion; it had been wrested away from them.

His harsher judgements were reserved for the English Catholics, over whom, he finally realized, his will would never prevail. 'I think he feels very much the sort of hidden antagonism to all his views which exists among the Catholic Upper Ten Thousand,' reported Mrs Crawford. 'He knows quite well that they only just tolerate him because they must and because they hope for better things.'

Indeed, Manning's death seemed to confirm English Catholics in their feelings of superiority. The poet Coventry Patmore reflected:

> Poor Cardinal! It is wonderful how he imposed on mankind by the third-century look of him, and his infinite muddle-headedness, which passed for mystery. I knew him well, and am convinced that he was the very minutest soul that ever buzzed in so high a place.

And a Jesuit, Father Forbes Leith, told an acquaintance: 'Your having known Manning intimately quite explains why you never became a Catholic.'

Yet surely now, 116 years after Manning's death, even the Upper Ten Thousand of English Catholics might allow themselves more generous judgements of an ecclesiastic who understood the vital importance of the Irish dimension to the faith in England, and who did so much to protect and nurture it.

As for the flaws in Manning's character, who is without flaws, and who can altogether eradicate them? In a sense Manning's achievements may be judged all the more praiseworthy because, while compassionate through upbringing, he was by nature so far from being a saint. Conversion, however, left him free – whether through divine grace, his own will, or both – to set his abilities at the service of his best instincts. The elegant Harrovian adopted the vulgar temperance crusade; the vainglorious Balliol First dedicated himself to the poor; the eager friend of Cabinet ministers became the leader of what was in England a despised religious sect; the Jingo developed into the champion of the Irish. These were not transformations which could have been achieved without suffering: the reward, on the other hand, was gathered in wide sympathies and beneficent works. And so, when the last sneer has been delivered at Manning's ambition and will to dominate, he remains not merely the most effective Catholic ecclesiastic in England since the Reformation, but also a noble witness to the transforming power of the Church.

Chapter 13

Hilaire Belloc

A. N. Wilson

Belloc's reputation today survives as the author of comic verses for children. He has been largely forgotten as a Catholic historian or controversialist. His friend Gilbert Chesterton has had many more books written about him, especially by those who see Chesterton as a Catholic thinker. This would have amazed, and quite possibly irritated Belloc, who liked to think of himself as the Catholic one in the famous friendship. Chesterton did not become a Catholic until 1922 – when he was forty-eight years old, and when most of his best books had already been written. (He died fourteen years later.) His friendship with Belloc had slightly cooled, and those who attended Chesterton's reception into the Church were amazed that Belloc did not even turn up for the ceremony. There was Father O'Connor, the original of Father Brown, who had just heard Chesterton's confession. There was Frances Chesterton, G. K.'s poor wife, weeping into a handkerchief. There was Father Knox. But as they looked at their watches in puzzlement, there was no Belloc. Nor did he ever offer apology or explanation for his absence. When Chesterton died there was a requiem in Westminster Cathedral attended by hundreds. Belloc had circulated during the Mass and by the end of it had managed to sell his 'exclusive' – 'My Friend G. K.' – to no less than four separate editors.

Belloc in the Catholic Cathedral at Westminster was a familiar sight, and the subject of many anecdotes. There was the story of his standing there during the Mass. It was his custom, learnt in France, to stand, even during the Canon. A fussy sexton approached. 'Excuse me, sir, it is our custom here to kneel', he whispered. 'Go to hell', said Belloc robustly. 'I'm so sorry, sir. I didn't realize you were a Catholic'.

Much of Belloc's work, as a Catholic apologist, and as a representative of the Catholic faith in a secularist-Protestant land, consisted of bluster.

> Noel, Noel, Noel, Noel,
> A Catholic tale have I to tell,
> And a Christian song have I to sing
> When all the bells of Arundel ring!

is how his charming carol begins – one of the songs for which he composed both words and music, and which remain forever in the listener's head, if they have heard his voice on the gramophone record he made. It ends

> May all good fellows who here agree
> Drink audit ale in Heaven with me,
> And may all my enemies go to Hell
> Noel, Noel, Noel Noel . . .

Such attitudes were comic. It would be cloth-eared not to hear that. But equally, Dante and Thomas More would have heard behind the merriment a perfectly sound doctrine. He who is not with me, is against me. The Christ of the Fourth Gospel tells His disciples that their authentic mark would be to earn the world's hatred; and what applies to them, applies to what Belloc calls 'The Catholic Thing' in modern times.

Yet this side of Belloc, his melancholy-cheerful acceptance of the absolute divergence between 'The World''s view of life and that of the Church, fell into disrepute during the changes before and after the Second Vatican Council. Then, Ecumenism began to teach all Christian peoples to put their differences behind them. And in a poverty-stricken, over-populated world, such papal doctrines as were contained in

Humanae Vitae sent many Catholics, and not merely those who left the Church, scurrying in the direction of an acceptance of secular values, greatly to the Church's undoing.

Of all Catholic writers who had been popular in the early twentieth century, probably none, in English-speaking lands, fell further from acceptance among his co-religionists than Hilaire Belloc. Indeed, he survives now, as a writer, in the public mind, chiefly as an author of incomparably funny verses for children, and his reputation as an historian, as a Defender of the Faith, as a serious poet, as an essayist, as a journalist, is not merely low; it is, in Catholic and secular circles, all but non-existent. The libraries of convents, retreat houses, Catholic schools and monasteries emptied themselves into the shelves of the second-hand bookshops, and even – to judge with the ease and cheapness with which I built up a collection of all Belloc's works – the junk-stall. His central contentions, repeated it must be said to the point of tedium in his many pot-boilers, were not what the Catholic hierarchy of England and Wales wanted to hear; or rather, they were not what these kindly men wanted non-Catholics, and especially non-Catholic fellow-Christians, to hear Catholics saying about the past. Those things, rooted in the Gospel, and confirmed by the socio-economic teachings of Leo XIII are, centrally and essentially these: that there is an absolute division between God and Mammon.

In the nineteenth century, the crisis of Capitalism led to some to think that there was a choice to be made between an acceptance of the Free Market, or a Socialist adjustment of it. But both these alternatives would lead to the enslavement of the human spirit which could alone find liberation in the Gospel and Church of Jesus Christ. The money-power, which had fed on usury and was based on an idea of property which was indeed theft had really been in control of England since Henry VIII appropriated the monastic lands. The Pilgrimage of Grace, in which the people of England marched against the tyrant to insist upon their freedoms, protected and enshrined in the Church, was an event in English life comparable to the French Revolution, a pivotal turning point which defined the rest of history. Political and economic history thereafter, with the triumph of the Whigs, the exile of the Stuart monarchy, the alliance of the English aristocracy with the money-power, with the exclusion of Catholics from professional and university life, with the Erastian state church holding on to the ancient seats of learning – above all of Oxford – was not just a tale of villainy, it was a story of the inevitable consequences of heresy.

> The moral is, it is indeed.
> You must not monkey with the Creed.

> The world is shrinking very fast, and neither exactly for the better or the worse, but for division. Our civilization is split-ting more and more into two camps, and what was common to the whole of it is becoming restricted to the Christian, and soon will be restricted to the Catholic half.

So he wrote at the beginning of that wonderful essay 'A Remaining Christmas'. It is simply an account of how the Belloc household celebrated Christmas down at King's Land, the curious warren of dwellings, next to the old mill, which Belloc and his wife Elodie made their home in 1901. He died there in 1953, falling into the fireplace as a muddled, bearded old gentleman, who had lost his wife nearly forty years before, and both his sons. Much of the house is extremely old, dating from the fourteenth century. Eleven gables make a chaotic zigzag along the roof. But the bulk of the house was built only sixteen years before the Bellocs moved in. And when they bought it, the room which is still the drawing room (it is inhabited by Belloc's great-grandson Charles Eustace) was the village shop. The room is still lined with old shop fittings, tiny drawers for spices and sugars, shelves for the packets and tins. In this room, each Holy Week, Belloc would pin up fourteen old French postcards of the Stations of the Cross. He would abstain from alcohol, a hellish deprivation ('Drink muck, think muck!'). And usually in Holy Week he would write one of his novels.

There are few houses in England, certainly few writers'

houses, which have a more potent atmosphere than King's Land, with its chapel on the first floor, where he so often prayed, and where the Mass was so often said. The wall is papered with those little cards given out at requiems, asking for prayers for the repose of the departed. And central to the chapel is the old piece of black-rimmed writing paper on which Belloc has inscribed his wife's name. It is grimy with his frequent fingering, for he touched and kissed it as often as he prayed here.

Shortly after I wrote my biography of Belloc in 1984, his grandson, Julian Jebb, a television producer who had grown up at King's Land, asked me to make a short film about HB. The camera crew came into the house. I felt awkward about their going anywhere near the chapel, but Julian, who felt in some degree oppressed by his grandfather, as by the Catholic faith, was all the more eager to bring to that hallowed place the glare of artificial light, and the intrusion of a microphone. However often they tried to make their electrical equipment in the chapel at King's Land work, it failed. Either the lights popped, or the sound failed, usually both. The electricity of HB and of Elodie was much stronger than the electricity of the BBC. I felt, too, not merely the Bellocs, but the old Catholic Thing fighting back against the intrusion of the modern.

So what survives of King's Land is not a short TV film, but Belloc's great essay on 'A Remaining Christmas', which describes how they decked the hall with holly and laurel from the nearby farm; then put up the tree and adorn it with candles; then invite in all the nearby children to be fed, and to revere the crib which had been set up beside the great fire in the hearth.

Those who were staying in the house would then have dinner and troop upstairs to squeeze into the chapel. 'And there the three night Masses are said, one after the other, and those of the household take their Communion.'

Then everyone slept in late, and ate a turkey dinner. (Elodie was American, and perhaps they were among the earliest to eat this American bird as their Christmas dinner rather than the more traditionally English beef or goose.)

This, which I have just described, is not in a novel or in a play. It is real, and goes on as the ordinary habit of loving men and women. I fear that set down thus in our terribly changing time it must sound very strange and, perhaps in places grotesque, but to those who practise it, it is not only sacred, but normal, having in the whole of the complicated affair a sacramental quality and an effect of benediction : not to be despised.

Belloc went to Mass every day of his life. He would rush in, and rush out, usually immediately after the priest's Communion. He seldom went to Holy Communion. He mistrusted sentiment. He thought that any priest who took longer than twenty minutes to offer the Holy Sacrifice excessive. His letters, and conversation, suggest a man who temperamentally had as much in common with the French sceptics of the eighteenth century as they did with the sometimes sugary pieties of his wife – an early devotee, for example, long before the canonization, of the Little Flower of Lisieux.

Yet, he kept the faith. Readers of his travel book *Many Cities* will recall the High Mass at Narbonne, when Belloc had just been on a tour of North Africa and came back, in glorious May sunshine, to Catholic Europe.

I must tell you that all this time the Blessed Sacrament was exposed above the altar on a very high place in a blaze of light. The Mass proceeded; the final prayers were said; the thing was over. If I could have got into that Nave of Narbonne all the starved, unbelieving men cut off from the past in the dissolution of our modern world, there would have come out some reasonable proportion restored to the traditions of Europe.

In his love of the Church, and his love of controversy, Belloc sometimes departed company from the young Belloc, who had been an historian who gained a First Class Honours degree in Modern History at Balliol College, Oxford, and who could, had circumstances been slightly different, have become an academic historian. There is something a little shocking about his disregard for the truth, especially when he was defending the faith against a figure such as G. G. Coulton, a medieval historian famous in his day who had an anti-Catholic bee in his bonnet. Surely, when crossing swords with Coulton, Belloc, whose professed aim was to defend the Church, had an especial duty to be careful. He was coming forward here not as a mere journalist, nor as a jester, but as a representative of Roman Catholics at a time when they were deeply disliked in many quarters in England. Coulton was a fanatic, who, in addition to his academic works, issued scores of pamphlets with titles such as *In Defence of the Reformation, Romanism and Truth* and *A Premium Upon Falsehood, dealing with Fr H. Thurston's attempted defence of Cardinal Gasquet.* He managed successfully to block the honorary degrees which Cambridge University was proposing to award to Cardinal Gasquet and Cardinal Bourne. In 1937, in the correspondence columns of *The Daily Telegraph*, Coulton entered into a controversy with Father Ronald Knox upon the subject of whether the Catholic Church had ever allowed divorce. Many thousands of words were eventually exchanged between Knox and Coulton, and then between Belloc (who weighed in on Knox's behalf) and the professional historian. Many of the words centred upon the Council of Arles in the year 314, which, it would seem, had authorized divorce in certain limited circumstances. Coulton eventually was able to come up with three popes and three councils or synods of the Church which had endorsed the Council of Arles, but Belloc by then would never answer Coulton directly. He took to publishing semi-defamatory articles about Coulton in Catholic periodicals such as *The Universe* and *The Month*, who in turn refused to publish Coulton's replies. Coulton issued yet another pamphlet – *Mr Belloc's Past Record* and to anyone who wishes to take Belloc seriously as an historian, it would make devastating reading.

What Coulton found shocking was that when actual mistakes were pointed out to Belloc, he never retracted them, or apologized. Among the many mistakes upon which Coulton gleefully seized were Belloc's appeal to Matthew Paris as an authority for the Battle of Evesham, which was fought after Paris's death; or his claim that the Black Death in Norwich had claimed 57,374 lives – a figure which was evidently invented. As Coulton, trained medievalist, could demonstrate, the population of Norwich at that date was nothing like 50,000. 'He therefore slightly abandoned the embarrassing 7,374; who too must too obviously be non-existent, and maintained only that 50,000 had died out of those 50,000 who were the most his fancy could create.' Belloc moreover, knew that he had become a sounding brass and a tinkling cymbal – though he would never admit it publicly to Coulton. There is the immensely sad story of Belloc coming upon a man in a railway carriage reading his *History of England*. He asked the man how much he had paid for the book, and when he heard the price, he shoved the money into the reader's hand, took the volume and hurled it out of the train window.

The development of modern history was one of the great achievements of the Enlightenment, and when we lie about the past, either as individuals or as societies, trouble ensues. One of the great distinctions between the free world and the rest in the twentieth century was between those who submitted to the academically demonstrable truth about their past, and those who merely feasted upon propaganda, whether in the Soviet Union or in Germany. Belloc had begun as a fine popular historian of France. His history of Paris, which he concludes before the Revolution, is very fine, and his early books on Danton and Robespierre can still be read today. It is not surprising, however, that after the Second Vatican Council, so many English convents and Catholic schools should have discarded wholesale those pot-boiling English histories which Belloc churned out so cynically – such as the life of James II, which he claimed to have scribbled out in eight days in a 'vile hotel' on the edge of the Sahara desert – at El Kantara. *How the Reformation Happened, The Life of Archbishop Cranmer, Characters of the Reformation*. They poured out of him. The paradox of things is such that, while most Catholics would shy away from these books today, academic history has moved since Coulton's day. There are many of Belloc's general 'positions' which would have a much more sympathetic ear in academic circles – his view that the Reformation amounted to an act of state theft, not merely of church property but of the personal rights of the people of England, for example.

If we were to imagine Belloc returning to England today, and attending Mass at a London church, his shock is readily imaginable. He would surely have sympathized with the cookery writer Jennifer Paterson who, when she first heard a priest say, 'Let us offer one another a sign of peace', raised two fingers slowly and solemnly in the direction of the altar. The man who had been born of a French father during the worst moments of the Franco-Prussian war, and who confirmed his own violently anti-German feelings when he himself served in the French army would have raised an eyebrow at the election of a German pope. (Belloc never spoke of Germany, always of 'The Germanies', thereby showing that he did not acknowledge the invention of a country called Germany in the year of his own birth. If anyone served him redcurrant jelly with his mutton he would snortingly refer to 'The filthy Prussian habit of eating jam with meat'.

Yet Belloc who became ossified in late middle age by a mixture of alcohol and disappointment should not be caricatured as a total diehard. He was a man on the move, and the centre of his existence was a belief in the Catholic Church as a living entity. His mother was inspired to join the Church by meeting Cardinal Manning. The Catholicism Belloc learnt was various. It was the Catholicism of Leo XIII and social justice – which Pope John Paul II very much revived during his pontificate. (The Belloc of *The Servile State* who found that Capitalism and Communism were equally at variance with the Gospel would have found much to feast upon in John Paul II's engagements with Communism and Globalized Capitalism.) It was also the Catholicism of post-

Renan, post Vatican I France. And that is a largely vanished Catholicism. It went underground after Vatican II and popped up as Lefebvreism, but Belloc would never have had any sympathy for a sectarian, which is what Archbishop Lefebvre became. For him, the whole point of Catholicism was that it spoke for Catholic Europe. 'The Faith is Europe, and Europe is the Faith', and in that spirit, Belloc would surely rejoice in the pontificate of Benedict XVI, who thinks the same, whether sailing near the wind in his discussions of Islam and the place of Turkey in or out of the European Union, or whether considering the rich, shared intellectual inheritance of Catholic Europe.

The Church was primarily for Belloc a place where the human spirit found 'hearth and home'. In *The Path to Rome*, he entered the Alpine village of Undervelier, and saw the entire population of the village go into church for the evening service. (He says it was Vespers, but given the hymn they sang, it must have been Compline?)

> At this I was very much surprised, not having been used at any time in my life to the unanimous devotion of an entire population, but having always thought of the Faith as something fighting odds, and having seen unanimity only in places where some sham religion or other glazed over our tragedies and excused our sins. Certainly to see all the men, women and children of a place taking Catholicism for granted was a new sight, and so I put my cigar carefully down under a stone on the top of the wall and went in with them ... All the village sang, knowing the psalms very well, and I noticed that their Latin was nearer German than French; but what was most pleasing of all was to hear from all the men and women together that very noble good-night and salutation to God which begins, '*Te lucis ante terminum*'. My whole mind was taken up and transfigured by this collective act, and I saw for a moment the Catholic Church quite plain, and I remembered Europe and the centuries. Then there left me altogether that attitude of difficulty and combat which, for us, is always associated with the Faith. The cities dwindled in my imagination, and I took less heed of the modern noise. I went out with them into the clear evening and the cool. I

found my cigar and lit it again, and musing much more deeply than before, not without tears, I considered the nature of Belief.

Chapter 14

Dom David Knowles, OSB

Abbot Aidan Bellenger, OSB

The 'bare ruin'd choirs' of the monasteries dissolved by Henry VIII in the sixteenth century stand as a melancholy monument to the religious revolution of the Reformation. The best of them, in the care of English Heritage and the National Trust, now form a component of the tourist trail, and one at least, Fountains in Yorkshire, is a UNESCO world heritage site. Evocative and magnificent as they still can be, even in their present patched-up and fragmentary form, they are a shadow of their former glory. The cathedral churches of such places as Canterbury, Durham, Ely, Gloucester, Norwich and Worcester, which retain not only their churches but their monastic buildings, remind us what the demolished monasteries once represented to a city or a locality, in town or country. Some of the modern monastic complexes, too, including those at Ampleforth, Buckfast, Downside, Mount Saint Bernard and Quarr, show the strong creative impact of a monastic settlement on the landscape of both the ground and the soul. The romantic, Gothic appeal of the monastic life has long been a part of English life, but making sense of monastic history and culture, demystifying, breathing life into the dry bones of the monastic past, was the achievement of Dom David Knowles, England's greatest modern monastic historian. His vivid and majestic use of language, sonorous and measured in its well-chosen tone, was given authority by his own experience and prayer as a Benedictine monk.

I selected David Knowles as my great English Catholic when I realized that some of my other choices – notably St Dunstan the monk primate – were known to me principally through Dom David's writings. So many of us owe a significant part of our knowledge of the monastic past and indeed the whole of the religious Middle Ages to Knowles that it became clear to me that Knowles, the Venerable Bede of our days, should be my choice. This is despite the fact that to some at Downside Knowles' monastic view – and attitude to his own community – still remains controversial.

Michael Clive Knowles (David was his given monastic name) was born in 1896 in the Midlands at Studley in Warwickshire, a Benedictine parish where his father, a prosperous industrialist, had settled. He was an only child and retained a self-contained air throughout his life. His dissenting forbears were men of independent thought and action and this, too, contributed to his personality. Knowles' parents were converts to the Catholic faith but familiar with the deep Catholic roots of an area so full of Benedictine echoes: Evesham, the two Malverns, Pershore and Tewkesbury, among others, not far away. It was an area, too, which while dominated by the growing urban might and blight of Birmingham, had strong recusant connections. Baddesley Clinton, Coughton Court, Harvington, Huddington were all nearby and the nexus of Gunpowder Plot families was still in place. The great recusant tradition of the Midlands and the Welsh Marches, easily accessible by the newly popular 'motor car', was being rediscovered during Knowles' childhood and celebrated by Dom Bede Camm in his *Forgotten Shrines* (1910). Camm was to spend the latter part of his life as a Downside monk. The young Knowles shared with his father a love of the countryside and old buildings and as a writer he displayed a great sense of place, second only in his writing perhaps to his description of character. In his unpublished autobiography it is the description of the special places of his life which remain in the memory.

He attended preparatory school at West House School in suburban Edgbaston, not far from home, but was sent as a boarder in 1910 for his public school education to Downside in Somerset. The school's origins were in the academy attached to the English Benedictine monastery of St Gregory the Great founded in 1606 at Douai in Flanders. The school and the monastery had been repatriated on account of the French Revolution and, after a period of uncertainty, were re-established at Downside House in Stratton-on-the-Fosse, a small village in the Mendips, twelve miles south of Bath. The Downside School of Knowles' day was a school in transition in every way. As it approached its centenary in 1914, the school buildings were being rebuilt in the grand manner to the designs of Leonard Stokes, the reflection of an internal reconstruction of the school's character as an English public school rather than a continental Catholic College. This owed much to its head master Dom Leander Ramsay, a convert Anglican clergyman who was determined to make Downside a great English school. It owed much, too, in its later stages (he was elected abbot in 1906) to Dom Cuthbert Butler who believed that education was an ideal work for monks, a work dependent for its success on collaboration and community.

Knowles espoused Downside to such an extent that he entered the monastic novitiate on leaving school in the summer of 1914. The celebrations of the Downside centenary in 1914 were crowned when one of the monks, Dom Aidan Gasquet was created cardinal, but were soon overshadowed by the First World War in which so many of Knowles' contemporaries and friends were to suffer and to die. Nineteenth-century Downside had been mission-centred. Most of the small resident community were waiting for the opportunity to go and work in the numerous 'missions' (the word used for 'parishes') as soon as one became available. In its search for fresh opportunities Downside had provided bishops for the new Australian Church. The great Downside missionary was William Bernard Ullathorne, pioneer in Australia, and first Catholic Bishop of Birmingham. It is significant that Ullathorne, with an eye to the future, considered the cloister rather than the mission to be the monk's true home and much encouraged those at Downside who favoured a more enclosed life. The young Knowles had presumably been impressed by the school but soon it was the monastic ideal which inspired him. Knowles' growth as a monk and as a scholar benefited from the presence within the monastery of a great and expanding library and the development and, to some extent, revival of a scholarly tradition, strong in the first generation of the seventeenth-century foundation but fading out in the eighteenth and nineteenth centuries. This revival owed much to two individuals: Edmund Bishop and Cuthbert Butler, both of whom were to have a strong influence on his work.

Edmund Bishop was a liturgical scholar of great originality who had tried his vocation as a Downside monk but had remained a layman. Professor Christopher Brooke, later Knowles' literary executor, described Bishop as 'one of the immortals', and although he was first known as a collaborator of Cardinal Gasquet (whose scholarly reputation is less well-respected) it was his own researches culminating in his seminal book *Liturgia Historica* (1918) which set him apart. Bishop's writing was distinguished by a precise accuracy (he was a stern critic of others less perfect than himself) and by a polished precision of language. Knowles learnt much from Bishop and more from Cuthbert Butler, his abbot from 1914 to 1922.

Cuthbert Butler combined pioneering monastic scholarship on the text of the *Rule of St Benedict* with the championing of a reformed, conventual monastic life within the English Benedictine Congregation. In the first quarter of the seventeenth century when the English Benedictine Congregation had been refounded it was a centralized missionary body with no immediate plans to live out the full monastic life in a resident community under an abbot which was the primary and traditional character of the Benedictine tradition. Cuthbert Butler was the most vociferous advocate of a return to monastic 'normality' and rejoiced at the new English Benedictine Congregation constitutions of 1899 which 'restored' the autonomy of the monasteries and upgraded Downside (alongside Ampleforth and Douai) to abbatial status. At the time Knowles was a novice Butler was putting the finishing touches to his most influential work. *Benedictine Monachism* (1919), which was both a work of sound historical scholarship and a manifesto for Benedictine reform and a return to origins. Knowles was to develop both these emphases. It may have been, moreover, Butler who first put Knowles in touch with historical research: the abbot, always keen that his monks should have ' a pot on the boil', as he described it, recommended Knowles to a study of Cluny, the greatest Benedictine monastery of the Middle Ages.

It was to the Classics, however, that Knowles was drawn both at prep school and Downside, and it was both parts of the Classical Tripos at Cambridge which he read from 1919 tp 1922. He was awarded a double first with a distinction in Philosophy in Part Two. That the greatest of Cambridge medievalists since Maitland should not have a degree in History is one Knowles' many singularities. He was a member of Christ's College, the fifteenth-century foundation of the Lady Margaret Beaufort and St John Fisher, but resided at Benet House, the Downside House of Studies in Cambridge, then in Park Terrace. This house was itself a symbol of the growing rapprochement between the English Catholic Community and the ancient universities, and allowed the young monks to continue their community life. While he pursued his classical studies Knowles completed his ecclesiastical formation. He had made his Solemn Vows on 18 October 1918, was ordained deacon on 25 September 1921, and priest on 9 July 1922.

Knowles' time in the school and monastery at Downside coincided with the completion of the abbey church which was a symbol of Downside's monastic integrity. Thomas Garner's choir, the decoration of the Lady Chapel by Ninian Comper and Sir Giles Gilbert Scott's nave, which became a memorial to the First World War, made the Downside Abbey Church what it had not been at Knowles' arrival: a full-scale setting for a monastic liturgy on the grand scale. It was possible to see on the Mendips not only Glastonbury restored but an English Cluny in the making. The ambition and beauty of the church remain inspirational.

Dom David spent a year at San Anselmo, the Benedictine College in Rome, from 1922 to 1923, a foundation very Germanic in its structures and culture. Here, as he recollected, he spoke German not Italian. He travelled to visit some of the great monastic (and classical) sites of Italy. He saw, close at hand, the growing power of Mussolini. Knowles, though European in his sympathies, was not a great traveller. He had monastic principles of stability to cope with and, the grand tour of youth excepted, it was not yet the age of mass tourism. Throughout the twenties, however, he often spent part of the summer in the chalet of F. F. Urquhart, the Catholic history tutor at Balliol, on the borders of France and Switzerland. Urquhart, a frequent visitor to Downside, always known as 'Sligger', invited many of the *jeunesse dorée* of Oxford (and beyond) to read, walk and talk in congenial company and surroundings, Among those he first met there was the young Kenneth Clark, whose vision of 'Civilisation' viewed the Middle Ages as one of the high points of European culture.

Knowles' first task as a young priest monk at Downside was as a teacher of Classics in the school (from 1923 to 1928). He enjoyed his work and the company of the young but as time progressed he sensed a growing contradiction between the career of a schoolmaster and the more austere priorities of the monastic life. He was relieved, soon after a serious traffic accident in July 1928, to be removed from the school and made temporary novice master in the monastery and from 1929 to 1933 junior master, responsible for the spiritual education of the young monks who had left the novitiate but had not yet been ordained. Given such responsibilities, Knowles was obviously highly regarded by his superiors, even an abbot in the making.

The crisis that followed was sparked off by Knowles' reflections on the clash between humanism and renunciation in his own life and in what he regarded as the essential further development of Butler's reforms. In 1929 he had approached Abbot Ramsay (who had succeeded Butler) about entering the Carthusians but this came to nothing with the death of Ramsay and the election of Dom John Chapman in his place. Chapman was a noted spiritual director and a man of genius, but he and Dom David were increasingly at loggerheads. Knowles placed increasing emphasis in his own life of mystical prayer, a practice much encouraged by Cuthbert Butler, and on avoiding contact with 'the world'. The shared liturgical life of the community was taking second place to his private devotions. His teaching and holiness made his juniors into zealous disciples and there was growing tension between him and his abbot. The monastery was overcrowded and the intention to make a foundation (ultimately Worth Abbey) at Paddockhurst in Sussex was made in 1933.

The foundation of Worth was the moment Knowles broke with Downside. It seemed to him that the proposed preparatory school at Worth meant that the Downside community were giving priority to the school rather than to the nurturing of the monastic life. For Abbot Chapman, who rejoiced in the paradoxical and the witty, Knowles' growing interest in the medieval monastic past was a diversion: 'the less we know about that, the better'. Knowles' response to the foundation of Worth was the request for another foundation totally dedicated to a simple, almost Cistercian rule of life. Chapman refused the foundation just before his death. While an appeal was made to Rome, Knowles languished in exile at Ealing, Downside's other priory, in suburban London. In July 1934 the Knowles foundation was rejected by the Holy See. Knowles had already made his last visit to Downside in April 1934 for the funeral of Abbot Cuthbert Butler.

Knowles had become a monastic fundamentlist and this was clearly apparent in his book *The Benedictines* (1929) which could be seen as a summary of his principles. He had been persuaded by his reading of the French Thomist R. Garrigou-Lagrange's book *Perfection Chrétienne* (1923) that contemplation was the only true work of the monk; all else was a distraction:

> Ordinarily speaking there should be ... no active work on which monks, as a body, can be called upon to spend themselves, nor was it the Founder's idea that the life within its walls should be such as to take a direct toll from all except the most robust ... the monk who in ordinary circumstances takes to any work with a zeal which absorbs all his time and energies and which burns out his fire of strength and health is departing from what is for him the way of salvation.

Knowles' circumstances were not, as it turned out, very ordinary, and the possibility of moving to a stricter monastic observance (he had read Garrigou-Lagrange at Quarr Abbey, on the Isle of Wight) increasingly unlikely. In 1934 Dr Elizabeth Kornerup had become the dominant person in Knowles' life and she was to remain so until his death almost forty years later. A Swedish doctor, a convert from Lutheranism, Dr Kornerup was seen by Knowles as a mystic and a saint, 'a perfect soul' living out the spiritual teaching of his hero St John of the Cross in her life. Knowles left Ealing and the regular monastic life in 1939, despite the best efforts of Abbot Sigebert Trafford to bring him back to Downside. He remained outside regular ecclesiastical jurisdiction as 'a fugitive monk' until 1957 when he accepted 'exclaustration'. During this period he suffered both from nervous exhaustion and from a growing certainty that although outwardly suspended, excommunicated and disgraced he was living – alongside Dr Kornerup – a true 'monasticism of the soul' far more elevated than anything the English Benedictines could offer. Knowles was an increasing embarrassment and cause for concern not only to his Benedictine superiors but also to the church hierarchy. The obscure monk was through his writings and academic career becoming one of the most eminent public figures in the English Catholic community.

Historians, unlike mathematicians, tend to be late starters when it comes to writing and this was exacerbated in Dom David's case because by training Knowles was a classicist and a philosopher rather than a historian. His first article, on Jean Mabillon, the pioneering monastic historian, was published in 1919 but, throughout the 1920s his only substantial piece was his first book, *The American Civil War* (1926) written clearly and with maturity but not obviously – except in its pen portraits – a preparation for a monastic historian. His work as editor of *The Downside Review* from 1929 to 1933 and his forays into the Downside monastery library suggested, that by 1929, he was looking, very seriously indeed, at medieval monastic history.

The Monastic Order in England, published by the Cambridge University Press in 1940, is his masterpiece and all the more remarkable because it emerged from the most troubled decade of his life. It presents the reader with the development of the monastic life in England during one of its most flourishing periods from the Norman Conquest to the thirteenth century. It is a thoroughly professional study with a strong narrative flow sustained by Knowles' thorough understanding of both content and sources. It tells its story beautifully and Knowles showed himself to be a great historical storyteller in the tradition of Macaulay and Trevelyan. It remains more than sixty years later a great mine of information as well as a deeply spiritual and personal exploration. The historian, he tells us, must assess the monks by

> The inward, spiritual achievement of their lives … by the abiding standards of Christian perfection … he must … resist with all his power the siren voice of romanticism. Few indeed who have written with sympathy of the monks of Medieval England have wholly escaped the spells of that old enchantress, who has known so well how by her magic of word and brush to scatter the golden mist of the unreal over generations of the past … By the prescriptions of [The Rule of St Benedict], understood not indeed with antiquarian literalness, but in full spiritual strength must the monasticism of every age be judged.

The Monastic Order allowed Knowles to embark on what rapidly became a distinguished academic career at

Cambridge. In 1944 he was elected to a fellowship at Peterhouse, thus becoming, with the exception of some short-lived appointments by James II, the first member of a Catholic religious Order since the Reformation to hold a fellowship at an Oxford or Cambridge college. Peterhouse, in Knowles' time, was a College celebrated for its historians and the fellowship included three knighted scholars. Sir Herbert Butterfield (like Knowles a fervent apologist for 'Christian' history), Sir Michael Postan, the pioneering Economic historian and Sir Denis Brogan, historian of France and political thought. In 1947 Knowles was appointed to the university's professorship of Medieval History and in 1954 he received a letter from Winston Churchill translating him to the Regius Chair, the senior professorship of the history faculty. Another Catholic, Lord Acton had already received this appointment. He received a Litt D. from Cambridge for *The Monastic Order* and later an honorary DD not only from Cambridge but from many other universities. He became a Fellow of the British Academy in 1947 and in 1956 became President of the Royal Historical Society. He was the first president of the Ecclesiastical Historical Society. He held a central position in the English historical community.

Knowles was a prolific writer. He continued, in the three massive volumes, the history of the religious Orders in England up to the Dissolution which he had begun in *The Monastic Order*. He is dominated by his sources in the first two volumes of the religious Orders which perhaps lack the overall distinction of his masterpiece, but he returned to form in the final volume, dealing with the Dissolution, which he approaches with balance and wisdom. His conclusion is memorable:

> At the end of this long review of monastic history, with its splendours and its miseries, and with its rhythm of recurring rise and fall, a monk cannot but ask what message for himself and for his brethren the long story may carry.
>
> It is the old and simple on; only in fidelity to the Rule can a monk or a monastery find security. A Rule, given by a

founder with an acknowledged fullness of spiritual wisdom, approved by the church and tested by the experience of saints, is a safe path, and it is for the religious the only safe path. It comes to him not as a rigid, mechanical code of words, but as a sure guide to one who seeks God, and who seeks that he may indeed find. If he truly seeks and truly loves, the way will not be hard, but if he would love and find the unseen God he must pass beyond things seen and walk in faith and hope, leaving all human ways and means and trusting the Father to whom all things are possible. When once a religious house or a religious order ceases to direct its sons to the abandonment of all that is not God, and ceases to show them the rigours of the narrow way that leads to the imitation of Christ in this love, it sinks to the level of a purely human institution, and whatever its works may be, they are the works of time and not of eternity. The true monk, in whatever century he is found, looks not to the changing ways around him or to his own mean condition, but to the unchanging everlasting God, and his trust is in the everlasting arms that hold him. Christ's word are true: he who doth not renounce all that he possesseth cannot be my disciple. His promise also is true; He that followeth me walketh not in darkness, but shall have the light of life.

Here, the historian in me sees clarity and understanding, the critic in me sees special pleading, and the Abbot of Downside in me sees admonition.

If the grand survey of the religious life in England is Knowles' principal memorial his other writings illuminated many other areas of medieval history. He had an abiding interest in architecture and topography and this was shown in his *Monastic Sites from the Air* (1952). He collaborated in producing handbooks to the monastic houses and superiors of the British Isles. He explored the background to the martyrdom of Becket. He introduced an informed readership to *The English Mystics* (1927) and *The English Mystical Tradition* (1961) and was a pioneer in the history of ideas. Knowles was one of the great formative influences on the new and burgeoning field of 'intellectual history'. His attempts to appraise and assess the leading characters of the past, an approach previously restricted to biographers, took medieval history away from narrowly textual and antiquarian concerns. His views on this methodology received their clearest expression in his inaugural lecture as Regius Professor: 'The Historian and Character'.

Knowles' vision was primarily that of an English Catholic who saw the great tradition of the English people neglected and ignored. In his saints and monks he underlined England's essentially Christian Catholic character. Not for him the broad European vision of his near contemporary Christopher Dawson but a strong English focus. In St Dunstan, Abbot of Glastonbury and Archbishop of Canterbury, he presents one of his monastic heroes as a wielder of national unity whose monasteries had been 'the soul of the country', 'the vital informing principle of life and unity'. Not for him, either, a 'little Englander' approach. Norman Bec was 'one of the most majestic peaks in the long range of monastic history' which showed a religious life lived 'in a perfection and purity as nearly ideal as is possible in things human'. Catholic England disappeared with a loss of faith and his last volume on the religious Orders has an elegiac tone. It is no surpise that in his last years Knowles was distressed by the loss of 'the old Mass'. He would have been encouraged by Benedict XVI's *motu proprio.*

In the early 1970s (Knowles died in 1974) I dined with Knowles in Peterhouse following a lecture to the Cambridge University Medieval Society of which I was then a committee member. I was struck by his physical frailty and by his clear, beautiful voice which reminded me of what I had heard said of Cardinal Newman. He was more than slightly deaf but he made conversation easily and we talked of R. H. Benson's writing especially his medieval novel *Richard Raynal, Solitary* and early twentieth-century Catholicism. The proceedings were brought to an end with the arrival of Dr Kornerup whom I assumed to be his nurse. I did not know about the depth of their relationship. I was in my early twenties then and he made a big personal impact on me. The meeting coincided with my first visit to Downside.

Knowles was perhaps the outstanding English Catholic public intellectual of the twentieth century. He was in many ways an Edwardian with a strong sense of the role of the educated elite in the proper ordering of society. His chronic status as a monastic rebel was not in tune with his overall outlook on life. He has little sympathy for modernism, in its cultural or religious sense, and for the watering down of values and culture. His was a clear and unmistakable contribution. As Maurice Cowling his Peterhouse colleague, and one of my historical mentors, suggested 'he came nearer than any twentieth-century English historian had come to finding a language through which to insert into the structure of a major work of scholarship conceptions of the reality of God, religion and eternal life, and this seems the more considerable an achievement once it is recognised that hardly anyone else has succeeded in doing it at all'. He remains, through his writings, a challenging figure: clearly anti-secular with a religious vision of society, demanding the highest ideals from all those who pursue the religious life, and setting the most exacting of standards to all those who study and write about the Catholic past.

Chapter 15

Leonard Cheshire

John Jolliffe

The Cheshire Homes for the Disabled, where they could live in small colonies in something like a family situation, instead of in large, inhuman soulless institutions, are one of the greatest of all charities, now operating worldwide. But there has always been more to them than that. Although no formal mission statement was ever issued, the intention from the outset was that a Cheshire Home should also be a place of spiritual encouragement, where residents could acquire a sense of belonging, by making whatever contribution they were capable of to the functioning and development of the Home; where they could help those even more handi-capped than themselves; and where confidence and greater independence could be gained, and interests and activities cultivated. To this day, they are havens of last resort for many thousands of severely disabled people; though in recent years emphasis has shifted, where preferable, to a system of care for the disabled in their own homes. Today, of the 21,000 people supported by the Foundation, only 10% are in the remaining residential homes. But who founded the organization, and how did he come to do so?

Leonard Cheshire has a strong claim to be the greatest Catholic layman of the twentieth century, possibly even the most admired individual, Catholic or otherwise. His earliest inspiration had been from C. S. Lewis's *Screwtape Letters*, and an important later source was Mgr Vernon Johnson's *One Lord One Faith*. He gradually came to believe that a man's life work is to mould himself into the individual masterpiece that God had intended; to develop his faculties and subjugate his emotions and passions to the rule of reason; and to harness reason itself to the infinite love and wisdom of his Creator. But he did not wish there to be a Catholic label attached to the Foundation, even though, as his life unfolded, the source of his inspiration and his strength became clear. His courage, determination and sheer stamina were developed in the infinitely testing circumstances of his wartime service. They survived periods of severe illness, and became legendary.

Born in 1917, he joined the University Air Squadron while studying at Oxford, and when the Second World War came he served with Bomber Command, and at twenty-five was the youngest Group Captain in the Service. He then took command of the famous 617 Squadron, the Dambusters. Altogether he flew in no less than 100 operations, including extremely dangerous raids on the heavily defended cities of Cologne, Brunswick and Munich. After being recommended for a third bar to his Distinguished Service Order he was awarded the Victoria Cross, but not, as is usual, for a single outstanding action. In fact, the 'Date of Act of Bravery' required on the recommendation was given as 1940–1944, that is to say for four years of sustained, exceptional courage, 'careful planning, brilliant execution, and contempt for danger'. This is not the place to record the details of his astonishing service career: they can be found in his biographies, first in *No Passing Glory* by Andrew Boyle, and also in *Leonard Cheshire* by Robert Morris. His general spiritual line is expressed in a book of short texts written by Leonard himself in his final illness, *Crossing the Finishing Line*, edited by Father Fuller.

The first atomic bomb was dropped on Hiroshima on August 5 1945, and shortly afterwards Leonard was invited to accompany, as an observer, the second raid, on Nagasaki, which led to the Japanese surrender. Unsurprisingly, what he then saw, and learned later, soon drove him to work for peace. But he later denied that it was the atomic experience which had led him to the creation of the Foundation. His first step was to organize a community for those who as a result of physical or mental disability, or homelessness, needed a breathing space before being fit to embark on a peacetime career. The site he found was a small estate at Le Court, near Liss in Hampshire, where he invited a series of disabled, unwanted or otherwise helpless individuals to congregate.

The prospect for the enterprise was grim, in some ways almost worse than wartime service, which was at least in an identifiable and obviously worthwhile cause. There was no staff, no money, no expertise, the buildings were in a bad state, and even if there had been money to improve them there were strict regulations forbidding repairs and improvements at a time when the building industry was exclusively commandeered for the construction of new houses to replace those destroyed in the wartime bombing. It was a time when numerous large houses, aesthetically more deserving than Le Court, were demolished by their despairing owners.

Financially, Le Court lived from day to day. Helpers often slept on mattresses on the floors, food rationing still applied, and the rations were cooked on paraffin stoves. After five years of war service in the front line, such conditions were all too familiar to many, but they could hardly have been endured in normal times of peace. Leonard led from the front. The *News Chronicle* reported him as 'scrubbing, painting, carpentering ... nursing, feeding, washing the helpless', until after a time his own health, obviously weakened by the stresses of war, collapsed. Le Court was then converted into a trust, with a management committee. It was the first of many occasions when Leonard, on top of all his other qualities, felt able to delegate control of a child of his brain and soul to other people, without either interfering or losing touch completely.

Leonard's conversion to the Catholic Church seems to have begun in a victory celebration in a London nightclub rather ironically called the Vanity Fair, a good example of the spirit blowing where it listeth. One of the girls in his party – he described her as 'not the sort who would fall for religion' – asked him 'What do you know about God?' He replied that 'God is an inward conscience, personal to us all, that tells us what we ought to do, and what we ought not.' To which she answered 'Absolute nonsense. God is a *Person*. And you know it as well as I do.' After much thought and study, he was received into the Church on Christmas Eve 1948. He had decided that he had two requirements from a church. First, it must speak with authority; and second, it must claim the power to forgive sins, as Jesus did. 'Is there a church which God founded and which He guarantees? If, not, take your pick of the the various churches in the world. But if there *is* something that meets the two requirements, then we have a duty to submit to it.' His extreme fairmindedness was later revealed in a letter to an Anglican ally:

> I acknowledge humbly that so far as the Reformation aimed at purifying and depharisaing (sic) the Roman Church it was right ... you on your side must try to realise that if Christ did not in fact establish an infallible Catholic Church which really holds the Keys of Heaven and wields power over sin and death, then the Apostles, the early Fathers and 1,900 years of saints have all been deceived and are proved wrong.

Few of England's great Catholics have stated the matter so clearly and compellingly.

Having successfully accomplished his first task of delegation, Cheshire agreed to join the brilliant aviation inventor Barnes Wallis, with whom he had of course worked in his Dambuster days, in a new project for supersonic flight. 'Wild Goose', as it was called, was not a success, but it took Leonard to Predannack airfield in Cornwall, where he soon also made plans for another project of his own, a second version of Le Court, in a derelict house on the perimeter of the airfield. There were no mains electricity, sewerage, or water; in other words, in Leonard's eyes, it was ideal. Under his usual inspiring leadership, colleagues from Vickers, airfield staff and other local volunteers came to paint, scrub, rewire and lay bricks. When a local lady asked what was most needed, and was told it was sheets, twenty pairs were delivered next day. St Teresa's was born, and the handicapped and the terminally ill began to move in; above all those who had nowhere else to go.

The combination of strains from these two forms of demanding work brought Leonard to the point of physical collapse, and he was found to have a large cavity in one of his lungs, which led to a stay of nearly two years in King Edward VII Hospital at Midhurst, and eventually to the removal of most of one lung, and sections of four ribs. Ironically, this appalling cloud nevertheless had a silver lining. Having to rely on the help of others, doctors and surgeons and nurses, taught him not to rely, egocentrically, on his own individual efforts, but to brief a series of helpers when he recovered, and thus eventually to achieve far more than would otherwise have been possible. One of the secrets of the later success of the Cheshire Foundation was that 'We stick to parcelling out the business and acting as if each particular bit is all that remains to be done ... The fatal mistake is to frighten off possible helpers by asking too much of them.' In other words, sufficient unto the day is the evil thereof.

But for this approach to work, Leonard needed ever increasing skills of coordination on top of the basic saintliness of his nature and of his power to recruit deputies at the various levels of management of the homes. But there was also another quite separate strand in his nature. He felt a strong inclination to join the Cistercian Order, 'partly because they are absolute in their standpoint and partly because I like very much their balance of life and its harmony between mental life, prayer and very hard physical work'. In the end he chose to remain outside the Order, not so much in order to reject the cloister as to embrace the world in the spirit of the cloister; and this was to remain his guiding principle in the long years ahead.

But first came another operation which left him immobile and in great physical pain, gazing at a reproduction of the Holy Face from the Turin Shroud. When he finally recovered, many other projects came and went. The Confraternity of the Holy Shroud; a biography by Andrew Boyle, much hampered by other cross currents, including a rival book by Russell Braddon. The Mission for the Relief of Suffering, which was even more widely framed than the Foundation itself. The Foundation's own pilgrimage to the world-famous healing shrine at Lourdes was of great importance to him, and there was also a scheme for airlifting people to Lourdes who were too ill or handicapped to go by train or coach.

The next improbable and problematic step was to buy the battered remains of Staunton Harold, a magnificent stately home in Derbyshire, on the brink of demolition and because of its layout quite unsuited to the needs of the disabled. (In Leonard's eyes, a mere detail.) Nevertheless, in spite of endless inconvenience to all concerned, many of the residents came to love it for its atmosphere and its history. Among other details, the fine church in the grounds was the only one to have been built under the Commonwealth in the seventeenth century, when, as a tablet on the outside proclaims, '*All thinges sacred were throughout ye nation Either demolisht or profaned.*' The church celebrated '*the best things in ye worst times*'. This certainly struck a powerful chord with Leonard.

At this stage it was not at all easy to track Leonard down, since he was of no fixed abode, but lived in a bus, adapted with a desk and with running water, in perpetual motion between the homes as they sprang up. He was not exactly a hard taskmaster, rather an elusive and confusing one. He felt that if all his affairs were conducted in a businesslike fashion, people would say, 'This chap Cheshire, he is such a good organiser that he doesn't need any help from us.' So he avoided being a good organizer, and it is not unfair to say that he largely left it to others to solve the innumerable problems and details which arose. But obviously it would have been quite impossible for him, as the Foundation grew, to deal with all the details himself. However, this could sometimes lead to feelings of neglect, resentment even, that had somehow to be soothed.

He also decided to set off at last on a long-intended trip to India. An important thread in his efforts to re-establish real peace after the war was his determination to confront suffering in the world. This had the additional advantage of distancing him for a time from the Foundation in England, so that it could learn to stand on its own feet and not rely on the personality cult of its founder. If homes were in difficulties, his view was that they couldn't be much good 'if they have to have me around the whole time'. In due course his faith in his followers was vindicated, but they had many anxious moments, and in 1956 the future of several of the homes was doubtful. (One pious but conventional senior banker who became a trustee was driven to distraction by his methods, or rather by the lack of them, and resigned in dispair. But needless to say, Leonard did not change his spots, and the show went on.) But as well as continuing to flit from one uncompleted scheme to the next, he did try to formulate a general principle for his future activities. There is among his papers the following note:

> To take them that are unwanted, and to make them wanted. Not to say to them 'Now just lie back and be comfortably sick for the rest of your life'; but to give them a purpose to live for, to give them the means of rising above their infirmity, to turn them into active members of the family, active helpers in the work that still has so far to go, so many countries to reach.

Consequently, ways were devised in the homes for teaching the handicapped to perform all kinds of activities of which they were quite unaware that they were capable, to their incalculable advantage.

He saw India as the ideal stepping-stone, 'a half-way house, Eastern but built on a British foundation'. He spent most of the years from 1955 to 1959 there, and it was from India that he considered he had 'an entrée really all over the world'. Certainly in the next three years a new Cheshire

Home opened somewhere in the world on average every three months. A letter survives from Nehru, emphasizing that whereas large, expensive schemes, tending to lose the personal touch, were suitable for governments to undertake, 'effective relief of suffering, 'without much fuss or expense', was of even greater importance, though on a different scale. After a teatime visit from Cheshire, introduced by David Lean, during which Leonard hardly spoke, except to say that he was taking the next bus back into town, Nehru said 'That is the greatest man I have met since Gandhi.' Back in England, Prince Philip later described Leonard's multiple achievements as 'the story of one of the greatest acts of humanity of our time', and many others have agreed that to meet him was to understand immediately how anyone even remotely interested in his mission (for that was what it was) would do their utmost to do anything he asked them. Leaving behind a cat's cradle of loose ends which were in one way or another all sorted out in the end, he remained in India for four years, bewildering the steady stream of well-wishers that was magnetically drawn to him, by always starting the next project before the previous one was finished. The volunteers were somehow inspired to regard the projects as their own, and to make them work. His great secret lay in the much misused word 'charisma', here correctly signifying a spiritual power given by God, and not just a generally persuasive personality. In 1958 he had the idea of founding the Family of the Holy Cross, in which individual families or groups were to join together for the relief of suffering, with the members working each for his own sanctification, and thus for the sanctification of the world. This was another project that he floated off, to sink or swim as the case might be.

A further project was inspired by his encounter, and eventual marriage, with Sue Ryder, who had worked as a very young girl in the war with Special Operations Executive, an independent commando-style force which achieved some sensational successes. Working chiefly among its Polish units, she became inspired, like others who became aware of the unique nature of what the Poles had suffered during and after the war, to do what she could to help them. Thousands of victims had been left homeless and helpless, survivors of concentration camps and forced labour, and they continued to be oppressed by inhuman Russian brutality. In 1958 there were 200,000 stateless persons living in Germany, under wretched conditions, and the generous worldwide campaign to end this scandal was characteristically, but in the end, unsuccessfully, resisted by the Foreign Office, 'for fear of its effect on Anglo-German relations'. Leonard and Sue began to devise a complex of homes for stateless Poles, one of them, perhaps surprisingly, in conjunction with lepers in India. This led to the creation of the Ryder-Cheshire Foundation, which arose largely because of an incident in India when a young boy had died. Leonard believed that this was because he had been unable to help him personally. He therefore wanted to start an organization in which he and Sue could have more personal involvement, rather than the usual process of delegation. It effectively began when they shared the driving in a tour of India covering several thousand miles, organizing, among other things, homes for many thousands of lepers. This was followed by a massive campaign against tuberculosis. And finally, the Ryder-Cheshire Mission organized a Family Week in Rome, attended by several hundred heavily disabled people from the homes all over the world, at which one and all received a special blessing from the Pope. This was also the occasion of the silver wedding of Leonard and Sue. As a result of the huge workload undertaken by each of them, more often than not in quite different parts of the world, little of their married life had been spent together, and this reunion was an even more special one as a result.

One might have thought that an overwhelming concern for the disabled would have been enough to keep anyone busy. But even on top of that he came to believe that 'the greatest affront to man's dignity, greater even than nuclear armouries, is our failure to act decisively against the poverty of developing nations', and never more so than when they are overtaken by terrible natural disasters. 1988 was a year especially notable for a succession of famines, floods and hurricanes. In September of that year Leonard attended a reunion of Commonwealth aircrews, and felt that the spirit of reunion could somehow lead to coping with these hideous new natural catastrophes. This led to the formation of a World War Memorial Fund for Disaster Relief, which came to be adopted all over the world, with particular support in Australia, New Zealand, Canada, Japan, Italy and several other European countries. The timing was excellent: the Fund was launched on 3 September 1989, the fiftieth anniversay of the outbreak of the Second World War, at the United Nations, who were to take charge of its distribution. There was to be a single campaign to end in 1995, of equal duration to that of the war itself. Sadly, for reasons too complex to go into in a short chapter, the project failed, perhaps because of the tension between Leonard's frugality on the one hand, and the practical demands of organizing a scheme to raise £500 million, for this was the target.

Leonard had put forward the name of Sir Peter Ramsbotham, a former ambassador to Washington who had become one of his closest admirers and confidants, to succeed the outgoing Chairman of the Cheshire Foundation itself. To his sorrow, the trustees decided otherwise. Till then, the succession had been virtually in Leonard's hands, and it was a cruel blow to feel that he had lost, in that respect, the trust that he had till then enjoyed. More happily, Ramsbotham remained one of Leonard's most intimate advisers, as well as being one of his greatest personal friends, becoming Chairman of the Ryder-Cheshire Mission instead of the Foundation itself. Leonard confided in him that the Memorial Fund had created an inner compulsion in him 'such as I have never felt even with the homes', no doubt because it covered not only the disabled but the victims of natural disasters whose sufferings were on an even wider scale. He wanted its organization 'to be as open as possible for the Holy Spirit to move our appeal strategy into whatever direction he wants'. As is almost inevitable in such a vast enterprise, especially when extended to the United States, costs escalated, supporting events went astray, and there was Leonard's old determination to keep ultimate control in his own hands. Long ago, his mother had considered that finance was not Leonard's strongest point. Not surprisingly, his health had already begun to suffer before the Fund was launched.

In 1981, he had happily accepted the honour of the Order of Merit, an award in the Queen's personal gift, needless to say only because it would confer even more prestige on the Foundation. In 1991 he accepted a life peerage, because of the possibility that his immense experience, combined with his unflagging determination to serve, could find a fruitful outlet in debates in the Lords. Sadly, in that year he fell a victim to Motor Neurone Disease, but mercifully died the following year. In her Christmas broadcast in the year following his death, though it was quite exceptional for her to mention an individual, the Queen had this to say:

> Just before he died, Leonard Cheshire came to see us with his fellow members of the Order of Merit ... suffering from a drawn-out and terminal illness. He bore this with all the fortitude and cheerfulness to be expected of a holder of the Victoria Cross. However, what struck me more forcibly than his physical courage was the fact that he made no reference to his own illness but only to his hopes and plans to make life better for others. He embodied the message in that well known line 'Kindness in another's trouble, courage in one's own'.

The way in which he met this cruel incapacity was movingly characteristic:

> The physical difficulties get me down – but it has given me a kind of inner joy. If you are a Christian then you have to believe that the Christian way is the Way of the Cross. I've had a good life. This is just something to be got round – a bit of flak on the way to the target.

If this is not the stuff that saints are made of, it would be interesting to know what is. Indeed, the author T. H. White, who had taught Leonard at Stowe, said of him 'He has all the characteristics of a saint: obstinacy, fanaticism, charm.' Surely a campaign for canonization cries out to be made. It might be difficult to pinpoint a single miracle for which he was responsible, but the massive total of his achievements over forty years in reducing the suffering of others is an uncanny parallel with the conspicuous valour over a long period in wartime which earned him the Victoria Cross. Indeed, there could be no better way of permanently filling the spare plinth in Trafalgar Square than by a figure that everyone could look up to, in every possible sense, namely Leonard Cheshire

He and Sue had begun their married life by composing together a prayer which ended as follows:

> To this we offer our all, our everything,
> To be consumed in the unquenchable fire of Thy love.
> To be generous as thou Thyself was generous,
> To give our all to Thee even as Thou hast given Thine to us.
> Thou hast called us, O Lord, and we have found Thee,
> In the sick, the unwanted and the dying,
> And there we will serve thee,
> Unto Death.

Few of the English Catholics celebrated in this book have expressed themselves more generously or more movingly.

Chapter 16

Cardinal Basil Hume, OSB

Archbishop Vincent Nichols

Basil Hume, OSB was Archbishop of Westminster from 1976 to 1999. When he came to that position comparatively few had heard of him. When he died he was acknowledged as the spiritual leader of the country, held in high esteem by all.

His funeral was attended by the Duchess of Kent and Princess Michael representing the Queen, by Cardinal Cassidy as the personal representative of Pope John Paul II, by the Prime Ministers of Great Britain and of Ireland and by people from every walk of life. Millions followed the funeral Mass on television. Everyone felt somehow personally close to him.

At his funeral Mass, Bishop Crowley spoke about the man he had known so well:

> For thirty-five years as a monk and for twenty-five years as Archbishop Cardinal Hume centred himself on God. And from that store of wisdom he fed us. Without ever seeking it, he became a spiritual beacon for millions of people. All the while, his deeply Benedictine soul propelled him towards balance – the common ground, the common good, and he did so without ever compromising the faith.
>
> He sought that common ground untiringly; within dialogue between churches, within the dialogue between different faiths, and within the Catholic Church, too.

One reason for this was that Cardinal Hume had a deep

understanding of weakness, of our human frailty. He was a realist who was never carried away with religious fervour. When he spoke he never minimized his own shortcomings and so found that common ground with others who were also struggling. Yet he also aspired to the highest calling of all human beings: that of knowing and loving God and living always in that knowledge and by that love.

In an age of uncertainty it was these qualities that made him a truly remarkable spiritual leader and an English Catholic hero.

When he had completed VI Form studies, George Hume joined the Benedictine community at Ampleforth in 1941, at the age of eighteen. This was the defining step in his life, for the routines of the Benedictine day and the spirituality of the Order of St Benedict (OSB) were to shape the rest of his life. It was within that pattern of daily prayer, work and community that George Basil Hume was to struggle and grow to the mature leader that he became. The Benedictine Order gave him his deepest identity and reinforced in him some of the deepest traits of his character.

St Benedict is rightly known as the father of monasticism and as one of the founding figures of European Christian culture. English monasticism from the eleventh century to today has been largely shaped by this Benedictine tradition and it was the monasteries that gave both stability and learning to this land in the centuries commonly called the Dark Ages. The Benedictine motto *Pax inter Spinas* (Peace among thorns) adopted by Cardinal Hume, indicates that the desire for peace will only be achieved through a genuine grappling with difficulties.

Basil Hume reflected many of these strands. He was a man who knew that community could be rooted only in prayer. He was recognized as somehow being quintessentially English, even though his father was Scottish and his mother French. He had a passion for 'fair play' and a love of competition, in rugby, football and cricket. He was a champion of education and knew that it was, at heart, a spiritual quest. He was a man of peace, yet not afraid to grapple with the thorny issues of the day and come out bloodied and scarred.

So it must have been a great relief to him to be told by Pope Paul VI, who had just appointed him to be Archbishop of Westminster, that he should continue to wear his Benedictine habit. He brought all the strength and resilience of that great tradition to the office of the Archbishop and to the role of Cardinal.

These are not easy roles to fulfil. As Archbishop of Westminster he had immediate responsibility for the 210 parishes of the Archdiocese and the 700 priests working there, of whom over 350 owed direct obedience to him. Within the Archdiocese were over 220 Catholic schools, as well as Allen Hall, the diocesan seminary for the education and formation of future priests. The diocese also included programmes for the adult education of its people, for the pastoral response to social need, to situations of injustice and racism. There were the universities, the hospitals and the prisons for which chaplaincies had to be provided. The direct oversight of all this Catholic life, with all the daily problems that arose, is task enough for anyone.

But, three years after his installation as Archbishop, Basil Hume also became the President of the Bishops' Conference of England and Wales, a post he held for the rest of his life. Now he became the public leader of the Catholic Church in these countries, responsible for giving shape to its public presence and voice. Gradually this led him into many high profile issues of public life, dealing directly with four Prime Ministers and their various cabinet members on a full range of delicate and controversial matters.

With his appointment as cardinal, also in 1976, he was drawn into the work of the Holy See, the ministry of the pope in governance of the Catholic Church throughout the world. For many years the Cardinal served on five of the Congregations or Pontifical Councils of the Holy See, as well as attending various meetings of the College of Cardinals. Most crucial of those were the two gatherings of cardinals, the Conclaves, he attended in 1978 for the elections of Pope John Paul I and Pope John Paul II.

These were exhilarating occasions when ceremonial is elaborate and speculation high. Cardinal Hume enjoyed telling of his amazement on seeing a police escort ready to accompany him on his journey into Rome for the first of these Conclaves. He was, after all, not just an elector of the next Pope, but also a candidate. He added, with relish, that no one was there to escort his car on its return journey to the airport, on his way back to Westminster.

As Cardinal and as President of the Bishops' Conference, he was also expected to attend the regular meetings of the worldwide Synod of Bishops. These Synods, or gatherings, took place more or less every three years and explored different aspects of the life of the Church in the light of the teachings of the Second Vatican Council. Cardinal Hume played a prominent part in these month-long meetings, which were very demanding. On one occasion he filled the key role of 'Relator', whose job was to summarize and guide the unfolding discussion. But his influence was often more personal, more charismatic than strictly structural. He had a great gift of expressing in imaginative and acceptable ways the anxieties or uncertainties felt by many.

When faced with iron certainty on the part of some insisting unflinchingly on the Church's teaching on sexual morality, whereas others were looking for recognition of heartfelt dilemmas and uncertainty, the Cardinal gave a remarkable speech in which he said 'It is sometimes better to dwell in the tents of Abraham than to sit secure in Solomon's temple' (14 October 1980).

Alongside these duties to the Holy See as Cardinal there was his constant rapport with the papal representative in London. The Apostolic Nuncio – or Delegate as he was until 1982 – has a double role: a diplomat representing the Holy See to the British Government, and the representative of the pope to the Catholic community of England and Wales. Throughout his time in office, Cardinal Hume took great care in working with the Nuncio in all manner of affairs.

There was one other layer of work that fell to him. Within Europe great change was taking place in the last twenty years of the last century. The European bishops of the Catholic Church used to meet regularly and formally as the Council of European Episcopal Conferences (CCEE). In 1978, Cardinal Hume was elected as President of this body, a position he held for nine years. During his presidency great efforts were made to bring together bishops from Western Europe, facing challenges of secularization and loss of faith, with bishops from Eastern Europe, whose churches were gradually emerging from a time of great suffering and martyrdom, impoverished but proud. Mutual trust was not always forthcoming, and Cardinal Hume's diplomacy and great tact helped to build bridges and overcome misunderstandings.

This range of responsibilities and tasks resulted in a heavy workload and a demanding daily routine. There was little free time in any day and the demands made on the Archbishop were incessant. Basil Hume brought to this position all his natural gifts of intelligence and wit as well as the fruits of his Benedictine formation and monastic life. Every day, following the monastic tradition, he rose very early and spent the first hours in prayer in the chapel in Archbishop's House. This was the foundation for everything. No matter the lateness of the hour at which his evening duties finished, he was up very early to find that necessary peace, in prayer, with the Lord. If he was not out on a public engagement, the guests soon realized that he would leave them by 9.30 p.m. to make his final prayers and start the silence of the night.

But no one should imagine that his praying was easy and rewarding. It was not. He would struggle in prayer, wrestling with the problems he faced, struggling with distraction, scribbling down words and phrases to keep his heart focused. 'Third Division', he would often describe himself to be.

This honesty and humility was, in fact, one of his greatest strengths. When he spoke, or wrote, of prayer he did so in a way that many could recognize and understand. For Cardinal Hume the struggle to know God, to live in God's presence, to trust in God's ways was as real as any difficult and rewarding friendship. It was a matter of the heart as well as the mind and, in his view, it was the most important relationship in every person's life.

Cardinal Hume understood how to speak about God in ways that were attractive and challenging, with words that had the ring of truth about them. This was based entirely on his own lifelong struggle to live a truly spiritual life.

In this lay his greatness. His first book, a collection of talks given as Abbot of Ampleforth, was entitled *Searching for God*, a title that, in fact, describes his whole life. He knew, and said so over and again, that this search was both frustrating and enticing; it was never accomplished except in rare glimpses and moments of consolation and inspiration. But he knew that God alone could satisfy his heart; God alone could be the foundation of his day and the source of energy for his efforts; God alone would be his reward, and most importantly, his judge.

Writing in 1994, Cardinal Hume gave an eloquent expression to the themes that were central to his life, his teaching and his Episcopal ministry. Using the image of an eagle hovering over its chicks in the nest, he explored our experience of God, of God's transcendence and immanence, of our freedom as human beings and our ultimate dependence. To understand him, these words must be pondered. He must speak for himself:

> Freedom is a priceless gift bestowed by God. Perhaps the most fundamental freedom we possess is that of choosing how we respond to God's love. It is freedom to explore a reality infinitely greater and more wonderful than we can ever imagine. Now love cannot be forced or coerced. It is of its essence a free choice. Having the capacity to love means we can choose not to. The eagle hovers, but does not overwhelm the eaglets. Furthermore, to be able to respond to the love of God by loving in return presupposes a certain distance between us and God.
>
> The existence of God is not obvious. The revelation of God in human history and in individual lives is not always so transparent as to compel us to acknowledge his sovereignty

and dominion over us. So we have to choose to bridge the distance that separates us from God, or, more strictly speaking, choose to respond to the initiatives which God takes to meet us where we are, that is, in the reality of our daily lives.

Now the experience of being touched by God can take many forms. The most direct we call mystical experience, a frightening word, no doubt, but one that describes a knowing and a desiring of God which has no other explanation but his action in our souls. It is more common than is often realized. There is also a yearning to seek a meaning and purpose to human life; the sense that the universe cannot explain either its own existence or its intelligibility; the awareness of moral obligation, of goodness, of beauty and of truth – these are some of the reasons that lead us to look beyond ourselves and our world, to One who can satisfy both an intellectual search for ultimate truth and a spiritual and emotional longing for love.

'The Hinterland of Freedom: Morality and Solidarity',
The Month, March 1994, p. 88–92.

These words and so many others like them, addressed the deepest experiences of people. Somehow Basil Hume had a knack of getting beyond the surface issues, the immediate news story, to gently probe these deeper, unsettling questions which we would rather push to one side or ignore entirely. And his probing was always gentle, full of respect not only for the freedom of the individual but more importantly for the freedom of God. The Cardinal's utter confidence in God never became a certainty about how God might touch another person's life. He was always the servant, and never dreamt that high ecclesiastical office gave him any hold over, or shortcut to, the workings of the Almighty in the soul of another person.

In he same article, he took his exploration of the spiritual life some steps further:

It seems to me that there are always hints and echoes of the divine which whisper to us and invite us to respond, for God is ever at work in human hearts … The eagle has not abandoned the nest but hovers, touching and not touching, coaxing us gently, individually and collectively, to respond with love, while always respecting our freedom.

Why is the existence of God not more obvious? One answer might be that it requires the deep engagement of the whole person before the question of God becomes real. What is obvious requires no engagement, no reflection, no struggle. To go in search of God, on the other hand, requires effort and a measure of self-discipline and self-denial. The voice of God does not speak dramatically, as in a hurricane, or an earthquake, or a fire, but calls to us gently in the very depth of our being. To hear the voice of God demands some solitude, silence and stillness. In our society today there is too much noise, both around and within us, and the quiet voice of God becomes stifled. But in a moment of gentle stillness, God not only reveals something of himself, but he transforms us too. So if God exists, it is the most fundamental truth of all. It changes everything. It cannot be both true and not matter.

Everyday it mattered to Basil Hume. His life cannot be understood without this first emphasis, this priority, this foundation. This search for God, this striving to respond to God's love, to allow the reality and certainty of that acceptance to shape every consideration and judgement lay at the heart of his daily efforts. The transparency of this priority was also the root cause of the appeal he had for so many people. He was evidently a man devoted to God. He was evidently a man whose compassion sprang from his experience of God's forgiveness, his anger from a sense of God's justice, his openness from an awareness of God's love for every human being.

But there was something else which was just as important. Cardinal Hume was not afraid to grapple with the harsh realities of life, and to do so in public. His was not a spirituality of an escapism, by which he might seek to excuse himself from the distressing conflicts and tragedies of human existence. Rather he held together the roughness and battles of life with the journey of prayer towards God. They were not alternatives. They went hand in hand. And this is what people saw. They saw a man of God who was also a champion of those suffering injustice, or caught in moral dilemmas, a man of prayer who would engage in a political scrap.

When priests in his care got into difficulties, they turned to him for support and acceptance. Many found strength in his compassion. He never turned away. Their burdens became his, for he recognized that bond between bishop and priest as being one like father and son. And when the bond was broken, he suffered and longed to see it restored.

The same was true of the broken bonds between the Christian Churches. He longed to see them healed, particularly with the Church of England. On the day of his installation he led the monks of Ampleforth to Westminster Abbey where they sang Vespers, the evening prayer of the Catholic Church. For Cardinal Hume these hopes for Christian Unity were dealt a serious blow when, in 1994, the Church of England decided to ordain women to the priesthood. Then he worked long and hard to secure a generous welcome in the Catholic Church for those clergy who, as a matter of conscience, could not accept the decision. The benefits of his work are evident in the Catholic community today.

Each day Cardinal Hume would view the world with a heart formed in prayer. His initiatives for all those caught in poverty or injustice were rooted in the compassion he saw in the heart of God. He helped establish the DePaul Trust and the Cardinal Hume Centre for young people at risk. He set up The Passage in a street alongside Westminster Cathedral. It is the largest day centre for homeless people in Britain. His practical involvement was evident. One day, walking across the front of the Cathedral, the Cardinal was spotted by a man from The Passage who called out 'Hi, Cardinal. I'm wearing your trousers!' His old clothes, with the label 'Basil Hume' still intact, had gone to the day centre.

In 1978 he visited Wormwood Scrubs Prison and met Giuseppe Conlon and the others convicted of the Guildford terrorist bombing. He came away convinced of their innocence. He could not rest. He then started a seven-year battle to win a review of their case, which eventually by February 1985 won them their freedom, although by then Giuseppe had died in prison.

The way this campaign was conducted reflected so many of the Cardinal's qualities. He knew he had neither the technical knowledge nor the political connections needed. So he invited the High Court Judge Lord Scarman and two former Home Secretaries, Merlyn Rees and Roy Jenkins, to work with him. They were joined by others and formed a formidable team. The Cardinal not only gave additional standing to the campaign, for his leadership made sure that its motivation – to right an apparent injustice – was not misinterpreted, but he also brought an unflinching determination. This was strengthened every morning in his prayer.

Within the life of the Catholic community remarkable events were also taking place. In 1980, the Catholic community embarked on a nationwide process of reflection and renewal under the heading of the National Pastoral Congress. It was fraught with difficulties of size, diversity and logistics. Aided by Archbishop Worlock, Basil Hume kept a steady head and was able to declare, at its final event in Liverpool Metropolitan Cathedral, that the work of the Holy Spirit was certainly to be found in its outcome.

This Congress was the foundation for the historic visit to Britain of Pope John Paul II in May 1982. This was the first ever visit by a pope to Britain; it was a massive undertaking for the Catholic community.

The visit was a great success, described as 'the healing of an ancient wound', enabling the Pope to reach many millions of people with his teaching and presence. It gave a great boost to relationships with other Christians. The Pope's visit to Buckingham Palace signalled a change in the public standing of the Catholic Church, one confirmed years later by the presence of Queen Elizabeth II at Vespers in Westminster Cathedral on 30 November 1995.

Yet at one point the visit was shrouded with uncertainty

when the Falklands war broke out at the beginning of May 1982. Only intense diplomatic activity, led by Cardinal Hume and Archbishop Worlock, ensured that the visit took place. These two events illustrated the partnership between the Cardinal and the Archbishop of Liverpool which characterized their years in office. It was a costly but highly fruitful partnership. The Archbishop was methodical, meticulous and dependable. The Cardinal was intuitive, charismatic and, at times, imperious. Both were strong-minded, deeply dedicated and very private men. They worked hard for each other and always for the good of the Church. They formed a trusted leadership of the Bishops' Conference.

During these years of leadership, difficulties constantly had to be faced. One, which stretched this partnership considerably, was the 1983 strike by Britain's coal miners. Bishops took up different positions, according to their situation and experience. The Bishop of Leeds, Gordon Wheeler, made strenuous efforts to support the families of striking miners, who faced increasing hardship. Archbishop Worlock attempted to explore the possibilities of reconciliation even though he was represented as trying to mediate between the miners and the Government. Cardinal Hume, closest to the Westminster Government, kept a more guarded distance. They were tense days during which the depth of each bishop's personal prayerful faith and commitment to the Lord kept them together.

Contact with the Government of the day was a regular part of the exercise of his office. Some was well known and documented: such as his discussions with Kenneth Baker in 1988 over the first of a long series of Education Acts. But he had more informal and less public contact with ministers, too, which were sometimes more effective. He met privately with Michael Howard, as Home Secretary, when anti-terrorist measures were presenting a legal threat to the inviolability of the seal of confession.

The declaration of war against Saddam Hussein in Kuwait also tested the Cardinal's leadership and his ability to find 'common ground'. Here again his pondering over the moral issues of the war became a constant part of his prayer. His instincts for peace, his abhorrence of violence had to be weighed against the cause of justice and international law. He felt deeply his duty of moral leadership towards the men and women of the armed forces.

For Cardinal Hume, moral dilemmas were never abstract. He always had in mind the person facing those dilemmas or moral difficulties. A deep concern of his, for example, was that persons of a homosexual tendency should not feel alienated from the Church by an insensitive presentation of its sexual moral teaching. He upheld the Church's teaching, but gave fresh emphasis to its forgotten esteem of the love of friendship. Often in confronting moral dilemmas he sought to uphold the greater good while never demeaning the lesser good, for example, individuals striving after the good of their family or facing the paradoxes of their human nature. He was a compassionate teacher, never forgetful of his own weaknesses and therefore sensitive to the vulnerability of others.

His own vulnerability came right to the fore when illness struck him in the early days of 1999. Shortly after Easter he was diagnosed as having terminal cancer. He immediately wrote to his priests in his inimitable way:

> I have received two wonderful graces. First, I have been given time to prepare for a new future. Secondly, I find myself – uncharacteristically – calm and at peace. I intend to carry on working as much and as long as I can. But nevertheless, I shall be a bit limited in what I can do. Above all, no fuss. The future is in God's hands.

With this firm and deep faith, he set about preparing for the most important step a person ever takes: that of dying. But one more public engagement intervened. He was informed by Buckingham Palace that the Queen was minded to make him a member of the Order of Merit, an exceptional honour in the personal gift of Her Majesty. He hesitated, for only one reason. His greatest desire, he explained, was to go to God empty-handed. He did not want to be filled with any sense of achievement. Only if he died empty-handed could he receive the greatest gift of all, that of God's mercy. He acknowledged the generosity of the Queen's wish, however, and accepted. But the award was not to be placed on his coffin.

It was with great pride, then, that on 2 June he went to Buckingham Palace to receive the Order of Merit from the Queen. For this, too, he is a Catholic hero.

He died on 17 June. The intervening days were spent peacefully. Those who were close to him tell of his continuing interest in them, their tasks, their families. And his sporting enthusiasms found their continuing place, too. Just as he taught us how to live, so he taught us how to die.

In the homily at the funeral Mass of Cardinal Hume, Bishop Crowley spoke of some of the Cardinal's last moments of prayer. These are the words on which to end for these sum up so much of his life, his desire, his faith. He was, above all, a man of faith. Bishop Crowley said:

> In those last days, he came to a fresh understanding of the Our Father.
>
> It was, he said, like discovering its inner meaning for the very first time. 'It's only now that I begin to glimpse how everything we need is right there in the Lord's prayer.'
>
> He then prayed the first three phrases of the Our Father, adding to each phrase a tiny commentary of his own. Sitting there and listening was somehow to understand afresh all that he stood for, to see again with great clarity why we admired him so much and loved him so deeply.
>
> 'Our Father who art in heaven, hallowed be thy name.' Then he added: 'to sing the praises of God, it is that for which we have been made, and it is that which will be, for all eternity, our greatest joy.'
>
> Then the second phrase. 'Thy Kingdom come.' The Cardinal added: 'The gospel values of Jesus, justice, love and peace, embraced throughout the whole world in all their fullness.'
>
> Then the third. 'Thy will be done on earth as it is in heaven.' Finally he added: 'That's the only thing which really matters. What God wants for us is what is best for us.'

In Westminster Cathedral there is a chapel dedicated to St Gregory the Great and St Augustine of Canterbury. It also commemorates other great fathers of the faith in this land: Aidan, Cuthbert and Bede all of them, like Cardinal Hume, Benedictine monks. It is there, in that company, that he is buried.

Notes on Contributors

Viscountess Asquith

Viscountess Asquith studied English at Oxford where she was awarded a congratulatory First. She worked in publishing, teaching and journalism before travelling abroad with her husband, who was posted to the British Embassy in Moscow in the 1980s and in Kiev in the 1990s. In 2000, struck by the similarities between censorship under communism and under the repressive regimes of Shakespeare's England, she published an article in the *Times Literary Supplement* on Shakespeare's poem, 'The Phoenix and the Turtle'. Since then she has written further essays on Shakespeare and Catholicism for various scholarly books and journals. Her book on Shakespeare, *Shadowplay*, was published in 2005. She lives in Somerset with her husband and five children.

Dom Aidan Bellenger, OSB

Dom Aidan Bellenger is Abbot of Downside. He has been a monk of the Benedictine Abbey in Somerset since 1982 and has served as Head Master and Prior. He is a much-published author on matters historical and has a special interest in the English Catholic Community and the medieval Church. He lectures on the Middle Ages at Bath Spa and Bristol Universities. A Cambridge Ph.D. he is a Fellow of the Royal Historical Society and the Society of Antiquaries.

Lucy Beckett
Lucy Beckett was educated at Cambridge University and taught English, Latin and History for twenty years at Ampleforth Abbey and College. She has published books on Wallace Stevens, Wagner's *Parsifal*, York Minster and the Cistercian Abbeys of North Yorkshire, as well as a collection of poems, a novel on the Reformation, *The Time Before You Die*, and a major study of writing in the Western tradition from Greek tragedy to Czeslaw Milosz, *In the Light of Christ*. Her new novel, set in Weimar Germany, *A Postcard from the Volcano*, will be published in 2008. She is married to the musicologist John Warrack and has four children.

Dr Andrew Breeze
Dr Andrew Breeze was educated at Sir Roger Manwood's School, Sandwich, and the Universities of Oxford and Cambridge. He is a Fellow of the Society of Antiquaries and of the Royal Historical Society, and since 1987 has taught at the University of Navarre, Pamplona. Married with six children, he is the author of the controversial study *Medieval Welsh Literature* (1997) and co-author, with Professor Richard Coates, of *Celtic Voices, English Places* (2000).

Robert Gray
Robert Gray was born in 1942 and educated at Winchester and New College, Oxford. Since 1990 he has been an obituarist for the *Daily Telegraph*. His publications include *A History of London* (1978), *Cardinal Manning* (1985) and *The King's Wife* (1990). He has a French wife and two children; and is a devoted Londoner.

Fr Bernard Green, OSB
Fr Bernard Green, OSB is a monk of Ampleforth and Fellow and Tutor in Theology at St Benet's Hall, Oxford, where he teaches patristics in the University. Having read history at Oxford, he subsequently took a research degree in theology at Cambridge, and later took a doctorate at Oxford on the theology of Pope Leo the Great.

Alex Haydon

Alex Haydon was born in 1963 and educated at Bedales School and Peterhouse, Cambridge. Since September 2004 he has been Research Assistant to Edward Leigh, MP. Before working for Edward, Alex's career included co-ordinating social policy in a Citizens' Advice Bureau; teaching remedial English as a private tutor; writing *Edmund Campion*, a life of the Elizabethan Jesuit martyr (Catholic Truth Society), and being Joint Editor of the Quarterly Journal-cum-Newsletter of the Keys (The Catholic Writers' Guild). As a freelance writer, he has published in the *Catholic Herald*. He is a member of the Parliamentary and Public Affairs Committee of the Catholic Union, and of its Council.

Hon. John Jolliffe

John Jolliffe was born in 1935 and lived as a child at Mells, where Mgr Ronald Knox spent his last years. He was Captain of the School at Eton College, and read Greats at Christ Church, Oxford.

He was for a time editorial director of Constable Publishers, and among other books has written a history of Glyndebourne, as well as editing two biographical collections. He has reviewed books regularly in the *Spectator* and *Country Life*, and is a contributor to the Catholic press. He served at one time as Chairman of the UK Board of Aid to the Church in Need.

Edward Leigh MP

Edward Leigh MP, was born in 1950 and educated at the Oratory School, Berkshire, the French Lycée, London and Durham University, where he was President of the Union Society. He worked in the private office of Margaret Thatcher from 1976 to 1977 as private secretary in charge of her correspondence as Leader of the Opposition.

In 1983, he was elected Member of Parliament for Gainsborough & Horncastle (since replaced by the new seat of Gainsborough). He has sat on many parliamentary committees, with interests in defence, agriculture and foreign affairs.

He has been Chairman of the National Council for Civil Defence and Director of the Coalition For Peace Through Security.

From 1990 to 1993, he was a Parliamentary Under-Secretary of State, Department of Trade and Industry. Prior to that he was a Parliamentary Private Secretary in the Home Office. Since July 2001 he has been Chairman of the Public Accounts Select Committee. In 2003 he founded the Cornerstone Group, a 'socially conservative' association of fellow Tory MPs: http://cornerstonegroup.wordpress.com/ He is a vice-president of the Catholic Union, a member of its Parliamentary Committee, and of its Council. He is the author of *Right Thinking* (1979), an anthology of Tory quotations, and *The Strange Desertion of Tory England: The Conservative Alternative to the Liberal Orthodoxy* (2005).

Archbishop Vincent Nichols

Archbishop Nichols was educated at St Mary's College, Crosby, at the Gregorian University in Rome, and at Manchester University and Loyola University, Chicago. After working as a priest in Wigan and inner-city Liverpool he was appointed to be General Secretary of the Catholic Bishops' Conference of England and Wales under the presidency of Cardinal Basil Hume. In 1992 he was appointed as Auxiliary Bishop to Cardinal Hume and continued in that role, working on a daily basis with the Cardinal, until 2000. He then took up the responsibilities of Archbishop of Birmingham along with national responsibilities for educa-tion and for the development of the work of child protection in the Catholic Church at a national level. He has published two books: one an exploration of the Mass entitled *'Promise of Future Glory'* (1997) and the second reflections on the priesthood under the title *'Missioners – Priests and People Today'* (2007).

Dr Roderick O'Donnell

Dr Roderick O'Donnell has published extensively on A. W. N. Pugin and his sons, notably *The Pugins and the Catholic*

Midlands (Gracewing, 2002) and in his introductions to the Gracewing reprints of Pugin texts – the series now comprising five of his seminal works. An internationally recognized authority on Catholic church architecture of the eighteenth, nineteenth and twentieth centuries in the English-speaking world, and a vice-president of the Historic Churches Preservation Trust, Dr O'Donnell has been an Inspector at English Heritage for over twenty-five years. He is a Fellow of the Society of Antiquaries.

Fr Peter Phillips
Fr Peter Phillips, a priest of the Shrewsbury diocese, is currently working as a parish priest in north Cheshire. He trained for the priesthood at Ushaw, John Lingard's college, and, after a number of years teaching both in secondary schools and in higher education, returned to the College to teach systematic theology and nineteenth-century church history. He has published a number of articles and books in these fields, recently completing a critical biography of Lingard which is to be published by Gracewing in 2009.

Dr William Sheils
Dr William Sheils is Reader in History at the University of York, where he teaches the history of post-Reformation religion, mostly focusing on Britain. He has published widely on English religious history in the sixteenth and seventeenth centuries, and was editor of *Studies in Church History* from 1981 until 1990. More recently he was Associate Editor of the *Oxford Dictionary of National Biography* (2004), with responsibility for priests and religious 1600–1640, and will be President of the Ecclesiastical History Society for 2008–9. He currently holds a grant from the Arts and Humanities Research Council for a research project on clerical taxation between 1173 and 1664, and is a Fellow of the Royal Historical Society.

James Stourton
James Stourton was educated at Ampleforth and read History of Art at Cambridge. He is proprietor of the Stourton Press and Chairman of Sotheby's UK. He is the author of *Great Smaller Museums of Europe* and *Collectors of our Time: art collecting since 1945.* He is a specialist in the history of collecting. He has written on the subject for *Apollo, The Art Newspaper, Country Life, The Independent* and *The Spectator* and lectures to Sotheby's Institute of Education and Cambridge University Faculty of Art History.

Fr Anthony Symondson, SJ
Fr Anthony Symondson, SJ is a Jesuit priest, writer, architectural historian, and conservationist. He taught at Stonyhurst College, Lancashire, and was curator of the college collections. In 2006 he published, with Stephen Bucknall, *Sir Ninian Comper: an Introduction and Gazetteer.* He serves on the Westminster Cathedral Art and Architecture Committee and is the representative of the Joint Committee of the National Amenity Societies on the Catholic Southern Historic Churches Committee. He is currently completing a study of the work of the church architect Stephen Dykes Bower, and a biography of Sir Ninian Comper.

The Revd Dr James Tolhurst
The Revd Dr James Tolhurst was a seminary professor and a parish priest. He is the Series Editor of the *Newman Millennium Edition* (Gracewing and Notre Dame) and author of *The Church ... A Communion in the Preaching and Thought of John Henry Newman*, as well as *A Newman Compendium for Sundays and Feast Days* and *Comfort and Sorrow* (Newman's letters and Sermons on the subject of bereavement) – all published by Gracewing.

A. N. Wilson
A. N. Wilson was educated at Rugby School and New College Oxford. As a non-Roman Catholic, he felt a little sheepish about writing the biography of Hilaire Belloc, which was

published in 1984. He is the author of twenty novels, and biographical studies of Sir Walter Scott, Milton and Tolstoy. He is also the author of the general histories, *The Victorians* and *After the Victorians*. He is about to complete the history of the last fifty years, entitled *Our Times*.

Lightning Source UK Ltd.
Milton Keynes UK·
UKOW020618081211

183413UK00001B/2/P